A Double Burden

SUNY series in National Identities
―――――――
Thomas M. Wilson, editor

A Double Burden

Israeli Jews in Contemporary Germany

UZI REBHUN, DANI KRANZ,
AND HEINZ SÜNKER

Published by State University of New York Press, Albany

© 2022 State University of New York

All rights reserved

Printed in the United States of America

No part of this book may be used or reproduced in any manner whatsoever without written permission. No part of this book may be stored in a retrieval system or transmitted in any form or by any means including electronic, electrostatic, magnetic tape, mechanical, photocopying, recording, or otherwise without the prior permission in writing of the publisher.

For information, contact State University of New York Press, Albany, NY
www.sunypress.edu

Library of Congress Cataloging-in-Publication Data

Names: Rebhun, Uzi, author. | Kranz, Dani, author. | Sünker, Heinz, author.
Title: A double burden : Israeli Jews in contemporary Germany / Uzi Rebhun, Dani Kranz, and Heinz Sünker.
Description: Albany : State University of New York Press, [2022] | Series: SUNY series in National Identities | Includes bibliographical references and index.
Identifiers: ISBN 9781438487892 (hardcover : alk. paper) | ISBN 9781438487908 (ebook) | ISBN 9781438487885 (pbk. : alk. paper)
Further information is available at the Library of Congress.

Library of Congress Control Number: 2022931953

10 9 8 7 6 5 4 3 2 1

Contents

List of Illustrations		vii
Preface		xiii
Chapter 1	The Migration Experience	1
Chapter 2	At Home in Israel	25
Chapter 3	Welcome to Germany	57
Chapter 4	Social Integration	99
Chapter 5	Construction of Identity	147
Chapter 6	Antisemitism: In the Eye of the Beholder	175
Conclusion		201
Appendix		207
Notes		209
Bibliography		213
Index		245

Illustrations

Tables

2.1.	Family Background Associated with Germany and the Holocaust (Percentages)	28
2.2.	Determinants of Reasons for Emigration from Israel	43
2.3.	Determinants of Choosing Germany	49
2.4.	Reaction of Family and Friends by Émigrés' Key Sociodemographic Characteristics (Percentages)	53
3.1	Sociodemographic Characteristics of Israeli Immigrants upon Arrival in Germany, Israeli Jews at Large, and German Population (Percentages)	61
3.2	Time of Emigration, by Reasons for Leaving Israel (Somewhat/Very Central)	70
3.3	Time of Immigration, by Reasons for Choosing Germany (Somewhat/Very Central)	73
3.4	Determinants of Time of Migration	74
3.5	Geographic Distribution and Internal Mobility of Israelis in Germany (Percentages)	77
3.6	Places of Settlement by Time of Arrival and Sociodemographic Characteristics (Percentages)	81
3.7	Places of Settlement by Reasons for Choosing Germany (Somewhat/Very Central)	85

3.8	Expected Place of Residence Five Years On, by Veterancy in Germany (Percentages)	87
3.9	Expected Place of Residence Five Years Later, by Reasons for Moving to Germany (Percentages)	92
3.10	Determinants of Future Place of Residence	95
4.1	German Language Proficiency by "Exposure" Factors (Percentages)	104
4.2	German-Language Proficiency by "Efficiency" Factors (Percentages)	109
4.3	German Language Proficiency by "Economic Incentive" Factors (Percentages)	111
4.4	Determinants of German-Language Proficiency	114
4.5	Marriage Composition by Family Background and Reasons for Migration (Percentages)	118
4.6	Marriage Composition by Migration and Settlement Factors (Percentages)	120
4.7	Marriage Composition by Sociodemographic Characteristics (Percentages)	122
4.8	Determinants of Marriage Composition	125
4.9	German Citizenship by Migration Characteristics (Percentages)	128
4.10	German Citizenship by Linguistic and Familial Characteristics (Percentages)	131
4.11	German Citizenship by Sociodemographic Characteristics (Percentages)	132
4.12	Determinants of German Citizenship	133
4.13	Homeownership by Human-Capital Characteristics (Percentages)	137
4.14	Homeownership by Immigration Factors (Percentages)	140
4.15	Homeownership by Macroconditions (Percentages)	142
4.16	Determinants of Homeownership	143

5.1	Indicators of Group Identification and Associated Facets	151
5.2	Transnational Identification among Israelis in Germany, Total and by Veterancy (Percentages)	155
5.3	Religio-Ethnic Identification among Israelis in Germany, Total and by Veterancy (Percentages)	161
5.4	German Identification among Israelis in Germany, Total and by Veterancy (Percentages)	165
5.5	Direction (Positive/Negative) and Magnitude of the Effects of Background Variables, Immigration Factors, and Sociodemographic Characteristics on Group Identity	169
6.1	Relations between Perception and Experience of Antisemitism (Percentages)	185
6.2	Perceptions and Experiences of Antisemitism by Integration Characteristics	187
6.3.	Determinants of Perceptions and Experiences of Antisemitism	194
6.4	Relations between Perceptions of Antisemitism toward Jews and Antisemitism about Israel among Israelis in Germany	197

Figures

2.1.	Importance of the Holocaust at Home of Upbringing, by Family Background (Percentages)	30
2.2.	Percentages Score of Reasons for Emigrating from Israel	34
2.3.	Reasons for Emigrating from Israel (Percentages)	35
2.4.	Percentages Score of Reasons for Choosing Germany	44
2.5.	Reasons for Choosing Germany (Percentages)	45
2.6.	Reactions of Family and Friends to Emigration from Israel and Settling in Germany (Percentages)	52
3.1.	Distribution of Israelis in Germany by Year of Immigration (Percentages)	64

3.2	Israeli Immigrants' Veterancy in Germany (Percentages)	68
3.3	Place of Current Residence by Expected Place of Residence Five Years On (Percentages)	90
4.1	German-Language Proficiency among Israelis in Germany (Percentages)	103
4.2	German Language Proficiency ("Good" and "Very Good") by Reasons for Immigration to Germany (Ratios)	110
4.3	Marriage Composition among Israelis in Germany (Percentage)	117
5.1	Mapping Sentence for Group Identification among Israelis in Germany	150
5.2	Structure of Group Identification among Israelis in Germany	153
5.3	Structure of Group Identification among Israelis in Germany with Tenure as External Variables	154
6.1	Perceived Extent of Antisemitism among Jews in Germay (Percentages)	183
6.2	Verbal and Physical Experiences of Antisemitism among Israelis in Germany (Percentages)	184
6.3A	Transnational Identification and Perceptions of Antisemitism among Israelis in Germany	190
6.3B	Religio-Ethnic Identification and Perceptions of Antisemitism among Israelis in Germany	190
6.3C	Local-German Identification and Perceptions of Antisemitism among Israelis in Germany	191
6.4	Group Identification and Experiences of Verbal Antisemitism among Israelis in Germany	192
6.5	Perceptions (Index) and Experiences (Percentages) of Antisemitism by Place of Residence	193
6.6.	Perception of Extent of Antisemitism about Israel (Percentages)	196

Photos

1	Israeli Passport with Stamp Prohibiting Travel to Germany	67
2	Cover Page of *Spitz* Magazine	105
3	Hebrew Library, Berlin	158
4	Interior View of the Burnt-out Israeli-Owned Bar "Morgen wird Besser"	181

Map

1	Map of Germany with Major Concentrations of Israelis	80

Preface

This book explores and depicts the migration of Israeli Jews to contemporary Germany. It is informed by a view among many Israelis that associates Germany with the most tragic chapter in Jewish history. Israel-Germany relations remain ambivalent and complex, as antisemitism in Germany—past, present, and "new"—filters into the attitudes of Israeli Jews, too. This historical but also current context is reflected in the considerations of Israelis who choose Germany as their destination country. It also underpins the reactions of family and friends as well as interaction with the native population, the local Jewish community, and Israelis on location after they arrive. As such, the story to be told in the following pages with the help of quantitative materials, in-depth interviews, and ethnography will illuminate the migrants' experiences in their own words, adding to what we believe will evolve into a new corpus of literature on Jewish life in the twenty-first century.

The study is historically anchored, calling attention to shifts in the discourse about emigration from Israel in general and relocation to Germany specifically; the policies that facilitate or deter migration to Germany; changes in Israeli Jewish society in regard to Germany; and how the changes above relate to the identity practices of Israeli migrants before, during, and after emigration. Our frame of reference is bordered by migration of Israelis to Germany from 1990 to the present, a period during which this flow increased significantly. We investigate the magnitude, motives, and ambivalence of this migration, the migrants' characteristics, their absorption into their surrounding society in Germany, the maintenance of Jewish identity and attachment to Israel, that is, the construction of identity, and finally their perceptions and experiences of antisemitism and hostility toward Israel. While a plethora of sources exists on remigration of German-born Jews ("*yekkes*" in the Jewish idiom) to Germany, almost nothing is known about contemporary migration from Israel to Germany.

Like any emigration of Israelis, emigration to Germany is contentious and inimical to Jewish-national (Zionist) ideals. We try to provide an understanding of the uniqueness of Israeli's migration to Germany in view of World War II and the Shoah because, unlike "neutral" receiving countries like the United States, Canada, or Australia, Germany—and a fortiori *emigration* of Israeli Jews to Germany—still triggers strong reactions in Israeli society. As Lapidot phrases it "Israelis who left Israel in favour of Berlin are, apparently, those who went the farthest from Israel, from the project of Israel, namely not just to another place but to the very place where the impossibility of its being home was the biggest ideological symbol of the Jewish state . . ." (Lapidot and Ilany, 2015: 4–5). We ask whether emigration to Germany is (still) a double offense or whether Israelis have changed their minds about the country. By researching migration to Germany, we produce outcomes that shed light on conflicts between national policies, in tandem with their ideological underpinnings, and the everyday practice of migration.

This study is the product of close collaboration among scholars from the origin country (Israel) and the destination country (Germany) vis-à-vis our researched population. Each scholar brought somewhat different qualifications and experience to the endeavor. The first author (Rebhun) is a native-born Israeli who speaks Hebrew and is hardly acquainted with German. He has published extensively on Jewish migration in general and on Israeli emigrants in particular, mainly to the United States; when he deals with other destinations, he lumps them into continents as opposed to individual countries. His main research tools are surveys composed of closed-ended questions and analysis of quantitative data. The two other authors live in Germany, or have lived in Germany for a significant part of their lives. The second author, Dani Kranz, is an anthropologist by training and an expert in Jewish Studies. She is a native speaker of German and English, and she has working proficiency in Hebrew. The third author, Heinz Sünker, is a philosopher turned pedagogue, researching interalia the socal history of National Socialism. Intensive interaction of all three authors through mutual visits, email, and joint attendance at conferences and workshops allowed us to carefully plan the data collection, discuss the findings, exchange insights, and mull their interpretation. We were privileged to have excellent research assistants, to whom we are most grateful: Dr. Maya Shorer-Kaplan and Dr. Nadia Beider in Jerusalem and Ms. Katja Harbi in Berlin.

This study was supported by a generous grant from the German-Israel Foundation for Scientific Research & Development.*

Uzi Rebhun
Dani Kranz
Heinz Sünker

---

*Parts of this research were carried out while Uzi Rebhun was a visiting fellow at the Simon-Dubnow Institute in Leipzig in the summer of 2017; and on summer sabbatical at Freie Universitate in Berlin in 2019.

Chapter 1

The Migration Experience[1]

The magnitude, directions, and characteristics of international migration change continuously, which affects the design and evolution of research and the research process. An additional precipitant of change is the flexibility that today's migrants, unlike those in earlier times, enjoy in managing the interplay of their ties with the sending country and those with their host environment. Having recognized migrants' far-reaching agency and recurrent involvement with their homelands, origin countries often develop programs to manage or engage their diasporas, meaning that they do not see migration as a one-way street. By virtue of these multiple actors, and the migrants' different trajectories, present-day research bridges diverse disciplines in the social sciences and acquires added richness and depth by using various complementary methods and empirical sources (Lee, Carling, and Orrenius, 2014).

International Migration Today

Data gathered by the United Nation's Population Division show that in 2015 there were a quarter of a billion international migrants in the world, that is, people living in a country other than their land of birth (United Nations, 2015). While some people move back to their home countries every year, larger numbers leave their native country to settle elsewhere—some because they prefer their destination country, others due to having sunk accidental roots, yet others because they cannot sustain themselves in their native country, and, in the worst case, as in the recent mass migration to Europe, many due to ongoing warfare or residence in failed/failing states. These migration flows take place between a diverse set of origin and destination countries, some in the same continent and others across continental borders (Arango, 2000). What some people see as sending countries are preferred destinations for others, as the case of Germany exemplifies (Statistisches Bundesamt, 2015). All countries around the globe participate in in- and out-migration (hence the "globalization" of migration), creating a complex fabric of sizes and directions of international population movements (Castles, De Haas, and Miller, 2009; Papastergiadis, 2000; Winders, 2014). Nevertheless, the main flow of international migration is from a large number of less-developed countries to selected industrialized and wealthy countries (South/East-North/West migration) (Czaika and De Haas, 2014; Morawska, 2012; Skeldon, 1997; Zolberg, 1999). The more developed a country is and the higher the standard of living it offers, the larger is the share of its foreign-born population (de Haas, 2010). In general, while in Oceania, North America, and Western Europe the foreign-born constitute between one-tenth and two-tenths of the local population, in Africa, Asia, and Latin America their proportion is less than 2 percent (United Nations, 2015).

Migrants are not cut from one cloth (O'Reilly and Benson, 2009; Cornelius, 1998; Higley and Nieuwenhuysen, 2009; Lee, Carling, and Orrenius, 2014; Luthra, Platt, and Salamonska, 2018; Martiniello and Rath, 2012). Some escape war zones and political crises; they form humanitarian intakes, including refugees and asylum seekers. Others are "guest-workers" who fulfill needs occasioned by labor shortages or take up jobs that natives find unattractive, for example, in services and manufacturing. Another category among migrants is that of skilled workers; found mainly in high-tech, medicine, and academia, they fill new openings in restructuring economies and are often sponsored by their new employers. There are also international students, business entrants, and people seeking an adventure or a new lifestyle who may initially move for a defined period of time but later decide to stay on, changing their status to permanent residents. Migrants may be accompanied by family members including spouses (or unmarried partners in some scenarios), children, or parents; they may arrive together or reunify at a later stage (family-reunification migrants).

The different types of migration overlap with broad binaries of "voluntary" versus "forced" (Yarris and Castaneda, 2015), legal versus illegal/undocumented (Caponi and Plesca, 2014; Fasani, 2015), temporary versus permanent (Khoo, Hugo, and McDonald, 2008), and untied migrants versus tied/trailing migrants (Clerge, Sanchez-Soto, Song, and Luke, 2017; Geist and McManus, 2012; McKinnish, 2008; see also Faist, 2000). Each type of migration is likely to involve different countries of origin and destination, different social classes, different relations with the host population, and different sets of economic opportunities encountered (Martiniello and Rath, 2012; Waldinger, 2011). Accordingly, today's immigrants are heterogeneous in gender, educational attainment, occupational profile, and marital status (Van Hear, 2014).

Resettlement opportunities vary in accordance with local immigration legislation. Each country or area has its own form of border control (Castles, 2004) and an immigration regime that reflects its national ethos (Joppke, 1999; Joppke and Rozenhek, 2002). Immigration policy is not static; it changes over time in response to demographic, economic, cultural, security, and political considerations (Castles, 2004; Hollifield, 2004; Zolberg, 1999); in the case of Germany, it remains impacted by the aftermath of World War II. Governmental policy, especially under conditions of mass immigration, is also sensitive to the stance of the native population (Portes and DeWind, 2007). Recently, countries have tended to harden their entry criteria by setting quotas on immigration at large and/or on immigration of specific types and characteristics (Avineri, Orgad, and Rubinstein, 2009; Bhagwati, 2003; Bonjour and Block, 2016; Joppke 2005; Yakobson and Rubinstein, 2008). Yet, other studies argue for the moderation of restrictiveness (de Haas, Natter, and Vezzoli, 2018) (see, also Beine et al., 2016). In some cases immigrants are admitted as part of intercountry acts of reconciliation, as in the case of family members of Jewish quota refugees to Germany, or due to specific moral obligations (Joppke, 1998). Once immigrants enter, each country sets its own criteria for the granting of citizenship (Castles, 2004; Harari, 2018). Sometimes governments roll out an amnesty to undocumented immigrants, legalizing their residency (Carens, 2010). Countries are not fully sovereign in matters of migration; in fact, they are largely subordinate to international treaties to which they are signatories (for entry applications) and human-rights regimes (for immigrants who have already arrived) (Hollifield, 2004; Macedo, 2007). Even so, they may turn immigrants away for specific local reasons (Kranz, 2016c; Masri, 2013) or as part of changes in the social and political landscape, as in the incidents along the US-Mexican border in the spring and summer of 2018.

Countries also differ in their philosophies of integration. Three prominent broad perspectives are assimilation, multiculturalism, and separation (Castles, De Haas, and Miller, 2009; Owen, 2011). A useful approach is that of Portes and Rumbaut (2006) who postulate a continuum from hostility to support in receiving governments' policies. In the modern era, Europe (Germany included) has evolved on the premise of mainly ethno-national nation-states (Alba and Foner, 2014; Tonkens and Duyvendak, 2016) while countries such as the United States or Canada have been largely immigrant receiving societies (Alba and Foner, 2014; Mollenkopf and Hochschild, 2010). Even in recent decades, relative to the United States, "European migration policies have been characterized by reactive, shortsighted measures with an emphasis on control" (Süssmuth and Weidenfeld, 2005: XI). Naturalization of (non-co-ethnic) immigrants remains problematic in Europe and the guiding principles of freedom of movement for European Union (EU) citizens within the EU remain multilayered and uneven (Favell, 2013; Kranz and Zubida, 2019). Immigrants may be expected to demonstrate strong loyalty to their host country, including, among other things, giving up their cultural and religious habits (Simonsen, 2018). The contents and structures of policy programs vary among specific facets of integration, for example, schooling, the labor market, political participation, national security, housing, religion, and sundry types of services (Huddleston and Niessen, 2011).

Accordingly, today's international migrants do not necessarily disengage from their native countries. Contemporary immigrants shape and preserve relations that connect their country of origin with their new place of residence in a way that exhibits transnational commitments (Basch, Glick Schiller, and Blanc-Szanton, 1994; Levitt and Glick Schiller, 2004; Portes, 1997; Smith, 2005; Vertovec, 2001; Waldinger, 2015). This is reflected, among other things, in frequent mutual visits of immigrants to their origin countries and of family and relatives to the immigrants' new country, taking advantage of cheap and convenient transportation (Brinkerhoff, 2009; Portes, Guarnizo, and Landolt, 1999). Likewise, new communication technologies allow immigrants to maintain frequent contact with people who stayed behind and to consume cultural products in their mother tongue, such as news, movies, and books (Kivisto, 2005; Levitt, DeWind, and Vertovec, 2003), leading to the creation of a home away from home (Cohen, 2008) or a third space anchored neither in the country of origin nor in the country of residence (Kosnick, 2007). These patterns are supported by both origin and host countries that recognize the transnational character of their immigrant citizens and are aware of the multiple spaces that they occupy including home country, host country, and often other countries where ethnic peers have settled (pan-ethnicity) (Gamlen, 2014; Sheffer, 2003). Moreover, immigrants today operate in social structures and environments that are increasingly tolerant of ethnic diversity, notwithstanding nationalistic backlashes across

European countries. Immigrants often join social networks based on common origin, establish ethnic organizations, lobby politically for their country of origin, and maintain religious and cultural practices in both the private and public spheres (Amersfoort, 2004; Hagan and Ebaugh, 2003; Hervieu-Leger, 2000; Levitt and Jaworsky, 2007; Sheffer, 2006). Some host countries permit their foreign-born population to hold dual citizenship (Bauböck, 2002; Castles and Davidson, 2000) upon naturalization; others construct highly restrictive legal frameworks that aim to force most naturalizing immigrants to relinquish their citizenship of origin (Faist, Gerdes, and Rieple, 2004).

Explaining Migration and Migratory Processes

Migration is not a one-off act; it plays out in several stages that evolve over time. Migrants first mull the possibility of moving and then make the decision. Next, they perform the physical act of travel and begin the settlement process in the new country, including the acquisition of human and social capital in order to maximize local opportunities and the shaping of group and national identities. Migrants may revise their original plans as they encounter the host environment directly. As it advances stage by stage, migration involves individual elements on the microlevel; structural political, economic, and cultural patterns on the macrolevel; and intervening mechanisms of migrant communities and social networks on the meso-level (Boyd and Nowak, 2012; Radu and Straubhaar, 2012; Czaika, Bijak, and Prike, 2021). Hence, migration explanations separate into a neoclassical functionalist approach, which relates to society as a system of individuals that acts to maximize social and economic utility, and a Marxist structural approach, according to which forces within the world system of countries and corporations determine individuals' behavior and are expected to create spatial inequality (Castles, De Haas, and Miller, 2009; Faist, 2000; Massey et al., 1993; Papastergiadis, 2000).

The neoclassical approach to human capital postulates that people move on the basis of the rational choice of an equilibrium between push factors at origin and pull factors at destination, which together make the latter attractive as a new home (Castles, De Haas, and Miller, 2009). For the migration process to manifest in a concrete act, the long-term benefits of migration must surpass their cost significantly (Borjas, 1989; Lee, 1966; Sjaastad, 1962). Among other things, people weigh up spatial variations in economic and cultural opportunities, health care, lifestyle, and political freedom. Cost-benefit considerations also take into account spatial transferability and convertibility of resources (Faist, 2000). Since migrants are often accompanied by spouses and children, the profitability of migration entails calculus of broad familial considerations, including the psychological price of rupturing long-standing contacts with relatives and friends (Massey et al., 1993).

Hence, the decision to migrate is not always made solely by individuals; instead, it flows from a joint consideration involving nonmigrant family or household members ("new economics of migration") (Boyd, 1989; Stark and Bloom, 1985). Under such circumstances, people act collectively not only to maximize anticipated income but also to minimize potential risks. From such a perspective, family resources may split, as some members remain in the local labor market while others move to foreign markets where they can improve their returns and send remittances to those who stayed behind. This model is most applicable for less-developed countries where neither governmental protective programs private insurance nor credit markets are sufficiently developed to allow economic initiatives, and where families and households are production and consumption units (Massey et al., 1993).

It is insufficient to view migration as a decision solely guided by individualistic or familial considerations of free choice. Migration is also affected by historical structural disparities of center/periphery distribution of political and economic power and recruitment of cheap labor (the "segmented/dual labor market," "dependency," or "world system" approaches) (Castles, De Haas, and Miller, 2009; Faist, 2000; Morawska, 2012; Piore, 1979). Where these disparities exist, people are forced to move due to interactions among economic structures and their fusion into global economic and political systems. Hence, while some migrants move from countries with ample labor supply to countries lacking laborers, migration in the opposite direction occurs as well: from countries with high human capital to poor countries that lack professionals such as engineers and managers and can offer them high returns for their qualifications (Massey et al., 1993). These worldwide systems are controlled by strong countries that have been shaped within the framework of the new capitalistic order of globalization (Castles, De Haas, and Miller, 2009; Morawska, 1990). Much migration in this world system moves from erstwhile colonies to former metropoles in Europe (Martiniello and Rath, 2012) taking advantage of cultural, linguistic, and administrative relations. Likewise, the world economy is managed in a small number of urban hubs, where major financial, administrative, and professional institutions are headquartered, making them preferred destinations for immigrants (Massey et al., 1993). When countries establish preferences for certain categories of immigrants, as they are likely to do, they also bear economic and security matters in mind (Faist, 2000; Massey et al., 1993) (see, also: Docquier, Peri, and Ruyssen, 2014).

To a large extent, what makes migration feasible and persistent are intervening agencies (Castles, De Haas, and Miller, 2009; Faist, 2000), including legal, illegal, and other actors, ranging from smugglers, labor agencies, aid organizations, and social network, to ethno-religious institutions (Cadge and Ecklund, 2007; Hirschman, 2004). Migration agencies ease the adjustment to the destination country, hence lowering the cost of migration. Where they are available, they tend to perpetuate migration, that is, broaden it into chain migration (Castles, De Haas, and Miller, 2009; de Haas, 2009; Massey, 1990). Insofar as migrants are pioneers of their ethnic group at destination, they lay social, economic, and communal foundations for additional waves of peers (Faist, 2000; Gurak and Fe Caces, 1992). This perspective has evolved into a "cumulative causation" theory, which postulates that such factors as remittances sent back home, successful integration into specific high-demand occupations, and attaining a substantial mass in the new country encourage others to move there as well (Myrdal, 1957). The flow of these migrants to destinations where ethno-religious communities already exist makes the destination more and more attractive as migrants successfully join its social and economic networks (Light and Gold, 2000), thus counterbalancing the affectively adverse aspects of migration, that is, loss of home, loss of familiarity, and homesickness in general.

Research on blue-collar migrant workers indicates that irrespective of their intentions upon migration—permanent or temporary settlement—these migrants initially become part of ethnic niche markets (Gilbertson, 1995). Not so is the situation for highly qualified individuals who are "on call" to commercial or state actors (Hannerz, 2004) and those who expatriate on their own account (Thorn, 2008). Given the temporary or undefined nature of their sojourn, typically they neither form ethno-religious networks nor assimilate into the local population (Fechter, 2007). In contrast, "life style migrants" (Benson and O'Reilly, 2016), although similarly privileged, may "go native" and assimilate into the local population with greater or lesser success (Amit, 2007; Benson and O'Reilly, 2016) or form ethnic or ethno-religious niches (King, Warnes, and Williams, 2000). Thus, all groups of migrants are at risk of emotional affects. Their ability to cope with these consequences is strongly impacted by intersecting factors such as motivation for migration, resources, education, gender, tenure, citizenship, age, and also personality (Kranz, 2019a; Luthra, Platt, and Salamonska, 2018).

We are not always able to draw fine distinctions among the micro-, macro-, and meso- structures of the migration process. They often intermingle and generally display interdependencies (Behar, 1996). Be this as it may, all three dimensions are required in order to explain why some people leave one country and settle in another (Castles, De Haas, and Miller, 2009; Faist, 2000; Massey et al., 1993), why others wish to do so but cannot, and why still others entertain no such wish or opt for transnational lifestyles. Still, as Castles, De Hass, and Miller (2009: 54) postulate, push-pull models seem useful in explaining much migration of educated people between welfare states, while the historical-structural paradigm is often appropriate for understanding geographical moves of poor and nonprofessional people as well as migration associated with political oppression. Even from the latter perspective, according to which migration flows are guided by the international system of states, individual migrants are likely to rationally consider the pros and cons of migration for themselves and for their family members.

Notably, too, migration does not flow along a hermetically sealed pipeline from one origin to one destination (Paul, 2011). People may circulate between two countries, stay in each for a certain time, and then move on to a third country without having "one single origin and a simple end" (Papastergiadis, 2000:4). Thus, they turn geographic movement into a way of life (Faist, 2000).

Immigration to Germany

Germany in its current form is the result of the unification of the Federal Republic of Germany (FRG, West Germany) and the German Democratic Republic (GDR, East Germany) in 1990. The consequences of the previous partitioning of Germany in 1949 remain palpable in terms of the identity composition of the local populations, the distribution of wealth and opportunities, and also the proportions of foreign residents—non-German citizens—and naturalized Germans in the respective sectors (Decker, Kies, and Brähler, 2016). Germany's foreign-born population is divided between 95 percent in the West and only 5 percent in the East (Foroutan, 2017). Expressions of xenophobia remain higher in the East than in the West (Decker et al., 2016), indicating that "diversity" is locality specific (Foroutan, 2017).

The largest groups of immigrants to postwar West Germany were *Gastarbeiter*, guest laborers, who were admitted in order to sustain the country's economic rebound. The idea was to rotate laborers between West Germany and the sending countries; permanent settlement, let alone naturalization, was not envisioned. Interstate treaties concerning these laborers were initiated at West Germany's request with Italy (1955), Spain and Greece (1960), Turkey (1961), Morocco and South Korea (1963), Portugal (1964), Tunisia (1965), and, last, the former Yugoslavia (1968). Many of the labor migrants who arrived under these arrangements came from poor areas and were unskilled or semiskilled (Aced et al., 2014). Due to the lack of interest from the German side, but also on the part of the migrants, who assumed that their stay would be temporary, integration into the host society was so slow that "parallel societies" began to emerge. They persist to this day for multiple reasons: Germany is an ethno-nationally based country and Germanness—a heavily contested concept—is conveyed by way of intermediary spheres (Preuss, 2003). Muslim migrants and those not perceived as white are particularly implicated. Their belonging to Germany is regularly debated and challenged, as much of the German population contests the notion of a "post-migration society" (Aced et al., 2014; Foroutan, 2017); although as has been argued and evidenced, empirically diversity is the norm in Germany (Czollek, 2020), and the more eager (former) migrants and their descendants want to integrate into German society, and the more active they become, the more conflicts arise (El-Mafaalani, 2018). This phenomenon has been dubbed the "integration paradox" by the teacher, cum professor of educational sciences, Aladin El-Mafaalani. Integration poses challenges, and it needs to be negotiated: Jews, and Jewish Israeli migrants, are faced with these challenges, too.

Religion is the key criteria for exclusion from German and other European mainstream societies (Kalmijn, 2015). Muslims in particular are affected; ongoing legislation concerning the headscarf is symbolic of this trend. Generally, Jews suffer from less exclusion, although bitter debates over male circumcision epitomize the construction of Jewish and Muslim otherness—currently (Doughan and Tzuberi, 2018; Yurdakul, 2016) and historically (Anidjar, 2003). This overarching trend is also evidenced in the relatively swift and easy integration of "guest workers" from European Christian majority societies. Thus, the social and legal integration of the majority of the labor migrants and their descendants remains problematic. They benefit neither from integration via religious homophily nor from the accession of their origin countries to EU membership, unlike in the cases of Italy, Spain, Portugal, and Greece.

The most populous group of labor migrants and their descendants are of Turkish origin and are impacted by the fraught German-Turkish relationship.

Like North Africans and other Muslim migrants and their descendants, they are affected by mass migration from countries of the Middle East (since 2015). The "refugee crisis," occasioned by that ongoing event, has allowed long-established but often hidden, structures to become visible, and to gain momentum (Decker et al., 2016; Kranz, 2018c; Schwander and Manow, 2017). Young men from any of these countries are unduly implicated, an objectified debate to date takes place mainly among experts and does not reach a wider audience (Lutz, 2017). Specific incidents are widely reported in the German media (Dietze, 2016) and acts of terror perpetrated by Muslims have led to the shorthand expression the "radicalization of Islam" instead of the "Islamization of violence" (Roy, 2017)—an infelicitous turn of phrase as the perpetrators had been criminal before "finding" Islam. These events have led to further polarization in German society and laid open the fact that Germany as a whole suffers from serious ethnic cleavages and badly managed previous migrations, and that integration needs to be seen on a societal, and not on a migrant-only, scale. Furthermore, social class needs to be filtered as the integration of skilled and highly skilled migrants (Grigoleit-Richter, 2017), and of global northerners (Klekowski von Koppenfels, 2014) shows.

Importantly, before the upheaval of German society in the wake of the "refugee crisis" that ensued in 2015, and continues at the time of writing, the 1990s also saw mass immigration to Germany. It is nearly forgotten that the Balkan wars brought record numbers of refugees to Germany, some of whom remained while others left or were forced out as section 16 of the Basic Law, which regulates asylum, was drastically amended in 1993. The early 1990s also saw antiforeigner violence on a scale not known before, as the Yugoslavian refugees entered alongside other groups of immigrants and refugees such as ethnic Germans and their families in the wake of the collapse of the Eastern Bloc (Panagiotidis, 2012). Altogether, about one million ethnic Germans (*Spätaussiedler*, late resettlers) entered the country under the provisions of German basic and citizenship laws, and received German citizenship on the basis of their ethnic descent in most cases (Panagiotidis, 2019). The existence of language and integration courses for this group gives further evidence that Germany wished to integrate those whom it defined as its own, whereas integration courses for other immigrants, including guest workers, were of little interest to the state and did not exist until 2005. Unlike the *Spätaussiedler*, who could immigrate along with their nonethnic German families, guest-worker migrants were allowed to pursue legal family reunification only in 1981 (Joppke, 1998). Until then, family unification took place de facto, and their integration was seen mainly as the personal concern of those involved.

Along with the ethnic Germans who immigrated in the aftermath of the collapse of the Eastern Bloc, some 220,000 individuals from the Former Soviet Union (FSU) entered Germany as Kontingentflüchtlinge (quota refugees) (Haug and Schimany, 2005). This number includes those permitted to enter Germany as Jewish refugees, and their non-Jewish and non-ethnic-German family members as a direct corollary of Germany's Nazi past. About 70,000 of these quota refugees became members of the *Einheitsgemeinde* (Unified Community), the umbrella organization of Jewish communities, while a much smaller number joined liberal Jewish communities that amalgamated under the aegis of the World Union of Progressive Judaism in some states, while in other states liberal and orthodox communities exist as part of the *Einheitsgemeinde* (Kranz, 2009). Yet, it should be noted that membership in any Jewish community is regulated by matrilineal descent, or by an appropriate conversion.

Like ethnic Germans, quota refugees attended integration and language courses. However, these populations are differentiated by the poverty levels of elderly FSU immigrants, which remains an issue as recurrent debates about their pensions indicate. For the *Spätaussiedler*, years worked in the FSU are counted toward pension contributions, for Jewish quota refugees they are not. The integration of those who arrived as adults is also problematic; young "Russian Jews," in contrast, perform well in educational and professional settings (Haug and Schimany, 2005; Körber, 2021). One may reasonably ask how "Russian" these "Russian Jews" still are, as most hold German citizenship. Defining them as "Russian Jews" reflects an intra-Jewish, but also a general, discourse that dwells on creating "others" within the categorical sphere of immigrants to Germany. Hegner (2015) stresses the political aspect of the term *Russian Jews*. In Germany they are defined by the language—Russian—in disregard of their FSU origin, while in the United States they are termed "Soviet Jews," indicating the relevance of the political system in the internal American discourse.

The sociologist Karen Körber (2021) shows that even those who came to Germany as children, or who are already Germany-born children, do not self-identify as Germans but as "passport Germans" (*Passdeutsche*). Their self-identification is based on holding German passports, but being nonethnic Germans. This self-identification still occurs, although the Russian Jews of the German discourse are typically naturalized in due time. Relative to guest laborers and their descendants, their access to German society is easier, causing aggravation among some of the marginalized guest population and its descendants (Mandel, 2008). In particular, guest workers from Muslim countries had turned from wanted guests to unwanted strangers (Kranz and Zubida, 2019). They had become ethnicized as part of this discourse, and also as part of the legal developments (Amir-Moazami, 2018). These developments evidence the past in the present in current immigration and integration in Germany. Jews from the Soviet Union were welcome to stay in Germany, as they were Jews, and the well-being of Jews and the nourishing of Jews is raison d'être of the Federal Republic (O'Dochartaigh, 2007), while (Muslim) guest workers, in contrast, were welcome to work but were then supposed to go home. In the same vein, Israeli Jews are welcome as Jews, while Palestinian Muslim migrants are less welcome (Kranz, 2018b; 2018c). Synagogues were renovated and rebuilt; the presence of mosques remains contentious.

With these historically entrenched constructions of categories of immigrants, tensions were unavoidable and persist to this day (El-Mafaalani, 2018; Czollek, 2020; Mandel, 2008). However, another group of migrants has been entering the country, namely, people whom Germany admits not due to its past but because of its present. They are part of the "Make it in Germany" campaign run by the Federal Ministries of Economics, as well as the Ministry for Labour and Social Affairs and the Federal German job services (*Bundesagentur für Arbeit*). By means of careful prescreening, Germany strives to attract skilled and highly skilled individuals to work—and settle—in the country. The policy includes family reunification and a path to citizenship (Kranz and Zubida, 2019). These immigrants are typically given "blue cards," a specific and relatively new visa category. How many of these blue card holders and their families will settle and naturalize as Germans remains to be seen, as highly skilled individuals are often characterized by strong mobility and global career trajectories (Näsholm, 2011).

Israeli immigrants to Germany cannot be seen as detached from the social history of the wider context of intergroup relations in Germany, and German migration policies. A number of Israelis have obtained blue cards on the basis of their professions. Some of them immigrated to Germany after being headhunted in Israel; they did so not because of family ties, an attraction to the country, or sheer curiosity, but simply due to better job opportunities than other places could offer. Others entered Germany on different kinds of visas for family reunification, as students, or on various types of business exchange and settled by chance. Still, others held EU or German citizenship. The number of Israelis who renaturalized as EU citizens had been increasing strongly since the late 1990s (Harpaz, 2012), and some of them have indeed used their EU passports to emigrate from Israel to the EU. Yet, the peak of potential naturalizations had been reached as EU embassies reported in Israel: Germany might become an exception as the country amended its citizenship legislation in 2020 and 2021. Since 1949, Germany has allowed individuals and their eligible descendants to renaturalize under section 116, point 2 of the (West) German Basic Law. Serious problems remain within the legal realm (Panagiotidis, 2019), and have been comprehensively addressed only in the most recent past. Israeli émigrés in Germany integrate more smoothly if they already speak German or have a German partner/spouse; those who lack both and come unprepared react to the country with puzzlement, as evidenced by Fania Oz-Salzberger (2001). A commonly encountered process, even among those who entered Germany as German citizens, is the shift from specific Israeli notions of Germany to an adjustment to the German reality (Kranz, 2018d), and the country's structures, intergroup relations, and everyday life (Kranz, 2018c). Being a *yekke* in Israel is very different from being a German citizen in Germany.

Jews in Post-1945 Germany

From the perspective of the German, non-Jewish, mainstream, Israeli Jews constitute an addition to the country's existing Jewish population. That the majority of Israelis in Germany feel at odds with the "local Jews" (Almog 2019; Kranz, 2016a; 2019b; 2020b) was initially glossed over. Lianne Merkur (2019) outlined this pattern in her comparative study of Israelis in Berlin and Toronto. She found that in both cities Israelis created structures that cater to their specific Israeli—and Jewish—identity needs, which they do not see fulfilled in the local Jewish structures. In Germany, the focus of our research, these differences have become known by way of the participation of Israelis in the public discourse, which goes hand in hand with their increasing integration (El-Mafaalani 2018). These Israelis do not adhere to the established pattern of confining dissent to the ears of the Jewish community (Bodemann, 2006), or Jewish groups (Khasani, 2005).

Owing to their position as a tiny minority in post-Holocaust West and East Germany and the extreme trauma that they had endured (von Baeyer et al., 1964; Platt, 2012), Jews in both parts of the country had developed identity configurations that differed from the German majority populations (Freker, 1998; Grünberg, 2000). The boundary to the outside was imperative guarded in West Germany (Grünberg, 1988), although intermarriage with non-Jewish Germans were common (Kauders, 2007). These intimate, familial transgressions caused tensions in families, and in the Jewish community (Rapaport, 1997) that oftentimes functioned like a quasi-family for the first, and the second generation of post-Shoah Jews (Kauders, 2007). This scenario was intensified by most Jews of the first and second generation being of Eastern European, displaced persons' origin in West Germany (Grossman and Lewinsky, 2012), and forming a close-knit community. To complicate matters, the initial official representation in West Germany consisted most often of surviving, or returning German Jews, who, in turn, were often married to other—non-Jewish—Germans (Geller, 2005; Kauders, 2007). The eastern sector of the country that was to become the GDR was dominated by Jews of German origin (Borneman and Peck, 1995). The official line was one of ideological remigration: going home to Germany for affective reasons was part of the private narratives of East German Jews. A significant number of those who returned to East Germany, and particularly to East Berlin, aligned to communist ideologies, and sought to build a better Germany (Borneman and Peck, 1995; Ostow, 1989). German Jews who returned to the West mentioned homesickness—publicly in their autobiographies, and in research (Blaschke, Fings, and Lissner, 1997). Some German Jews who returned to what was to become West Germany were political remigrants and some became well known public figures, for example, the prosecutor Fritz Bauer; Josef Neuberger who became a minister of justice of the (new state of) North Rhine-Westphalia (Schmalhausen, 2002); and the philosophers Theodor Adorno and Max Horkheimer. If, and in how far any of them self-identified as German, or now West German Jews, is debatable: ethno-histories that seek to understand a Jewish perspective from the inside out, such as *Jewish Salonica* (Naar, 2016), are to date few and far between. The historic work of Anthony D. Kauders (2007; 2010) constitutes a rare exception but it fills in only so much; the sociologist Lynn Rapaport (1997) evidenced an ethnicized boundary for second-generation Jews in Frankfurt, West Germany, where she conducted qualitative research work in the mid-1980s, and again in the mid-1990s. The literature scholar cum ethnographer Jeffrey M. Peck (2006) avers her finds. Yet, besides Kauders', this output is written in English and never reached larger audiences in Germany: it never became part of German discourse. More common are depictions such as those in *Geschichte der Juden in Deutschland von 1945 bis zur Gegenwart* (History of Jews in Germany from 1945 to the Present) (Brenner, 2012), which in style also owns up to the specific style of writing history in German and in Germany that differs very significantly in style, scope, and personal engagement from English or Hebrew language historiography.

Be that as it may, Bauer, Neuberger, Adorno, and Horkheimer had experienced pre-Shoah Germany as part of the German mainstream. This set them far apart from the majority of East European displaced persons (DPs) who found themselves in a new society that did not welcome them and was alien to them (Bodemann, 2008). As Jay Howard Geller (2005) outlines convincingly, surviving German Jews maintained their in-group status in Germany despite all odds because they were German by way of language, culture, and habitus; they were natives among other natives. Furthermore, a significant number of them were married to German non-Jews, which had insured their survival, and given them access to a vast, non-Jewish, German family network that oftentimes supported them.

While the ideological nuances that exist within the population of Jews of German background are important to bear in mind, they should not deflect from the fact that most Jews in West Germany, as well as the vast majority of all Jews in the country, were displaced persons from Eastern Europe (Poland, Hungary, Romania), who for various reasons remained in West Germany. Immediately after the Holocaust, many survivors fled to the British, French, and American occupation zones in the hope of safety and also for a chance to migrate to one of these or other countries. The number of Jewish DPs in postwar Germany was as high as 250,000 (Geller, 2005). With changes in US visa regulations (Geller, 2005) and the foundation of the State of Israel in 1948, most of them left Germany. When the last DP camp closed in 1956, a tiny fraction remained in West Germany (Geller, 2005). The first membership count of the West German communities, including West Berlin was 15,920 (Scheller, 1987); the number grew, and stagnated at about 30,000, until the immigration from the former Soviet Union (FSU) after 1990. The number of Jews in East Germany is estimated to be around 8,000 (Ostow, 1989). The demographic increase in the West German community should be attributed to immigration, as the population was ageing, as evident in the figures of the community membership of the central welfare offices of the Jews of Germany—an adjacent body to the *Einheitsgemeinde* (Scheller, 1987). Jews returned to West Germany from the British Mandate of Palestine, and after 1948, from Israel (Webster, 1995). As they had become Israeli citizens by default, these German Jewish returnees were the earliest Israelis migrants to West Germany (Webster, 1995). A significant number entered West Germany after the Luxemburg Treaties, hoping to gain restitution—and leave again, which many did not. Whether a similar movement took place in the GDR cannot be established. Yet, emigration from Israel to Poland occurred (Silber, 2008), and indeed "emigration" from prestate Israel and early state Israel existed (Yehudai, 2020).

The traumatized DP survivors who remained, or who arrived, formed the core of the Jewish communities (Brumlik et al., 1988) in West Germany. Unlike most surviving Jews of German origin, they had been orthodox in practice and much more marginal in their countries of origin than German Jews had been. The latter had become part of the German mainstream despite recurring antisemitism in the Weimar Republic (Barkai, 2002; Hecht, 2003). They spoke German, not Yiddish, natively, and they intermarried in high numbers (Meiering, 1998; Meyer, 2002). These differences triggered a clash of identities in the early postwar/post-Holocaust period already. Hoping to organize the remaining Jews and bridge the identity issues, the American Jewish Joint Distribution Committee supported the refoundation of a Unified Community (Einheitsgemeinde), which adopted an orthodox form of praxis (Geller, 2005). The idea that this mode of praxis would allow any Jew to be included remained a compromise unfulfilled. Filtering into the trauma that lay at the core of the community was an evolving "contaminated intergenerativity" that had dire effects on second-generation Jews (Grünberg, 2007).

The commandment to migrate to Israel became a central element within the self-concept of Jew in Germany (Schütze, 1997) that collided with the reality of many second-generation Jews who had German friends (Rapaport, 1997), not to mention German business partners and spouses (Grünberg, 2000; Rapaport, 1997), but, as stated earlier, these ties were contentious even though they were common (Kauders, 2007). Their ambiguous integration into the texture of German society as well as the ongoing struggles over the shape of the Jewish community, its form of practice, and its effectively boundaries were indicative of the permanence of a Jewish presence in Germany (Geis, 1996), which evolved into an identity matrix of extremes for the second generation. Wedged between their own wishes to leave Germany and move to Israel (Maor, 1961; Oppenheimer, 1967), their extremely strong bond with their parents (Löw-Beer, 1996), and their German partners/spouses, these second-generation Jews in Germany were often left in limbo; for many, it took half a lifetime to come to terms with their identities and find a place to settle (Speier, 1988).

The situation for second-generation Jews in East Germany was no less complicated, even though their parents had—ostensibly—returned to the country for ideological reasons. While officially victims of the Nazis among various other groups, GDR Jews suffered from the uneasiness of an ethno-religious collectivity in an atheistic country (Ostow, 1989), in which antisemitism prevailed despite officials claims to the contrary (Benz, 2020). While the parents may have remigrated for ideological reasons, their children were trapped in a challenging situation that was different from that of their West German counterparts: unlike the latter, they were not geared at migrating to Israel. What is more, amid the imposition of "anti-antisemitism" on the general society, Jews could obtain a pension from the state. In reality, however, GDR Jews were exposed to an antisemitism that existed side-by-side with (state-sponsored) philosemitism: while it is beyond the scope of our work, a historic account that compares the ambiguous tropes of antisemitism and philosemitism in East and West is lacking to date.

Against this background, it is still surprising that Jews from Israel were one of the largest groups of Jewish immigrants to West Germany in the years the country was separated from the East (Webster, 1995). While some of them were of German origin, other "Israelis" were Jews of East European origin who had not managed to make a good life in Israel. The historian Moshe Zuckermann (2007) is the son of such East European migrants to West Germany and he, like most "Israeli children," resented his parents' decision (Maor, 1961; Panagiotidis, 2015). Despite their umbrage, however, a share of these and other second-generation children remained in Germany. The Jewish population of the two Germanies stagnated at 30,000 in the West and slumped in the East, evidencing that in particular immigration contributed to the number of Jews in West Germany. Jewish immigration post-1945 and pre-1990, which has been oddly overlooked by historians so far, is not a new issue.

The late 1970s and early 1980s marked the coming of age of the second generation. Second-generation Jews who remained in the country but were at odds with the Jewish community began to set up Jewish groups in which they met to discuss social issues, Jewish ontology in Germany, and Israel (Khasani, 2005). They founded the periodical *Babylon*, which acted as a forum for debates of current issues, and which included contributions from non-Jewish interlocutors and experts. In other words, a German/Jewish dialogue had begun to take shape, which was fraught, as some of the missiles evidence. "Israel" was particularly problematic for these so-called critical Jews (Grünberg, 2000) within the realms of the Jewish community (Kauders, 2007) but also beyond it as *Babylon* also evidences. While critical toward Israel and Israeli policies, they remained supportive of the country. Furthermore, while having decided to stay in Germany or to return to Germany (often from Israel), they had learned from experience that criticizing Israel could very easily be taken out of context (Kranz, 2009), and that "critic of Israel" might begin with life-worldly, ethnographic depictions of Israeli reality such as poverty (Zimmermann, 2008). This placed them in a paradoxical situation vis-à-vis non-Jewish society, which considered Jews as victims and at the same time Israelis as perpetrators of occupation (Atshan and Galor, 2020). In other words, the German Middle East conflict had begun to take shape (O'Dochartaigh, 2007; Ullrich, 2008), impacting on Jews in Germany, and increasingly on Muslims (Atshan and Galor, 2020), based on the permanence of their presence. To complicate matters further, Jews who wished to engage in (critical) debate were confronted by the highly cohesive and imperatively pro-Israel Jewish community (Kauders, 2007). Bodemann (2008) argues that despite these tensions, one may speak of a Jewish renascence from the mid-1980s onward, as Jewish diversity became public again. That Jews were living and not just sojourning in (West Germany) is epitomized in oft-quoted line by Salomon Korn, on the opening of the new community center in Frankfurt, Main, in 1986: "Wer ein Haus baut, will bleiben, und wer bleiben will, erhofft sich Sicherheit." ("The one who builds a house wants to stay, and the one who wants to stay hopes for safety.") (Frankfurter Jüdische Nachrichten, October 1986, S.4; https://www.fr.de/frankfurt/salomon-korn-nimmt-ehrung-trotz-boykott-aufrufen-10997223.html). Korn, born in Lublin (Poland), entered Germany with his family as a child DP and held, as well as still holds, a number of official functions within the structures of the *Einheitsgemeinde*.

The—unexpected—Jewish renaissance did indeed happen, albeit on a small scale: Jews did become publically noticeable again—not as victims but as active players as Jews and as Germans, although the mating of the two remains an issue. The dual, if not dialectic relation, of being Jews and Germans, coupled with the matter of Israel, has created a double bind as Jews are regularly confounded with Israelis (Kranz, 2018c). While the share of respondents who hold antisemitic attitudes remains stable at about 20 percent in representative samples of the German population (Decker et al., 2016), negative attitudes toward Israel are on the rise (Hagemann and Nathanson, 2015). The Israeli/Palestinian conflict, the settlements, and right-wing Israeli policies are the key factors that alienate Germans (Hagemann and Nathanson, 2015), even as most Germans have little actual knowledge of Israel, the conflict, and the region (Kranz, 2018a; 2018c), and antisemitism had been existing independently of Israel. The Palestinian American anthropologist Sa'ed Atshan, and the German-born and -raised

Israeli American archaeologist Katharina Galor sought to untangle some of these issues in *The Moral Triangle: Germans, Israelis, Palestinians* (2020), as they realized that "things to do with Jews," including Israel, carry a specific moral currency. Their contribution seeks to understand the multiplex intergroup relationship and evidences just how complicated, convoluted, and conflated issues are around Israel, and Palestine, in the country; although, unfortunately, key contributors who wrote in German about these issues, and who lift the local discourse, such as Alexandra Senfft or Peter Ullrich, have not been integrated into their work. These two authors, who know the local discourse and its intricacies, and how to contribute to it forcefully, make abundantly clear that Israelis cannot be considered separately from the local Jews (however much these groups are at odds) and Palestinians from the local Muslim populations (even if they are not Muslims). Thus, while their work is a first attempt that will reach English-speaking audiences, it does not satisfy the complexity that characterizes the writing of Ullrich (2012) and Senfft (2020), who engaged with this phenomenon, or of Lianne Merkur (2019), who outlines Israeli Jewish misgivings about the Israeli state of affair in fine-tuned, ethnographic detail.

Consequently, Jews in Germany, be they of German, DP, FSU, or Israeli origin, act against a historically and presently fraught background. The majority of Russian-speaking Jews who immigrated to the country did so between 1990 and 2004, at which point migration was nearly shut down. Latvia, Estonia, and Lithuania joined the EU that year and the legal framework for the remaining FSU countries tightened as the migration to Germany had caught the attention of the Israeli government (Kranz, 2016a). By then, however, the Russophone newcomers had become the numerical majority in the "German" Jewish communities, both East and West (Kessler, 1997). The ambiguous minority of resident Jews was supposed to integrate them—begging the question of what these Jews were supposed to be integrated into (Kessler, 1997), as the small existing community was just slowly coming to terms with being residents, and not sojourning in Germany themselves. A significant number of Jews still dwelled on the myth of packed suitcases that reified the trauma underpinning the symbolic—and actual—packed suitcases, ambiguities that persisted in the third generation (Brumlik, 1998).

Symbolic or actual, the third generation of locally raised Jews evinced higher rates of psychopathologies than did their non-Jewish peers (Frerker, 1998). Even those unaffected by psychopathologies were of two minds about whether they were living in Germany or just sojourning (Ranan, 2014). Some left for Israel or other countries (Kranz, 2015a); others felt at home in Germany (Kranz, 2016a; Mendel, 2010). Relations between "locally raised Jews" and "Russians" are sometimes tense as the two populations entertain different notions of Jewishness in a reflection of their collectively infused and individually different biographies (Kessler, 2002). As these groups exist side by side, Jews from other countries are finding their way to Germany. The most significant group among them is the Israeli one, most of whose members belong to their native country's third generation and whose identities diverge from both groups previously mentioned, as our research found. Generally speaking, Jews in Germany have begun to show their diversity and vitality publically to an extent not evinced since the Nazi devastation, if not the Weimar Republic period, as intra-Jewish tensions over community membership or burial provisions may even find their way to courts of law.

Methodology

Our study of Israeli migrants in Germany relies on information that we collected using an online survey, face-to-face semistructured interviews, and ethnographic methods, including participant observation of individuals, groups, and social gatherings, ranging from family events to public, religious, and cultural ones. The integration of quantitative and qualitative data has been gaining strength in social science research, and in our case it prompted us to question the term that we initially used, *Israeli immigrants*, as we learned that immigration, emigration, and (ambivalent) migration coexist. This allowed us to adopt an approach that combines the best of both major methodological schools and mitigates some of the weaknesses associated with using only one of them (Bryman, 1988). The quantitative and qualitative data were collected simultaneously between the autumn of 2014 and the autumn of 2015; qualitative data were gathered on an ongoing basis. Our study focuses solely on native-born Israeli Jews.

The questionnaire used in our survey was uploaded to the web through the use of Qualtrics software. It comprised seventy-five items that were introduced under nine major headings (in the following order): *personal characteristics* such as year of birth, gender, country of birth, and marital status; *education*, referring to studies both in Israel and in Germany, as well as area of specialization; *language and culture*, that is, proficiency in Hebrew, proficiency in German, and consumption of Israeli press and websites; *employment*, mainly focusing on employment status and occupation; *geography*, at both origin and destination and including changes in place of residence after settlement in Germany; *familial and social ties* such as the frequency of telephone and electronic contacts with family and friends in Israel, frequency of visits to Israel, ties with Israeli family members and friends who reside in Germany, relations with local Jews, as well as with non-Jewish Germans; *reasons for immigration and identity* be it Israeli, Jewish, or German identity; *satisfaction and well-being*, which distinguishes between questions relating to Israel and others relating to Germany; and, finally, *political worldview and religio-ethnic identification*, reflecting attitudes and behaviors.

We used several methods to spread the word about our study and encourage Israelis in Germany to visit the website and fill in the questionnaire: placing an advertisement in the most important magazine of Israelis in Germany *Spitz*; social networking on Facebook; personal approaches by the principal investigators and their assistants (i.e., using "organic social networks," cf. Noy, 2008); and a "snowball" technique among respondents who gave their email addresses and were asked to encourage their Israeli friends to fill in the questionnaire. In total, over the course of a year, 603 people took the questionnaire. We excluded 8 of them from our analysis because they indicated that they were not Jewish (under the Law of Return provisions) and 11 because they had immigrated to Germany as minors. Hence, our quantitative findings pertain to 584 respondents.

The research employed a range of qualitative methods. We worked within the framework of multi-sited ethnography (Marcus, 1995), a conceptualized method that implies working in/out of the world system (Wallerstein, 1974) and gathering any kind of data, regardless of its initial nature. Data are collected across the whole spectrum, and it does not privilege micro or macro structure (Behar, 1996). It may be described as opportunistic (Anderson, 2013), as it seeks underlying structures but does not superimpose them.

This approach also implies that neither macro nor micro structures are privileged; they are seen as mutually dependent (Behar, 1996). What this meant for us is that, apart from ethnographic observations and interviews, we had to complement the research by consulting archival, legal, and historical sources, alongside digital anthropology (Horst and Miller, 2012) focusing specifically on social media (Facebook, in particular), and analyzing any kind of available print and online media. We conducted media searches on the basis of key words to tackle specific issues; read daily, weekly, and monthly publications in Hebrew, English, and German indiscriminately; and checked sources that the research participants sent us or to which they referred us.

The families and friends of the two field anthropologists of this project were involved in the fieldwork, a common practice among anthropologists (Cassel, 1994). The difference was that the anthropologists who wrote essays in the Cassel collection traveled abroad to their fieldwork location, while the two anthropologists who conducted ethnographic fieldwork on this project worked in their country of permanent residence, as well as within their cities of residence. By that token, they never left the field, but conducted fieldwork at home (Okely, 1996). They used their personal networks to generate contacts and, due to their different personal positioning within the broader Israeli (Jewish) society, these networks overlapped only in small part. Despite these differences, both did their fieldwork within the idiom of anthropology of experiences (Rosaldo, 1988). The fieldwork was conducted in Hebrew, German, and English, the choice of language usually being negotiated within the fieldwork situation. To attract respondents, both anthropologists posted calls for participation in social-media outlets and distributed flyers that describe the research project. This amplified the heterogeneity of the research participants and surmounted the homophily that commonly attaches itself to organic social networks (Noy, 2008). One of the anthropologists also participated in conferences, public plenaries, and other events to publicize the project. Thus, she gained contacts with Israelis across Germany and earned the trust of local gatekeepers who had been out of reach until then.

Even though the ethnographic data retrieved were very rich and complemented the quantitative outcomes, the research team also decided to conduct semistructured open-ended interviews across Germany. The large majority of these interviews took place in person, at a location chosen by the participants, and all were transcribed. All interviewees had participated in the survey and knew about the research project before being approached for an interview.[2]

Plan of the Book

This book is set within the thematic context of present-day international migration in general, and migration to Germany in particular. It concerns itself with Israeli Jews who left their homeland, Israel, where the national ideology—Zionism—is a paramount component of group identity and solidarity, and where the dynamic process of nation-building, including its security, economic, cultural, social, and legal realms, still continues. Further, it attempts to explore these migrants' choice of Germany as their destination and to probe their integration into the society of a country that the Israeli collective memory still associates with the most traumatic event in Jewish history and a rather recent one at that—the Holocaust, an inescapable theme in the everyday Israeli discourse (Cohen and Kranz, 2017; Lustick, 2017). At the same time, the history of National Socialism—as the German form of fascism—is still both the biggest challenge in German history and the history of 'the' Germans, especially with respect to its founding ideology of *Volksgemeinschaft* (Sünker, 2006), and 'the' challenge in politics and pedagogy to prevent Auschwitz again as Adorno called or phrased it (Sünker and Otto, 1997). Hence, Israelis in Germany carry a "double burden"—having left Israel and having reached out to Germany and Germans. This is somewhat of a paradox, as a number reported having left Israel out of conviction (Amit, 2018) or based on a general feeling of unhappiness and inability to accomplish within the Israeli structures (Merkur, 2019), yet they mourned and lamented (Dekel, 2020), evidencing just how ambiguous migration can be, and that a migrant might encounter a permanent feeling of out-of-placeness (Merkur, 2019).

This book is composed of five chapters, each incorporating both quantitative and qualitative materials. These five chapters reflect our analysis of migration and potential integration into a host society as a multistage process. To a large extent, each stage lays the foundation for, and affects, the succeeding one, yielding a comprehensive analysis of the issues discussed. The Conclusion advances and discusses several synthetic conclusions.

Chapter 2 focuses on the background of the migrants in their country of origin, Israel. It describes and investigates their familial extraction, including that associated with Germany and Nazi-occupied areas, reasons for leaving Israel, reasons for choosing Germany as their new country, and the reaction of family and friends to their decision to move to Germany. Chapter 3 looks at the migration and settlement process. We examine the sociodemographic characteristics of Israeli migrants on their arrival, trace the chronology of migration, their spatial dispersion in Germany, and plans for the future, namely, to stay in Germany, return to Israel, or move to a new country. We also assess the extent to which the background factors determine the settlement patterns and sociodemographic characteristics of our immigrant population. Chapter 4 calls attention to integration into the general society, using such dimensions as proficiency in the local language, citizenship, ownership of property, and, for those who are married, whether their spouse is German or not. We evaluate the effect of major factors associated with the two earlier stages—background and migration and settlement, on integration. We find what appears to be some order among the dimensions of integration, such as language and citizenship, playing a role in shaping the others. Thereafter, chapter 5 discusses identity and identification. Attention is paid to each of the migrants' three identities—Israeli, Jew, and German. To make these inquiries, the data are treated by several different but complementary approaches, including analysis of the structure of group identification, descriptive analysis of the strength of identity and identification, and analysis of the determinants of group belonging and commitment. This investigation, of course, is reinforced by insights from the in-depth open interviews with our Israeli informants in Germany. The last empirical part, chapter 6, inquires into Israeli migrants' perceptions and experience of antisemitism and how they assess the hostility toward Israel in present-day Germany.

Each empirical chapter concludes with a summary of its main findings. The Conclusion synthesizes the analyses and discusses the meaning of the observations regarding trends in Israeli society, the encounter of the Israeli migrants with the history of the host society, and the significance of the newcomers for Jewish life in Germany seven decades after the Holocaust. *En passant*, it also illuminates the unique contribution of this study to the existing corpus of knowledge on Israeli-Jewish/German-non-Jewish relations, as well as to the literature on modern Jewish migration, transnationalism, and diasporism.

Chapter 2

At Home in Israel

The Interplay of Motivation and Rejection

Voluntary migration between developed countries involves ongoing deliberation of gains and losses. The balance between push factors at origin and pull incentives at destination does not always maintain equilibrium. This is mainly true when one takes into account not only economic and professional considerations but also of the social and cultural difficulties that arise when the primary migrant and his or her accompanying family members attempt to adjust to their new environment. Likewise, under conditions of free flows, migrants can always return to their home country (Lee, 1966; Massey et al., 1993; Wolpert, 1965).

People may also assess alternative destinations from historical, ideological, political, and religious perspectives. If a certain place has been seared into the collective memory of a people as the site of persecution, alienation, and mass violence, members of this people may feel uncomfortable migrating, returning to, or settling there. Likewise, people who reside in their homeland, especially if it is in the midst of a nation-building process, may be exposed to ideologies and social attitudes that stigmatize or single out those who leave the country and may interpret their act as the prioritization of personal and material cravings over the public welfare and collective commitment (Sobel, 1986).

Insofar as a country is in an ongoing conflict with its neighbors, the threat to personal safety may constitute a push factor for migration. Concern about acute religious coercion may encourage citizens to seek a more tolerant and open environment. Conversely, individuals who define themselves as belonging to a specific ethnic or ethno-religious group may wish to reside in what they construe as their homeland, where peers constitute the majority of the population and determine the local culture and way of life. This dovetails with the concept of social capital (to which we add cultural capital), namely "migrant networks . . . of interpersonal ties that link migrants, former migrants, and non-migrants in origin and destination areas through the bond of kinship, friendship, and shared community origin" (Massey, 1988: 396).

This combination of economic and lifestyle considerations, on the one hand, and particularistic group factors, on the other hand, is typical of the migration of Israeli Jews to Germany. Below, we portray the familial background of Israeli émigrés in Germany and ask whether it is associated with World War II Germany or other Nazi-occupied areas in Europe; the role of Holocaust memory in the home where they were raised; reasons for emigrating, in general, and the specific choice of Germany as their destination, in particular; and the reaction of family and friends to these decisions. Analysis of the survey data and our respondents' remarks and expressions, complemented by primary materials from the Israeli media (both in Israel and in Germany), yield insights into background characteristics and their interrelations.

Family Background

The Jewish population of Israel is very heterogeneous. It is comprised of people from many ethnic and national backgrounds, reflecting immigration from dozens of countries in Europe, America, Oceania, Asia, and North and South Africa. Jews from Germany migrated to British Mandate Palestine even before the State of Israel was founded. One rather small wave of 2,000 to 3,000 immigrants arrived before 1933, as part of the Yishuv (the organized Jewish presence in the mandate area) (Worman, 1970). A sizable wave of around 53,000 people, emigrated—or, to be more precise, fled—from Nazi Germany between 1933 and 1941 (Lavsky, 2011)—some 10 percent of the Jewish population in Germany at the beginning of this period (Bodemann, 2008). German-born Jews continued to move to Israel after statehood was declared: slightly more than 20,000 between 1948 and 2014 (Israel Central Bureau of Statistics, 2015). This paltry migration over such a lengthy time owes itself to the very few Jews who had remained in

Germany after the foundation of the State of Israel and after the United States liberalized its visa policies.

As the refugees/immigrants from Germany aged and many died, the most recent Israeli census carried out in 2008 found 25,004 people who had been born in Germany. Many more, 82,240, while not born in Germany, indicated that at least one of their parents had been born there. Overall, we estimate more than 100,000 people of German background in Israel today. If we had information on grandparents' place of birth, we would find even more Israeli citizens who are related to someone of German extraction.

Between 2000 and 2010, 25,051 Israeli citizens were renaturalized in Germany (Kranz, 2016b); in 2016, some 1,080 more followed suit (Destatis, 2017a: 71). Among them, eighty-seven (Destatis, 2017a: 98) were descendants of German citizens, indicating that Israelis in Germany itself obtain German citizenship even if they are not descendants of German Jews under the entitlement granted to them by section 116 of the Basic Law (1949). In an interview in 2015, the German Embassy in Israel estimated that 100,000–200,000 additional Israelis can naturalize as German citizens. As it turned out, after new directives came into place in late 2019, more potential German citizens emerged than expected, meaning the number of Israelis with German ancestry is higher than estimated. The directives regulate the details of renaturalization. Besides the Basic Law, an applicant must be eligible under the subordinate Citizenship Law. The application of the latter is guided by specific directives, issued by the Federal Ministry of the Interior that regulates citizenship issues. Three hundred individuals applied through the Tel Aviv Embassy in the first months of 2020; overall the response to new directives was overwhelming, according to interviews conducted in 2019 and 2020, with the Embassy and the Federal Ministry of the Interior. Some of the applicants had been declined before, others had never applied, and still there were those who would have satisfied the old, more stringent, legal requirements but had reservations about applying.

Notably, a sizable number of Israelis who hold German citizenship reside in Israel. One of them is Adi Birk, whose parents provisioned her with a German passport some thirty years ago, when she was a young child. She received citizenship due to her grandfather being a German citizen. Her father was born in Germany and was raised there until he moved to Israel in his twenties. For Birk, German citizenship is part of an identity that was passed on to her from home. As she describes it, "Unlike other families that came from Germany and boycotted German products, we always bought Bosch. Germany was [my grandmother's] home, her culture of origin, along with our being Israelis. I feel that it's part of my identity" (Noyman, 2013: 4). Birk's son acquired German citizenship by descent because female German citizens have been able to confer on German citizenship since 1975. Thus far, Birk has not put her German passport to special use and does not know if and when it may help her in the future (Noyman, 2013).

In addition, Israel has a large population of Holocaust survivors. The latest report of the Foundation for the Benefit of Holocaust Victims in Israel estimated their number at 190,000 in 2015. This group includes any individual who lived in an area that had been under Nazi rule or who was directly affected by the Nazi regime at any time between 1933 and 1945. Also included are people who were forced to leave their homes because of the Nazi regime (Jewish Displaced Persons [DPs]). Accordingly, this number takes into account German Jews who reached Mandate Palestine in the years immediately after the Nazis rose to power. Clearly, if the survivors' children and grandchildren were taken into account, the number of Israelis who fall within the multigenerational bracket of Holocaust survivors, or have a close relative who is a Holocaust survivor, would be much larger.

The findings of our study show that very few Israelis in Germany today are offspring of someone who was born in Germany: only 4 percent of our respondents identified one or both of their parents as natives of Germany (see table 2.1). An even smaller proportion, 1 percent, were raised in a home in which German was the main vernacular. The majority of Israelis in Germany, some two-thirds, are the second generation of native Israelis. Looking at the extended family, however, about one-third (31 percent) of Israelis in Germany have a relative who was born in Germany (most likely a grandparent but possibly also including partners and children). This meshes with Gad Yair's description of his informants, "many [of whom] returned to

Table 2.1. Family Background Associated with Germany and the Holocaust (Percentages)

German/Holocaust Background	Yes	No
Parents (at least one) born in Germany	3.8	96.2
Mother tongue German	0.7	99.3
Family member born in Germany	30.6	69.4
Parents/grandparents Holocaust survivors	55.0	45.0
Family received compensation from Germany	62.9	37.1

Germany with German citizenship—a present from a grandfather or a grandmother who exiled from there during the Holocaust" (2015: 19).[1] A larger proportion, 55 percent, indicated that they have a parent or a grandparent who is a Holocaust survivor. The last-mentioned groups probably overlap, that is, some of those who are Holocaust survivors were born in Germany.

A more comprehensive assessment of family background associated with the Holocaust in general and Germany in particular may be provided by the proportion of those whose families received compensation from West Germany (most likely within the framework of the 1952 Luxemburg Reparation Agreement between the State of Israel and the Federal Republic of Germany, which provided monthly individual compensation for loss of income and property caused by Nazi persecution and genocide). Nearly two-thirds (63 percent) of Israelis residing in Germany indicated that their families received this kind of financial support (see table 2.1). Notably, about half of our respondents did not reply to this question. It is common in surveys that a large share of respondents refuses to answer questions related to earnings and income. It stands to reason that the families of a large proportion of the refusals did receive compensation but preferred not to confirm it. In the case of German reparations, however, the motive may have been psychological and shame-based, since reparations remain a fraught area (Slyomovic, 2014). Overall, we postulate that the familial background of a majority of Israelis in Germany is strongly rooted in Europe of the Nazi regime and World War II.

Not only does family origin connect the individual with Germany and its Jewish past—another important element is the extent to which the memory of the Holocaust was significant at home during childhood. Several studies show that this memory remains a paramount factor of Jewish identity in Israel. For example, in a survey from 2009, 98 percent of respondents termed it very or somewhat important for them to remember the Holocaust as part of their Jewish and Israeli identity (Israel Democracy Institute, 2011). The anthropologist Carole Kidron (2004) refers to the prevalence of such a memory as a manifestation of cultural trauma, which the sociologist Gad Yair (2015) considers essential to understanding the formation of the Israeli national character, while the political scientist Ian S. Lustick (2017) defines it as the interpretive template of political life in Israel. Similarly, two-thirds of respondents in a survey on religiosity in Israel in 2013 defined remembering the Holocaust as essential for the meaning of Jewishness to them personally; this indicator ranked highest among seven indicators of Jewish identity (which included living in Israel and observing Jewish law)

(Pew Research Center, 2016). We phrased the question slightly differently because it was our purpose to assess the extent to which the Holocaust was essential to the Jewish identity of the home in which respondents were raised. We found that a majority (59 percent) were raised in homes where the Holocaust played a very or somewhat important role in their Jewish identity (see figure 2.1).

Substantial differences exist according to familial experiences during the Holocaust. The Holocaust is most central for Jewish identity among people whose close family members are Holocaust survivors: more than one-third (35 percent) of people from such a background indicated that the Holocaust was somewhat important and another 42 percent that it was very important, as against 21 percent and 15 percent, respectively, of respondents who numbered no Holocaust survivors among their kin. That about half of the Israelis in Germany have family who are Holocaust survivors, and that among most of them the Holocaust was an important component of Jewish identity during childhood, suggests that moving to Germany may impose a special burden on top of that of leaving a home country and adjusting to a new environment.

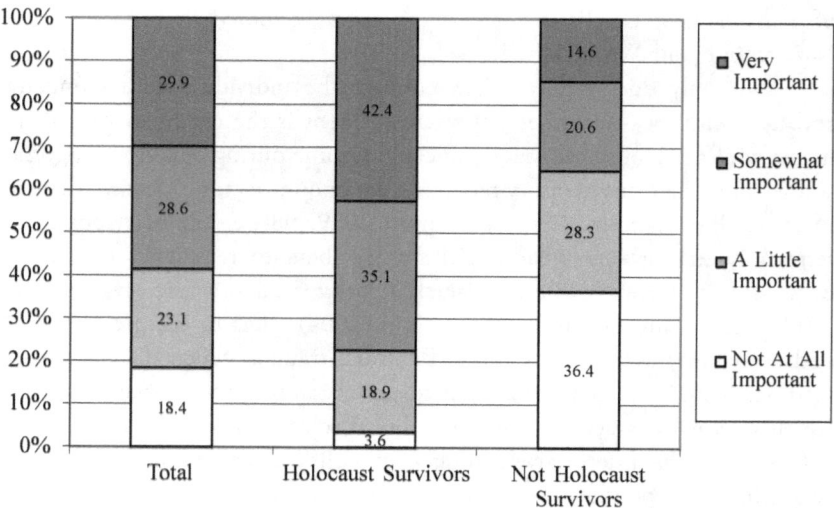

Figure 2.1. Importance of the Holocaust at Home of Upbringing, by Family Background (Percentages).

When the role of the Holocaust was investigated in our interviews and, more so, in our ethnographic fieldwork, a highly nuanced picture emerged: respondents connected the history of the Jewish people to themselves as growing up as Israeli Jews in Israel and being exposed to the Holocaust in their families, among their peer groups, and at school, as well as in their migration to Germany. The key difference lay in previous interactions with all things German, which occurred not only among the descendants of *yekkes*, as Germany had been running a vast array of cultural and educational programs in Israel and for Israelis. Our interview partners as well as other research participants who had taken part in educational exchanges such as ConAct or specific scholarship programs, related differently to Germans and, in particular, to the sounds of the German language, which to them was not the shock factor that it was to Israeli Jews who had not interacted with German speakers before (Katz, 2011; Oz-Salzberger, 2001; Yair, 2015). That both Germany and Israel are supportive of these contacts and exchange programs is evident in the establishment of a new youth-exchange institution per agreement between the relevant German and Israeli ministers in November 2018. Even though the absolute number of participants in these programs is small, they act as multipliers. Two of us, Dani Kranz and Heinz Sünker, gave evidence of this through their involvement in the Short Term NRW Scholarship Program in which the Bergische Wuppertal University takes part, sponsored by the Ministry of Culture and Science of the German State of North Rhine–Westphalia.

Even so, the individual and collective trauma of the Shoah has left its traces, some of which are evidenced surprisingly in the émigrés' perceptions, that is, their navigation of a mythical time (Kranz, 2020b) that bears traces of trauma (Kranz, 2018d; 2020b). As most of the émigrés fall into the age bracket of third-generation Holocaust survivors, they had not expected to have such strong, emotional reactions to what was experienced as random triggers. Trains, for example, could trigger reactions and turn from trivial means of public transportation to "those trains," meaning trains used for deportation, or perfectly polite conduct (by German standards) could be interpreted as "cold." What was experienced as "German efficiency" could be related to the mechanisms that facilitated deportations, while the restitution of German citizenship, a highly complex, fraught, and legally dynamic area that contains serious obstacles could lead to frustrated outbursts—"They killed my family, give me back *my* citizenship!"—while legally, the German administrator concerned simply followed law, procedure, and binding directives. A particular pointed matter was their being surrounded by the sounds of the German language, as Guy Katz (2011) illuminated in his research on German/Israeli business negotiations. While rationally the migrants realized that German is merely the language spoken in Germany, its sounds triggered specific reactions and reminded them of what they had heard about Germans while growing up in Israel. Still, most of the interview and fieldwork partners adjusted to the foreign sounds rather quickly. Typically, reactions to the German soundscape served as a trigger in the very first phase only. Gad Yair (2015) refers to the perception of Germany by Israelis as "through scratched eyes," but not only the eyes but also the ears and indeed the whole body were affected. As stated before, Israelis who had interacted with Germans and had heard German before did not react in this manner because their relations with Germans had taken place in more diverse and often personal ways. To these Israelis Germans, and Germany, were not alien.

Israelis whose partners and spouses are German—most often German non-Jews—stand out in this regard: they had already accustomed themselves to the sounds of the German language and lived in intimate contact with Germans. The prominence of the Shoah varied among these couples; it was more dominant if the Israeli partner was Ashkenazi (of European extraction) than if he or she was Mizrahi (of Asian or North African origin; cf. Shohat, 1999). Thus, while data collected in Israel indicate that the Shoah is a strong point of reference for the Israeli Jewish population, in general, the different family histories of Ashkenazim and Mizrahim point to different long-term effects (Goodman and Mizrahi, 2008); Tunisian and Libyan Jews might be an exception, as these countries were occupied by Germany and/or Italy (Boum and Stein, 2018). This is to say, our data confirms the existing trend but as the overall amount of self-identified Mizrahim in our sample was small it needs to be treated with caution.

Interestingly, the perception of the German language, possibly coupled with anxiety over not understanding it and being foreign in Germany, was much stronger among the émigrés than was their reaction of the numerous memorials all over Germany in the initial phase, although the language issue ebbed away fast. The memorials registered with them even though they did not necessarily catch on because they were designed according to the German memorial culture. Visits to memorial sites were most often limited to requests by visiting family or friends. The émigrés themselves hardly frequented the memorials unless their jobs touched on German/Jewish or German/Israeli matters, memory studies, history, or the like. This finding is not counterintuitive: had their transmitted trauma of the Shoah been too pronounced, they would have not emigrated to Germany to begin with.

However, individual Israeli émigrés occasionally tell Shoah jokes as a coping mechanism (Kranz, 2020a) when they feel overwhelmed by their migration situation or when they experience a strong and unexpected issue that raises the Shoah as a point of reference, as evidenced from a snippet of a fieldwork conversation during the so-called refugee crisis in the summer of 2015: "The Germans are so good at managing stuff. All these refugees [. . .] it's like back in the day of the camps. They just get things done." This and similar quotes indicate intersections: of "the refugees" and being a migrant in Germany, of being descendants of Jewish refugees to Palestine/Israel and the notion of "camps" as part of the transmission of the trauma. Our interview partner witnessed what is perceived as the immense efficiency that constitutes part of a disembodied bureaucracy (Graeber, 2012; Herzfeld, 1991) and remains central in the way Israelis imagine—and experience—Germany. This construction, in turn, is also prevalent in perceptions of bureaucratic experiences of Germany: the narratives vary between the poles of the "evil, unwelcoming, cold" bureaucrat and a system "where things are clearer. The forms are annoying, but it is clear what they want from you," which this respondent contrasted with bureaucratic experiences in Israel. Thus, in rather impersonal encounters with Germans, the Shoah, an event typified by depersonalization and deindividualization (Bauman, 1991), gained momentum, while in personal encounters it was less commonly an issue. The latter tendency relates directly to age, as most participants were third-generation Israelis who may have had personal encounters with individual Germans in exchange programs or with German tourists in Israel. Indeed, some Israelis recounted friendly encounters with German tourists, volunteers, or participants in programs run by the German Academic Exchange Service (Deutscher Akademischer Austausch Dienst [DAAD]) or the Goethe Institute.

Why Did They Leave Israel?

People migrate for different reasons that one may group in rubrics such as economic factors, family and social considerations, and political unrest. In addition, personal considerations associated with biography may drive spatial relocation for some while others turn to migration in search of lifestyle changes. Often, migration is not explained by one factor but by many factors, ranked in importance variously in view of individuals' demographic and socioeconomic affinities.

Such is the case among Israeli émigrés in Germany. We presented our respondents with a suite of six reasons for leaving Israel that relate to the situation in their home country: political security, inability to progress professionally, inability to progress economically, search for better educational opportunities, resentment of the religious establishment for its involvement in everyday life, and being tied to a family member and/or friends. The respondents were asked to rank the centrality of each reason in their decision to emigrate, from not central at all (0) to a little (1), somewhat (2), and very (3). Thus, the sum of scores for the six reasons together ranges from 0, for those who attribute no centrality to any of the reasons in their decision to emigrate, to 18, for those who judge all six reasons to be very central. Notably, the respondents could also opt to mark "other."

For 16 percent of Israelis in Germany, none of the specified six reasons had anything to do with the decision to emigrate (see figure 2.2). Some chose "other"; if they specified, they offered a variety of reasons, including climate, dislocation, mentality, and stressful environment, among others. Those who scored 1–3 (8 percent) either indicated one reason that had a very central impact on their decision to leave Israel or mentioned two or even three reasons, each of lesser centrality. Clearly, those with scores of 4 or higher left Israel for more than one reason; they constituted the majority

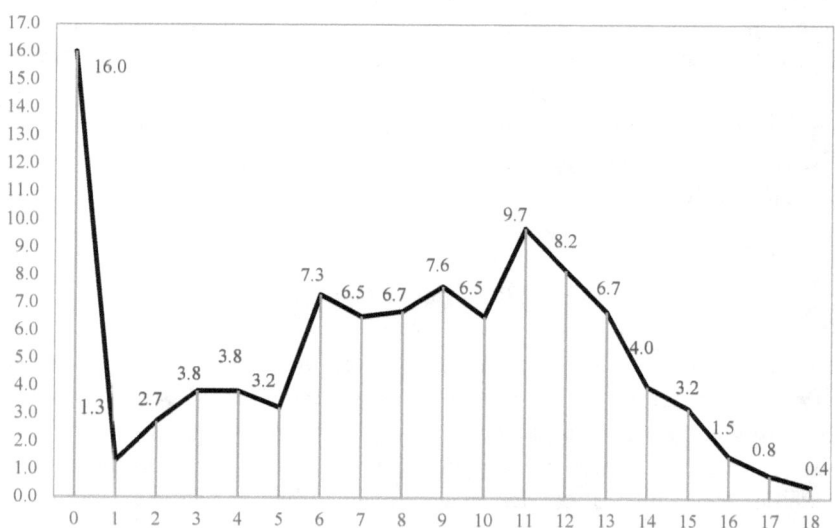

Figure 2.2. Percentages Score of Reasons for Emigrating from Israel.

(nearly three-fourths) of émigrés. The approximately 6 percent who scored 15 or higher ranked five of the six reasons as "very" central.

With the exception of joining family or friends, a majority indicated that each reason had at least a little centrality (little/somewhat/very) in the decision to emigrate (see figure 2.3). The paramount reasons are economic and professional: four out of ten specified the lack of opportunities for economic development as a very central consideration and another two in ten ranked this reason as somewhat central (63 percent together). Only slightly behind was the inability to progress professionally: approximately one-third assigned it much central and slightly more than one-fifth considered it somewhat central (57 percent together). Almost half (46 percent) ranked the involvement of the religious establishment in life in Israel as very or somewhat central in their decision to leave the country. Slightly less salient but nevertheless significant were educational considerations, which 42 percent judged to be a very or a somewhat central reason for their leaving Israel; and the political-security situation in the country (42 percent). Ten percent of the émigrés were very or somewhat tied to a family member or friends.

Interestingly, neither the interviewees nor the Israelis in fieldwork conversations had to be prompted to talk about the reasons for their emigration. Having been raised on the Zionist ideology of Israel's being the Jewish state

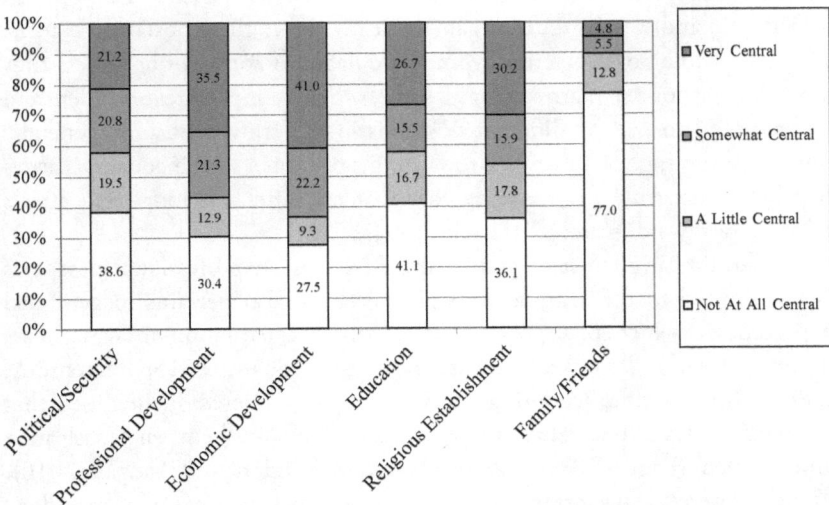

Figure 2.3. Reasons for Emigrating from Israel (Percentages).

and of their being part, as Israeli Jews, of the Israeli Jewish collective that is responsible for its survival, reasons or justifications for leaving surfaced immediately. The way these reasons were framed, however, differed in accordance with the perception of the interviewer, indicating that emigration is emotionally charged and that the narrative of leaving Israel was coded to match the interviewer's expectations (Cohen and Kranz, 2017). In this sense, the migration/emigration/immigration narrative constitutes an emotional currency that takes a personalized shape and at the same time documents the interaction of the encounter with the researcher (Angrosino, 1989). It is true that no somewhat neutral formal or informal interview took place, but the nonneutrality yielded decisive insights into the émigrés' emotional landscapes. Yet, we did not seek migrants with specific profiles in terms of, say, age, gender, and political attitudes to understand a narrowly defined group such as political emigrants (Amit, 2018).

Economic and professional factors were mentioned as key reasons for leaving Israel. The cost of living relative to income was experienced as suffocating. This is all the more striking because the majority of our respondents classified themselves as Ashkenazi, meaning they had access to the white privileges and high educational attainments, which are associated with Ashkenazi Jews. Even so, their privileges and educational accomplishments reached only so far; they were limited not only by social structures but also by the structure of the Israeli labor market, which is impacted by the country's geopolitical situation (Hever, 2014). Israel is a militarized society and individuals' postings in the army affect their postarmy careers. However, while both men and women are liable to conscription unless they are ultra-Orthodox, married, or in some other exempt category, men and women tend to occupy different positions in the army, with men generally obtaining the higher and more rewarding positions. This inequality carries over into postarmy life, meaning that woman suffer the long-term effects of their "army non-careers" (Izraeli, 2004).

The limiting effect of gendered differences on professional prospects is not limited to the army and its aftermath. It also pertains to gendered expectations, which place women in a particular situation in which caring, marriage, and motherhood are expected (Donath, 2015; Remennick, 2002). This specific gendering reflects unique gendered inequalities that sociologists relate to as religiously enshrined inequality between Jewish men and women (Fogiel-Bijaoui, 2016; Halperin-Kaddari and Yadgar, 2010). These gendered expectations are also reflected in Israeli women, regardless of their ethno-religious group, birthing nearly three children compared to fewer than two children per woman in Germany (OECD, 2018). The weight of this "gender role," motherhood, and Israel-style inequality was experienced as particularly onerous by female migrants who, as one put it, "opted out." By the same token, female Israeli migrants in Germany fit into a pattern that was discovered among Israeli émigrés in the US (Rebhun and Lev-Ari, 2010) and in global, comparative data as a general trend (Gold, 2002).

Gendered issues, however, were not the only reasons for the émigrés' limited career prospects in Israel. The specifics of the Israel labor market, which directly relate to the country's geopolitical situation, have repercussions in the importance of the high-tech sector. This sector benefits from the experience that conscripts in specific branches of the army amass during their service, creating a feedback loop among the army, the business, and the labor market. This means that specific skill sets that match the demands of the high-tech sector and related professions (such as economics and other life-sciences as well as law) benefit only individuals who have specific training, expertise, and degrees. The majority of our respondents and interview partners did not fit these parameters: they held degrees in the social sciences and the humanities, which are in much less demand, creating a lack of career opportunities for them (Cohen and Kranz, 2017).

The small size of the Israeli population and economy places limits on options by default. The size of the German population, roughly ten times that of Israel's, makes for a very different labor and consumer market, offering niche products and giving individuals who hold non-high-tech degrees more and better opportunities. The nexus of the Middle East conflict, Israel's militarization, and the structure of the Israeli economy and labor market sometimes untethered itself only after emigration. "In Israel, you are in this bubble," one respondent said. "Everybody reads *Ynet* and talks about it," reasoned one interview partner. Another offered a contrasting perspective: "I couldn't deal with the situation [*ha-matsav*] anymore, it disgusts me. Actually, many of us left in disgust." These quotes indicate that despite the prevalence of the combined economic and professional factors, the awareness context (Glaser and Strauss, 1965) of these two Israelis, who share the same sociodemographic, educational, and gender profile, is different. The second respondent used an Israeli Hebrew figure of speech, *ha-matsav*, as a discursive shorthand with which he pinpointed the effects of the Middle East conflict. The first respondent, in contrast, came to understand the social structures—and *ha-matsav*—only upon emigration.

Much like the mix of professional and economic issues, the political situation of the country and the role of religion there were regularly conjoined. Most of our research participants were born after 1975, and many remembered the first Palestinian uprising ("Intifada") in the late 1980s, and described the period of the Oslo accords as an "era of hope." Subsequently, they rued the collapse of that hope with the second Intifada in the early 2000s, the intensification of warfare, the hardening of political lines, and what was experienced as an increasingly tight grip of the Orthodox religious establishment on the public sphere. As one Israeli who works in human-rights law in Israel bitterly remarked, "Civil society? We've been losing it" (quoted in Kranz, 2018a: 57). Even though these parameters are interlinked, however, they need careful untangling in view of the research participants' biographical background. Most of the participants and their interview partners described themselves as Ashkenazi, secular, and politically moderate to left, which means they constitute a minority of Israeli Jews in the country (Wright, 2018), but are also the descendants of the established Ashkenazi elite, whose power and influence are declining (Fischer, Hotam, and Wexler, 2012; Harpaz, 2012; Shenhav, 2008; Yadgar, 2010). These descendants are faced with a changing social and political landscape in which Mizrahim and religious Jews, and more so national-religious Jews (Hotam and Wexler, 2014; Scham, 2018), have attained political and cultural hegemony. This changing landscape was referenced in strong terms in some of our fieldwork conversations in Germany, in which individuals complained acridly about what was happening to "their" country, meaning one with an Ashkenazi-dominated secular society. This argument is somewhat paradoxical, as some of the strongest drivers of Israel's political Judaization are Ashkenazim. A prime example is Benjamin Netanyahu (Likud), who since the mid-1990s has been stressing the importance of "what's good for the Jews" as opposed to what is good for the Israelis (Abulof, 2009). Another Ashkenazi, Naftali Bennett first prominent in the Jewish Home party, now in the religious-secular New Right party openly embraces Judaism and Jewish values (whatever these are), West Bank settlements, and other rather nationalistic policies that clash with the political attitudes of the majority of our sample population.

Overall, our respondents experienced these political developments as part of a sense of being squeezed into a corner in terms of their self-identity configuration. This experience was exemplified by a statement made in the course of a fieldwork conversation: "Jerusalem [the respondent's hometown] is getting blacker and blacker. Berlin is so liberal by comparison." Black, in the Hebrew discourse, is a code for "religious" because ultra-Orthodox men typically wear black suits or coats. This "blackness," or metaphorical darkness, was contrasted to Berlin, which was experienced as liberal. Again, however, context is needed. This research participant had been living in Berlin for less than three years and, although his German-language skills were developing, they were not developed enough to allow him to pick up on specific figures of speech and social trends. In particular, the general polarization and radicalization of German society that were already under way in Germany at the time of the meeting (late 2015) did not figure into his experience of Berlin: the *Alternative für Deutschland* (*AfD*, Alternative for Germany) that had started as an anti-Euro, anti-EU, nationalist conservative party was morphing into a fully anti-immigration, anti-Muslim, anti-EU/Euro party that carried strong antisemitic undertones. Founded in 2013, it found repercussions on the street, with *Patriotische Europäer gegen die Islamisierung des Abendlandes* (PEGIDA), Patriotic Europeans against the Islamisation of the Occident, which appeared in 2014 in East Germany, and spread to the West. In the 2017 federal election, the *AfD* came out as the third largest party; it also gained very significantly across state and communal levels. This radicalization shifted the German political landscape as well as daily discourse to the right: things could be said in public that had been unimaginable only a short while earlier, and which includes antisemitic tropes (Wodak, 2018).

However, this research participant, like the majority of our quantitative sample, experienced himself first and foremost as Israeli and not as Jewish. Although he is Ashkenazi, the same was observable among the—ostensibly—more religious Mizrahim, who indeed fell into the same parameters as those who self-identified as Ashkenazim, calling into question the utility of the Ashkenazim/Mizrahim binary. "I could only emigrate," one respondent said. "I mean, I'm gay, secular, Mizrahi, from Petah Tikva, and I voted for Meretz" (a left-wing social-democratic party). His comment suggests that the Ashkenazi versus Mizrahi parameter, which remains an emotional Israel-infused currency, may be fallacious, or at least change its meaning, in the diasporic situation in Germany. This finding was all the more incisive when individuals across our sample stressed the role of religion in their daily lives in Israel as a negative factor, suggesting that an unmodified Israeliness (Shoshana, 2016) that unites Israelis exists even as the country undergoes such rapid Judaization (Ghanem, 2011) as to prompt some social scientists to depict its society as a postsecular one (Hotam and Wexler, 2014).

A mixture of reasons for emigrating from Israel recurs in other studies. Amit (2013), for example, cites Yael (not her real name), who claims that life in Israel is difficult and that she has no more energy to struggle with Israelis' aggressive manners. Nonheterosexual or queer Israelis lack a sense of belonging to the Israeli collective and experience continual discrimination and humiliation (Amit, 2018). Gender identity, however, does not stand alone; many members of the queer community belong to the radical Left and are frustrated by their inability to influence and bring hope for a solution to the Israeli-Palestinian conflict (Wright, 2018). In fact, their political activism, which is often anti-Zionist and anti-Israeli in nature, continues after they settle in Germany (Shapira, 2014). Stauber (2017: 180) reports on Yoav (Sapir), a student in Israel specializing in German history and literature, who in 2003 received a fellowship to travel and study for one year in Berlin. Sapir turned down the offer, claiming that he was psychologically unable to go to Germany. Politically active in the right-wing Likud party, he was heartbroken after Israel unilaterally withdrew (disengaged) from the Gaza Strip in 2005. Physically sickened and deep in emotional crisis, he felt unable to continue connecting with the country. Therefore, he applied for a second round of fellowship and was invited to study first in Vienna and then in Berlin (see also, Golan, 2014), where he remains. At the other end of the political spectrum is Ido Porat, a member of the young-activist circle in the Meretz party. Although coming from "an anti-German home, especially because of my mother, whose parents are from Poland" (Stauber, 2017: 181), he attended a German-Israeli-Palestinian student-exchange program in Germany—where he discovered young Germans who expressed interest in the Shoah and acknowledged responsibility for Germans' past crimes. In 2005, he traveled to Germany and spent the next three years in Berlin, studying German and getting better acquainted with German culture. After returning to Israel, he enrolled for graduate studies but also married a recently arrived immigrant from Austria. Together they came to the conclusion that Israel was unwilling to absorb immigrants from anywhere other than the former Soviet Union, and that he would find it more appropriate to study abroad (Stauber, 2017). Some Israelis, especially those of former Soviet origin, felt ambivalent about their Israeli-Jewish identity and their contrasting European cultural orientation (Stauber, 2017). Still others just wanted to be "released from Israel" (Yair, 2015: 75).

The range of reasons for emigration is also documented in the "Packing Alone" section and standalone articles in *Spitz*, the magazine of the Israeli community in Berlin, which published twenty hard-copy issues in 2012–2016. Each iteration of "Packing Alone" told the personal story of an Israeli who had moved to Germany. The first person interviewed, Michael Rimel, was awarded a fellowship for training in the German parliament and was then offered "a position as parliamentarian assistant to the President of the Bundestag, and remained" (Sapir, 2012a: 8). Tal Shaham "wanted to pursue a Master's degree abroad and chose Berlin" (Sapir, 2012b: 10); Micha Kaplan moved to Berlin to learn to play the contrabass (Sapir, 2013b); and Nirit Ben-Yosef, who studied cinema at Tel Aviv University, visited Munich in 1986 to attend a film festival, met a Berliner, and decided to try life in the city (Sapir, 2014b). A love affair was the paramount reason for Albers Ben-Hamo's emigration to Germany (Sapir, 2012c) and for Dorit Levita-Harten's (Saberdlov, 2013). Others, such as Liat Tal, moved because of her work (Sapir, 2013a). There are Israelis who searched for adventure (Onger, 2013; Sapir, 2013c) or left Israel with a friend for a two-month visit, like Yoav Shavit, but was eventually affected by "the knowledge that my friend is here to stay" (Golan, 2015a: 16). Other articles in the magazine broadened the spectrum of factors for leaving Israel, including Israeli political and social circumstances, a general wish not to live in Israel any longer (Shavit, 2012), and an aspiration to greater affluence (materialistic reasons that were emphasized in the 2011 unrest over the high cost of living in Israel and the 2014 "pudding protest") (Lapidot and Ilany, 2015).

From this standpoint, the intra-Israeli differences continued in Germany. The émigrés' situation in Germany was complicated by the strong emotional currency of the Israel/Palestine issue in that country (Atshan and Galor, 2020; Ullrich, 2010). Amid a plethora of pro-Israel and pro-Palestine groups there, Israelis who voiced their opinions encountered the problem of being interpreted through the filter of the German discourse, which is different from that in Israel. Some Israelis were aware of this issue and sought out like-minded individuals to pursue their agenda, while others were caught off-guard. The Israeli émigrés spanned the whole spectrum of political views, from supporters of the Boycott, Divestment, Sanction (BDS) movement to centrists, backers of right-wing policies in Israel, and even exponents of the right-wing AfD, which lobbies against migration and Muslims and depicts itself as "protecting Jews" from Muslims while indulging in historical revisionism about the Nazi era. Indeed, a report by the German domestic intelligence services (*Verfassungsschutz*) highlights the right-wing antidemocratic and antisemitic stances of *AfD* members (Ulrich, Amann, and Knobbe, 2019). Operation Protective Edge in the summer of 2014 raised questions among some respondents about their being away in Berlin while their home country was fighting a war that included missile attacks on its civilian population. For others, this military clash reinforced their conviction that they did not want to live in Israel. For yet others, it substantiated their stance that Israel was using excessive means. Between these contradictory stances—supporting Israel and being ashamed of their Israeliness—the vast majority were trapped in the middle, struggling with ambivalent feelings toward their peers in Israel and toward local Germans (Alon, 2014); the anti-Israeli stances expressed in street protests contributed to this predicament.

To what extent are sociodemographic characteristics associated with each of the push factors? To answer, we interpret our quantitative data through multivariate analysis. This approach assesses the net effect of each sociodemographic variable on a given reason for leaving Israel with all other variables held constant. An allied metric is the power of the overall model to explain variation in the specific reason under investigation (see table 2.2).

Only a few of the preemigration individual characteristics are significant in explaining differences among people in their motivation to leave Israel. The most salient pro-emigration determinant is employment. Those who had worked in Israel before emigration were more likely than the others to cite some of the six reasons as central in their decision to move. This is especially significant for push factors such as the political/security situation, which was found to be significant for émigrés in all types of occupations (but especially among those who had held professional or technical posts or had been artists in Israel), lack of opportunity for professional development, and the religious establishment's involvement in daily life in Israel. Notably, Israeli artists were the most critical of the situation in Israel, with positive and significant effects on four of the six reasons for leaving the country. People who had lived in the West Bank did not leave the country because of the political/security situation in Israel or the power of the country's religious establishment. Similarly, those from northern Israel were not troubled by political/security considerations. While for West Bank settlers this may be explained by a right-wing political orientation and a strong Jewish identity (even if they are not religious), for those who lived in the north it likely reflects geographic distance from areas of security tension, which in the past decade has been concentrated largely in the south, facing Gaza, and in terrorist acts in major cities in the center. Another major finding is the positive relation between young age and the desire to acquire higher education. People who had already earned a bachelor's degree in Israel, compared to those lacking an academic diploma, were more likely to leave the country because of political/security considerations and seek more educational opportunities abroad. The insignificance of many of the independent variables suggests that other factors, unrelated to such characteristics as age, gender, education, place of residence in Israel, or employment status, are

Table 2.2. Determinants of Reasons for Emigration from Israel

Preemigration Sociodemographic Characteristics[a]	Reasons for Emigration					
	Political/ Security	Professional Development	Economic Development	Education	Religious Establishment	Family/ Friends
Age 18–24	0.152	0.483	−0.255	1.686*	0.102	−0.778
Age 25–29	−0.391	0.418	−0.363	1.198*	0.050	−0.403
Age 30–34	−0.212	0.247	−0.336	0.588	0.169	0.023
Age 35–39	−0.353	0.065	−0.203	0.089	−0.383	−0.322
Female	−0.020	0.213	0.293	0.261	−0.103	0.221
Other	0.338	1.089	1.907[i]	1.543	10.929	0.944
Matriculation	0.353	0.373	0.059	0.597[i]	0.056	−0.411
Post-secondary	0.727	0.452	0.125	−0.097	0.219	−0.527
BA	1.112*	0.282	0.291	0.609[i]	0.434	−0.227
MA+	0.263	0.322	0.018	0.946*	0.042	−0.518
North and Haifa	−1.060*	−0.276	0.006	0.132	−0.340	−0.474
Tel Aviv and Center	−0.078	−0.311	0.222	−0.079	−0.080	−0.133
South	−0.041	−0.511	−0.236	−0.751	−0.998[i]	0.243
West Bank	−1.603[i]	−1.110	−0.222	−1.220	−1.996[i]	0.055
Professional	1.071*	0.966*	0.478	0.761[i]	1.108*	1.970*
Management	0.853[i]	0.237	−0.114	0.365	0.921[i]	1.521
Technical	1.130*	0.549	0.577	0.594	1.494*	1.727
Sales and services	0.844*	0.562	0.494	0.661	1.061*	1.634
Arts	1.357*	1.537*	1.111[i]	0.595	1.598[i]	1.155
Blue-collar	0.838[i]	0.570	0.217	0.630	0.613	2.004*
Explanatory Power	10.4%	5.6%	4.0%	12.8%	7.1%	5.8%

*Significant at least at the 0.05 level; [i] significant at $P < 0.10$.

[a]Reference categories: age at immigration—40+; gender—male; education—no diploma; area of residence—Jerusalem; occupation—did not work.

more important for understanding why Israelis leave their country. In other words, people with different sociodemographic characteristics who leave Israel do so for much the same reasons.

The efficiency of the sociodemographic characteristics in explaining variations in reasons for emigrating from Israel is especially strong in seeking educational opportunities (13 percent explanatory power) and concern about the political/security situation in Israel (10 percent).

Reasons for Choosing Germany

The choice of Germany as the destination country was also made for other reasons, including opportunities to acquire education, cultural activities, professional and economic mobility, German background, having a German partner, and seeking a challenge. About one in ten (12 percent) expressed a reason other than those mentioned above (see figure 2.4). Those who gave more specific information emphasized the extent of freedom in Germany, a place that is easy to move to, high quality of life, and having German citizenship, which makes the move easier and entitles the new citizen to the full package of benefits that citizenship assures. However, Israelis do not move to Germany to become rich. Germany is not constructed as a land of unlimited opportunity (as many Israelis view the US). Germany

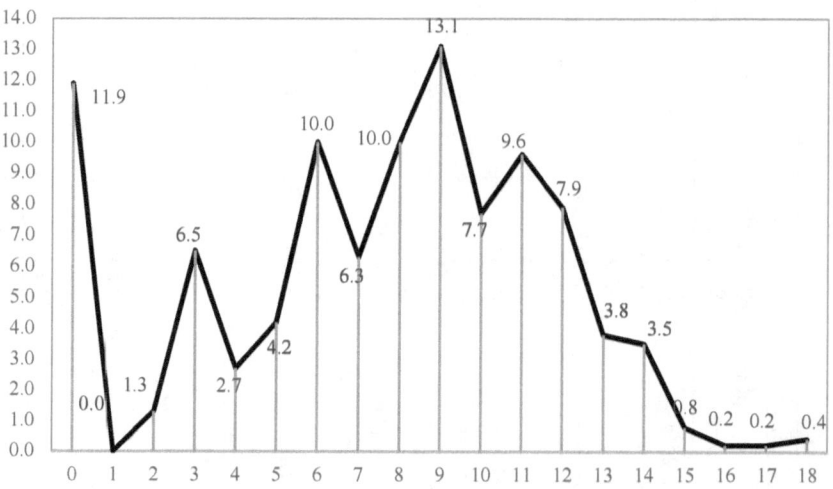

Figure 2.4. Percentages Score of Reasons for Choosing Germany.

does not have a magic pill that enables people to get by easily. One has to work in Germany. In certain occupations, it is true that even noncitizens may receive some supplemental income from the government (Amit, 2013). These opportunities often pertain to funding for the arts or state support for self-employed EU citizens whose earnings fall below a certain threshold. This support for EU citizens is specific to EU treaties, which makes Germany attractive to Israelis who hold German or other EU citizenship in the unlikely event of a crash landing. The Israeli émigrés are knowledgeable about funding and regulations that would allow access to supplementary income, as our ethnographic fieldwork and analysis of social media reveal.

Much like the reasons for emigrating from Israel, 8 percent of those who chose Germany had either one strong reason or as many as three less-central reasons. Slightly more than three-fourths indicated at least two reasons (a score of 4 or higher). Less than 2 percent of the Israelis were attracted to Germany for five reasons, each of which played a very central role (scoring 15+). Judging by the proportion of respondents who scored 15 or over, we postulate that push factors were more decisive in the emigration of Israeli Jews to Germany than were pull factors at destination.

Professional and economic considerations not only explain why people leave Israel; they are also pivotal in attracting them to Germany. As many as 42 percent of respondents specified this as a very central reason and another one-fifth saw it as a somewhat central reason for choosing to

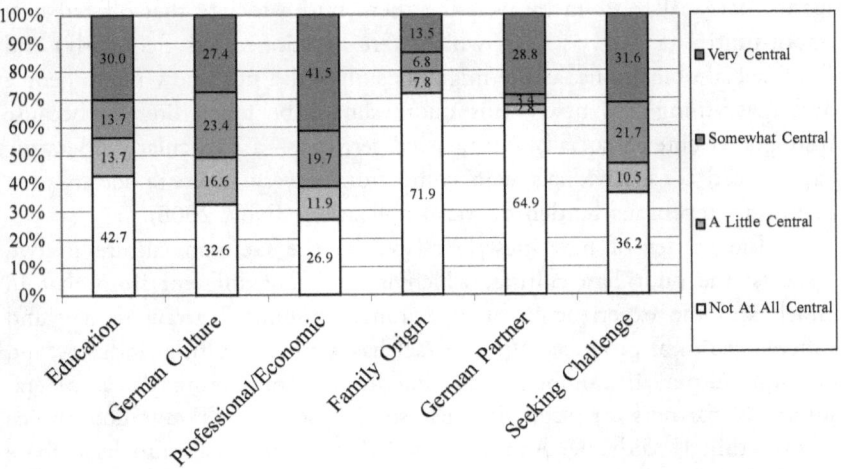

Figure 2.5. Reasons for Choosing Germany (Percentages).

settle in Germany (see figure 2.5). Interestingly, the second most important factor was the search for a challenge, with more than half of the Israelis ranking this reason very (32 percent) or somewhat (22 percent) central. A slightly lower proportion was attracted to Germany because of its cultural opportunities. The remaining reasons—education, family origin, and German partner—figured much less centrally in the decision to move to Germany. Still, more than one-third of respondents had a German partner who had at least some effect on their decision to settle in Germany.

Our respondents described the move to Germany as smooth; it was also aided by the plentiful youth and educational programs that target Israel citizens (Heil, 2011) and specific advantages for Israeli passport holders that ease their way to visas and work permits (Bundesagentur für Arbeit, 2017). This specific blend of factors made Germany an attractive and easy-to-get-to migration destination. Germany was also hyped among Israelis in social media and in conversations among Israelis at home and abroad. "When are you finally going to take me to the [sic] Berlin?" was the rather straightforward demand of an Israeli in Israel to an Israeli who had a (partial) base in Berlin.

Lifestyle issues such as vivid cultural landscape and adventure were brought up in interviews and fieldwork conversations. Adventure in particular may ring oddly in regard to a country such as Germany but as one research participant remarked, "It's like an adult summer camp" (quoted in Cohen and Kranz, 2017: 330). Leaving Israel increased the research participants' personal freedom by ushering them into a society that offered new opportunities (as well as risks, which were mentioned less frequently) and fewer social obligations, as the migrants simply did not know many people and "everything was new." This quote should be taken literally because immigrants enter a socially unchartered territory—a particularly liberating experienced for individuals who come from a very intimate society that carries an enormous burden of social obligations (Noy, 2008).

The matter of new lifestyle related to the German culture in two respects: the quotidian culture, which is markedly different from that in Israel, and the experiencing of a seemingly unlimited array of new and different cultural products. While Israel has a sizable cultural industry and cultural output, it cannot match the diversity of Germany's, as several interview partners stressed. "It's just so diverse. There's so much choice of everything!" said one. Another noted that his son "can also have these multicultural experiences that he wouldn't have in Israel" due to the very different cultural composition and broader diversity of the German population, tracing to the very different migration histories of Germany and Israel.

While Germany experiences permanent migration of individuals who are related neither by kinship nor by ethnicity (Kranz, 2017), Israel knows this kind of migration only marginally (Kemp and Kfir, 2016). However, spatially these "others" are concentrated in the former West of Germany, and in the urban areas including Berlin, where most Israelis live, which means that Israelis experience a very specific kind of Germany. Historically, Germany made a point of attracting "guest laborers" with the intention of rotating them. Many, however, remained in Germany and used chain migration to establish large groups of first-, second-, and third-generation migrants of Turkish, Italian, or Moroccan background who had no historical connection to Germany. The West German city of Düsseldorf homes very significant Moroccan and Japanese populations, for example: many Japanese companies are headquartered in Düsseldorf area, while Moroccans came to the city via chain migration. Cologne and the Rhine-Ruhr area became home to a significant batch of Italians, the documentary *Wie die Pizza in Ruhrgebiet kam* (How Pizza Came to the Ruhr Area, Wilczynski, 2012) depicts the history of a very early Italian restaurant in Gelsenkirchen, a city that lived of heavy industry, which in turn led to the migration of guest workers. Israel did not seek out foreign laborers until the aftermath of the first Intifada; those whom it admitted entered on time-limited visas by default, were not intended to become permanent immigrants, and were not eligible for family reunification. Thus, while an appreciation of the historic German culture existed among our research participants, they were not homesick *yekkes* (Panagiotidis, 2012; Webster, 1995), but third-generation Israelis who wanted to discover their new Germany with its culturally, ethnically, and religiously heterogeneous population.

The two key reasons for emigration to Germany—professional advancement and personal challenge—sometimes became one, when succeeding in Germany was deemed a professional and personal challenge. One Israeli émigré who works as a lawyer outlined the course that he had followed: he had qualified as a lawyer in Israel and then obtained an LLM from a (private) German university on a scholarship, which in turn helped him to get a job with a very prestigious law firm. He felt that he was amassing professionally accomplishments and "learning the whole time." He experienced professional development in parallel with personal development, which handed him a challenge, albeit a positive one. His remarks resembled those of other Israelis who sought to combine personal and professional development.

Partner and spousal migrants experienced this challenge differently. They chose Germany not for individualistic reasons but because their significant other was German. While this gave them a "migration assistant" who could admit them to the social networks of their partner/spouse, they had to negotiate a relationship in a foreign country. Some partner/spousal migrants fared better in this scenario than others. One female partner migrant who was visibly upset stressed that "I have been here for more than fifteen years. I still don't have permanent residence and I have three kids here. I speak German. But really, I don't have anything here but him," underlining that her lack of permanent residence bothered her and that she felt still alien in Germany. Her husband, listening in to the interview, was puzzled; he had thought that she felt fine in Germany, as they had bought a house together and their three fully bilingual children were living with them. His wife mused about her persistent sense of alienation, which was now underscored by the rise of the new right. (The interview was conducted in the summer of 2016.) Still, she remained in Germany because her German spouse and her children were there. Other partner migrants felt differently, at home in Germany and even content to live in the small rural villages whence their German spouses had come. What the overwhelming majority of these partner and spousal migrants shared, however, was partnership/marriage to German or other non-Jews, a complete oddity among Jews in Israel, who in their majority reject marriage to non-Jews (Burton, 2015).

We also examined the relation between each reason for leaving Israel and each reason for settling in Germany. This was done by means of a Pearson test, which yields scores from 1 (a perfect positive correlation) to −1 (the strongest negative correlation), with a value of 0 attesting to no correlation at all. The findings in the Appendix show much consistency between push factors and pull factors. The strongest relation is between leaving Israel in search of educational opportunities and choosing Germany because of the educational programs it has to offer (0.815). Strong coefficients were also found for economic and professional push and pull factors: between each reason concerning inability to develop professionally and economically and opportunities in Germany for professional and economic mobility ($p = 0.653$ and $p = 0.643$, respectively). Another robust relation is between dislike of the involvement of the religious establishment in the way of life in Israel and the German culture (0.415), which is known for official, if incomplete, separation of religion and state.

Young people, respondents who defined their gender as "other," those who held a matriculation certificate or an advanced academic degree, and those who had had professional jobs in Israel were strongly attracted to Germany because of its educational opportunities (see table 2.3). Relative to Israelis who lived in Jerusalem, those who originated in the West Bank were not drawn to Germany for any of the six reasons suggested to them, least of

Table 2.3. Determinants of Choosing Germany

Preemigration Sociodemographic Characteristics[a]	Education	German Culture	Reasons for Immigration Professional/ Economic	Family Origin	German Partner	Seeking Challenge
Age 18–24	1.466*	0.538	0.722[i]	-0.405	0.381	-0.157
Age 25–29	0.956*	0.184	0.335	-0.170	0.212	0.199
Age 30–34	0.272	0.076	0.341	-0.119	0.567	-0.281
Age 35–39	-0.014	-0.331	-0.038	-0.033	-0.499	0.137
Female	0.072	-0.207	0.050	0.203	0.088	0.083
Other	2.292i	0.627	1.530	-0.379	1.501	0.927
Matriculation	0.794*	0.162	0.421	-0.655[i]	-0.433	0.199
Post-secondary	-0.097	-0.027	0.434	-1.033[i]	-0.038	0.067
BA	0.610[i]	0.022	0.525	-0.641*	0.051	-0.219
MA+	0.823*	-0.354	0.761*	-0.426	-0.141	-0.139
North and Haifa	-0.074	-0.591[i]	0.287	-0.175	0.143	0.510
Tel Aviv and Center	-0.366	-0.216	0.045	-0.221	-0.068	0.381
South	-0.760	-0.146	0.334	0.004	-0.412	1.288*
West Bank	-20.466*	-1.627	-0.259	-19.622*	-19.902*	-1.708
Professional	0.944*	1.450*	0.546	0.676	-0.028	0.043
Management	0.554	1.386*	0.807	0.628	0.162	0.159
Technical	0.283	1.168*	0.680	0.079	-0.115	0.988*
Sales and services	0.593	1.203*	0.109	0.466	-0.85	0.124
Arts	0.527	2.037*	1.498*	0.024	-0.107	0.892
Blue-collar	0.713	0.785[i]	0.007	0.651	-0.091	-0.11
Explanatory Power	*15.3%*	*8.8%*	*5.9%*	*4.1%*	*5.2%*	*7.0%*

*Significant at least at the 0.05 level; [i] significant at $P < 0.10$.

[a]Reference categories: age at immigration—40+; gender—male; education—no diploma; area of residence—Jerusalem; occupation—did not work.

all educational opportunities, family background, and partner/spouse. Those who had worked in Israel were powerfully attracted to the German culture; judged by the size of the coefficients, these relations were strongest among those who worked in the arts. Young age (18–24), advanced education, and having been employed in the arts were also good predictors of moving to Germany for its economic incentives. By contrast, higher education was negatively associated with moving to Germany due to having a German background; expressed differently, those who lacked a high school diploma (the reference group) tended more to move to Germany due to familial background at destination. It is possible that these people have German citizenship and assume that they will have better social, economic, and cultural opportunities in Germany than in Israel. However, these Israelis typically do not feature in the German media, which is dominated by depictions of Israelis who are artists, academics, and other high achievers. Overall, the demographic and socioeconomic characteristics were especially useful in deciphering variations among Israelis in the extent of centrality of educational opportunities in deciding to move to Germany (15 percent explanatory power). For all the other reasons, the explanatory power of the individual variables was half as strong or less.

The personal interviews revealed that migration to Germany offered a particularly favorable window of opportunity to some specific migrants who were especially driven to obtain more education or who had a high level of education and wanted more. Concurrently, highly educated individuals who felt professionally limited in Israel felt that Germany presented a viable chance to develop their careers further. This nexus applied in particular to Israelis who had moved to a specific location to pursue their careers. "I was head-hunted," said one. "I wanted to leave Israel anyway, but it could have been to Amsterdam or some other city. It just happened to be Munich." The respondent had migrated to Germany on a work visa while her husband, who held dual Israeli and Polish citizenship, followed her to Germany. Due to his citizenship combination, however, he was not a tied spouse and he opted to pursue his career successfully, too. Interestingly, this couple also practiced "nontraditional" gender roles par excellence: it was the husband who followed and the father who took over more parenting duties for his more career-driven wife. For these two and their son, the move to Germany offered the pursuit of a specific lifestyle and, as they were not Germans, their nontraditional lifestyle raised no eyebrows. This finding is all the more interesting because gender inequalities, although different from those we depicted for Israel, also persist in Germany. Women earn on average 21 percent less than men (Eurostat, 2017)—a sticky disparity—and childcare remains a major issue that deters mothers from paid work and career progress (Bund, Geisler, and Kunze, 2019). Even though Germany was a good fit for their lifestyle, that it would remain their permanent place of residence was not certain. Another Munich-based Israeli recounted a similar story, although she, unlike the other respondents, made it clear that Munich—and Germany—was just one step in a global career (what Paul [2011] termed "stepwise migration"). Her engagement with German society was extremely limited; she lived in what she called "an international bubble where everybody speaks English." This contrasted with the other two still-indecisive migrants, who learned German, interacted with their German surroundings, and stressed their wish to be able to help their son with his homework and take part in his school activities. Their pursuit of their "careers" was linked to "personal developments" such as acquiring a new language and amassing cultural capital.

Notably, in addition to the various social, economic, and cultural incentives that Germany offers, the migration stories described above would not have been possible if Germany had not been interested in having Israelis come and stay. The presence of Israeli Jews in Germany confirms that the country has changed, and Israelis become smoke screens in a German identity play of mirrors (Kranz, 2018c). *Ad imago*, Germany reverts to an allegedly glorious past that had been before the "catastrophes of the twentieth century" (Lapidot and Ilany, 2015: 3).

Reactions of Family and Friends

People who consider moving to another country often consult with family and friends about it. Close confidants are expected to contribute honest information and emphasize the pros and cons of migration, generally, and of the specific destination, particularly. Given the intimacy of their relations, the views of kin and friends are likely to have a meaningful influence on potential migrants' decisions on whether or not to go ahead with their plans.

In the past, Germany seems to have evoked a rather strong sense of revulsion among Israelis. Dorit Levita-Harten has resided in Germany since 1980. Both her family and friends were negatively disposed to her move. "Germany was then at the most disadvantaged place on the exilic hierarchy. If you moved here, you were an outcast. To her last day, my mother was ashamed of me for having married a German; she kept telling people that I'd married a European" (Saberdlov, 2013: 27). Daniel Norman suspects that if his grandfather, who had served in the Red Army and fought against the Germans, had lived to see him moving to Germany, he would probably have asked him if he had gone mad. He would have said that it is totally unacceptable to live among Germans, work for Germans, and learn their language. Concurrently, Daniel Norman could also see his grandfather acknowledging the personal aspects of the matter, that is, his grandson having established himself, advancing professionally, and living in a safe place (Sapir, 2014a). Anat Ziv also experienced a negative reaction. She was born in Israel to a German-born Jew who had left Germany on the eve of World War II and returned afterward for several years of study. She herself moved to Germany in 1972 to study graphic art and later went on to artistic photography. After several successful exhibitions, her family approached her: "That's okay, wonderful, but now come back." She refused. Her father implored her to live with an Israeli or at least with a Jew; she rejected this as well. Although her father did not raise the subject again, she realizes that it hurt him badly (Golan, 2015b: 12).

Our émigrés, who moved to Germany after 1990, received stronger moral support from their families (see figure 2.6). Slightly more than 60 percent indicated that their families strongly supported or supported their decision to leave Israel. Another 15 percent said their family took a neutral stance. Less than one-fourth had to confront opposition or strong opposition. Close friends were even more supportive: 65 percent strongly supported or supported and only 16 percent opposed the move to one extent or another.

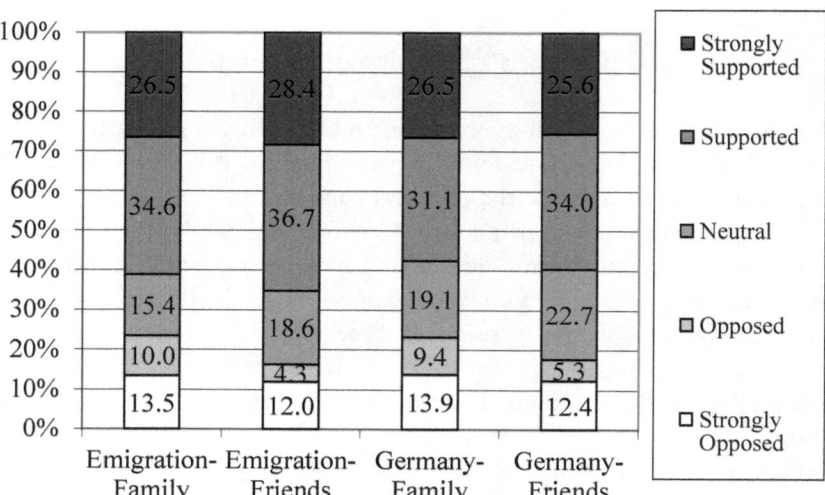

Figure 2.6. Reactions of Family and Friends to Emigration from Israel and Settling in Germany (Percentages).

When the choice of Germany as the destination country was explored, the support weakened although it remained robust: 58 percent received support or strong support from their families and 60 percent received this level of support from their friends (see figure 2.6). Apparently, most of those who supported emigration from Israel but opposed Germany as the destination expressed a neutral view but did not reject Germany altogether. Thus, all things considered, most Israelis' decisions to emigrate to Germany were sympathetically received by their dear ones. This is quite consistent with earlier observations. Already in 2001, Oz-Salzberger told the story of N., whose parents encouraged him to travel to Berlin. It was not only him, however, but also relatives of his family who sent their children to study in the city (138). Or Yael (not her real name), who stated that her parents are very satisfied with her being in Berlin and that her mother, if asked, would probably say that it is not worth her returning to Israel (Amit, 2013: 18).

The extent of support from family depends on the emigrants' characteristics (see table 2.4). People below age forty-five received more support

Table 2.4. Reaction of Family and Friends by Émigrés' Key Sociodemographic Characteristics (Percentages)

	Emigration from Israel			Settlement in Germany		
	Strongly Oppose/ Oppose	Neutral	Support/ Strongly Support	Strongly Oppose/ Oppose	Neutral	Support/ Strongly Support
Age						
18–24	15.6	15.6	68.9	17.8	11.9	71.7
25–34	24.6	13.5	61.9	23.1	17.7	59.2
35–44	22.2	16.2	61.7	24.4	18.5	57.1
45+	28.3	21.7	50.0	25.0	33.3	41.7
Gender						
Male	23.6	15.4	61.0	24.8	15.7	59.4
Female	23.7	16.7	59.6	22.3	23.6	54.1
Other	70.0	10.0	20.0	60.0	10.0	30.0
Education						
No Diploma	35.8	20.9	43.3	37.3	17.9	44.8
Matriculation	21.3	15.3	63.3	23.3	18.0	58.7
Post-secondary	18.2	21.2	60.6	18.2	27.3	54.5
BA	22.4	14.8	62.8	21.3	20.8	57.9
MA+	22.2	11.1	66.7	19.0	16.0	65.0
Family Holocaust Survivors						
No	36.4	13.0	50.6	33.9	18.0	48.1
Yes	12.9	17.4	69.7	14.2	20.1	65.6

than did their older peers, both for leaving Israel and for choosing Germany. We postulate that the younger migrants left more recently and that the somewhat more sympathetic reactions reflect longitudinal changes in the way the Israeli public views emigration; it also attests to the thawing of Israelis' attitudes toward Germany. Stauber (2017: 44) suggests similarly that the criticism of moving to Germany, especially from family and friends, has gradually eased over the years. Educational attainment is positively associated with receiving support. Relatives of highly educated migrants acknowledge the professional and economic advantages of life outside of Israel. Still, they are less definite about whether Germany is the appropriate place to benefit from their qualifications.

Significant differences exist between émigrés whose parents or grandparents are Holocaust survivors and those who are not. Somewhat surprisingly, the former received stronger support for their move. Our interpretation is that these survivors are highly sensitive to personal safety; given the complex security situation in Israel and the as-yet unsolved conflict in the Middle East, they may see a better future for their offspring elsewhere. Being of European background enhances their acquaintance with the continent, including the changes that German society has undergone over the years, and fosters feelings of reconciliation and openness toward Germany. Some of the elderly relatives may have pre-Shoah memories and it is likely that their experience of Europe at that time was positive.

"When I told my survivor grandmother that I was going to move to Germany to study, she was supportive of my decision. She told me that Jews had been living in Europe for centuries and we've been in the Middle East for only two generations." The interview partner recounted this conversation as decisively clearing up his ambiguity about moving to Germany. He was returning to the continent where his Ashkenazi family had originated. Respondents whose families had come from Europe had positive pre-Shoah memories, had emigrated—as opposed to fled—from Europe, and had experienced less persecution felt less averse to their grandchildren returning to Europe than those who had suffered severe persecution, experienced trauma, and survived the camps (Kranz, 2016b).

"I really can't stand it when people [his family in Israel] ask me when I'll be coming back. Or if Germany is good for me," stated a Berlin resident. "They just don't get it." When he was asked who in particular bothered him, he revealed that it was members of his family in Israel, mainly uncles and aunts of the second generation. His family originates in Yemen, meaning that no ancestral connection to Germany or direct loss of family members in the Shoah existed. By inference, acceptance or rejection of migration to Germany is a more complex matter than the parameter of Shoah and ancestry can capture. This complexity, which we found in our qualitative fieldwork, ties in with our quantitative findings. This respondent's friends—third-generation—did not take issue with his moving to Berlin; on the contrary, they considered it "a great opportunity for him" and were happy to visit him. Similarly, when he was offered a job as first violin with the Berlin Philharmonic Orchestra, Guy Braunstein received many positive reactions of the sort of his being in the right place and the right job, with one of the best orchestras in the world. For some, it sounded alarm bells in view of the orchestra's historical background; for Braunstein, it did not raise any second thoughts or hesitations (Oz-Salzberger, 2001: 143).

In sum, many Israelis who moved to Germany have a family background associated with the Holocaust. They carry with them a strong awareness of Jewish history in general and Holocaust history in particular, the Shoah often having been an important component of identity in their upbringing. Furthermore, they are sensitive to many things that are German, such as the sound of the German language (Katz, 2011), what is perceived as a strict order, and chilly personal demeanor; this was especially salient among Israeli émigrés of European background shortly after their arrival in Germany. When Israelis decide to leave their home country, they bring many factors into play—professional, economic, political, educational, and cultural. These reasons for emigration are spread quite evenly among different demographic and socioeconomic strata of the émigré population. Nevertheless, young Israelis in Germany emphasized the lack of educational opportunities in Israel, women speak vehemently about difficulties in professional advancement, and people who had worked in Israel complained mainly about professional distress, the political and security situation, and the influence of the religious establishment on life in Israel. Similarly, Israelis chose Germany because of various incentives and exhibited strong harmony between the factors that pushed them out of Israel and those which attracted them specifically to Germany. The attitudes of family and close friends, which often straddled the aspiration to emigrate and its implementation, were not serious impediments; emigrants received strong support even when they were plainly heading for Germany. Sympathy was especially strong among those who had immediate relatives who had survived the Holocaust. It seems, then, that about seventy years after the end of World War II and the establishment of the State of Israel, many Jewish Israelis, of European background or not, place the welfare of their children, grandchildren, or close friends above national collective considerations and their personal feelings toward Germans and the German state. As Ilany suggested, "Ultimately, immediate life is more important than memory, history, and myths" (Lapidot and Ilany, 2015: 3). This point is also averred in strong terms by the sociologist Larissa Remennick, according to whom, "on a deeper level this wave of emigration often reflects feelings of resentment and hopelessness as to their future in Israel. It signifies the arrival of a pragmatic, post-Zionist generation that is no longer willing to tolerate under-employment, high living costs, ineffective government, security threats, and the ongoing demise of the social fabric in their homeland" (2019: 105). Lianne Merkur (2019) offers yet another explanation, which bases more on personal ethics of those who choose to leave: "The marginalized may be Muslim and Christian Arabs or Palestinians situated geographically on either side of the Green Line, in addition to Druze, asylum seekers, foreign labourers, and non-Jewish partners of true-blue Israeli citizens. This can perhaps most dramatically be evidenced by the full government-approved privileged status extended to Jewish families who live in the West Bank, compared to the complete denial of civil rights experienced by their non-Jewish neighbours" (2019: 265).

Chapter 3

Welcome to Germany

Settling in a New Land

Flows of people between developed countries within Europe as well as overseas, have accelerated powerfully in the past two decades (Raymer, 2016). They are but an expression, albeit a major one, of wider processes of globalization and more convenient access to areas by means of speedy and inexpensive air transportation, advanced technology that enables immigrants to stay in regular touch with their home countries, and increasing similarity of cultural and consumption patterns across countries, all of which mitigate spatial movements (Ostergaard-Nielsen, 2012). Intercountry migration is facilitated and at times even encouraged by the easing of legal restrictions, including, among other things, free movement among EU member states under the Schengen agreement and the option of citizenship in EU countries for previous residents as well as their descendants (Guild, 2012; Voutira, 2012). Likewise, the growing propensity to multiculturalist agendas and/or engagement in diversity management in many countries allows newcomers to maintain particularistic group identities more easily than before (Castles, De Hass, and Miller, 2009; Bloemraad and Wright, 2014; Portes and DeWind, 2007)—although this process is neither smooth nor conflict-free, as the rightward lurch of various European countries evidences clearly. From the migrants' side, the growing emphasis on individualism and self-fulfillment (within the general structural context in which they operate) (Hirschman, Kasinitz, and DeWind, 1999) softens the decision to leave a home country in favor of social and economic opportunities elsewhere. These developments have dictated the generally rising angle of the immigration slope.

Unrestricted migration is often guided by search for professional advancement and a new lifestyle. Typically, young, highly educated, and economically active people are overrepresented in these flows (Castles, De Haas, and Miller, 2009). Their migration may be conceptualized as lifestyle migration (Benson and O'Reilly, 2016) and relates to mobility in that they can opt to be mobile as opposed to being forced to leave a place for sheer survival. Such migrants are extensively exposed to the world outside their place of residence, and their spatial awareness transcends their local economic system; hence, they have greater possibilities of mobility among international labor markets than do other migrants (Ritchey, 1976; Wolpert, 1965). They expect their new country to provide them with better living conditions and economic status than their old country had furnished. Destination countries, in turn, often privilege such people with assistance in legalizing their permanent settlement due to their good professional skills and potential contribution to local technological and economic development (Iredale, 2001). Home countries, recognizing this trend, are investing more and more in diaspora management institutions (Gamlen, Cummings, and Vaaler, 2017) in order to maintain contact with their self-selected migration populations and enjoy the advantages of brain circulation.

Immigrants tend to settle in gateway cities and in close proximity to ethnic and national peers. As their "veterancy" in the new country grows and they improve their qualifications, information about opportunities, and human capital, they are likely to indulge in internal migration (Fang and Brown, 1999; Gurak and Kritz, 2000). Studies on social networks propose that migrants are reluctant to resettle if they reside in ethnic communities that provide a sense of security and assistance in finding permanent housing and work (Gurak and Fe Caces, 1992; Newbold, 1996; Rebhun, 2006). Conversely, the foreign-born show high levels of internal migration when they believe it necessary to strengthen ethnic concentration (Rogers and Henning, 1999). Immigrant groups, however, differ in the importance they attach to nativity concentration, resulting in diverse patterns of resettlement (Bartal and Koch, 1991; Moore and Rosenberg, 1995). Sociodemographic characteristics are also important determinants of internal migration (Kritz and Gurak, 2015; White and Mueser, 1994). Obviously, area contextual conditions of wage and employment opportunities, climate, crime rates, and the like affect immigrants' desire to stay in their initial place of settlement or move elsewhere (Cadwallader, 1992; Clark and Maas, 2015; Michalos, 1997). Middle- to upper-class immigrants are likely to settle in areas where jobs have been arranged for them beforehand—often in major metropolitan areas, high-tech hubs, and university towns. Hence, they are less inclined to move internally, although they may relocate from a rented house to a dwelling that they own.

Migration is a long and multistage process (Docquier, Peri, and Ruyssen, 2014; Lee, 1966; Paul, 2011). Its well-established pattern begins with passing thoughts, exploration of costs and benefits, and establishing the desire to move; it continues with acquiring the requisite documents, arranging housing and work, and physically making the move; and it ends only several years later when the decision to stay permanently or return to the origin country (or, in some cases, to move to a third country) is made (Ravenstein, 1885; White and Johnson, 2016). In an alternative pattern, individuals who never thought about emigrating may leave their native country if they fall in love in the new country and decide to join their partner or spouse (Mai and King, 2009), possibly bringing an array of personal and professional consequences to bear (Riano, 2011). Be the primary factor that initiates the migration trajectory as it may, uncertainty about the permanence of migration may inhibit integration into the new environment—a process also affected by the migrants' legal status, naturalization options, and/or legal restrictions that force them to remain foreigners (Amit, 2001; Faist, Gerdes, and Rieple, 2004). The mechanism at work may also operate in reverse, namely, social, economic, or cultural incompatibilities and failures enhance the likelihood of returning home. Depending on the motivation and the initial reasons for emigrating, return migrants may represent success or failure from their subjective point of view (Ben Yehuda-Sternfeld and Mirsky, 2014; Gmelch, 1980). In any case, return migration is not evenly dispersed across migrants and is strongly tied to familial background and individual sociodemographic characteristics (Bocquier, 2016).

This chapter explores major aspects of immigration and settlement of Israelis in Germany. Attention is first directed to the Israelis' sociodemographic profile upon their arrival, comparing them with two groups: the sending society (the Israeli Jewish population) and the receiving society (the German population at large). Next, the chronology of Israeli immigration to Germany is traced in a manner that also investigates veterancy, probably a pivotal factor in further stages of the immigrants' overall social integration and their reconstruction of group identity. Third, we look at the Israelis' preferred places of settlement and the rhythm and direction of their internal migration within Germany. Finally, we analyze their expectations of remaining in Germany for the foreseeable future.

Demographic and Social Portrait

Israelis who reach Germany are young: one in five is age eighteen to twenty-four, another one in three in his or her late twenties, and one in four are in the thirty- to thirty-four-year-old bracket (see table 3.1). Thus, nine out of every ten Israelis who settled in Germany did so before reaching the age of forty. As Tal Alon described in her contribution to the debut issue of *Spitz*, "Among the many young people and students who have come here in the past few years, Berlin has a growing Israeli community composed not only of people in their twenties [. . .] but also of families" (Alon, 2012: 2). This has yielded specific dynamics in migration trajectories and specific social structures. Likewise, looking at the age profile of the Israelis who were interviewed for the "Packing Alone" section of various issues of *Spitz*, we found that all had moved to Germany before the age of thirty-eight, and the overwhelming majority did so in their twenties—a much younger group than the overall Israeli Jewish population and that of the host society, among both of which fewer than half were younger than forty (see table 3.1). Detailed information, not presented here, suggests that every fifth Israeli in the eighteen to twenty-four age group who immigrated to Germany was actually twenty or younger upon arrival. In Israel, this stage of the life cycle overlaps with mandatory military service—a civic obligation that these people may not have fulfilled.

Israeli men and women participate almost equally in migrating to Germany (see table 3.1). The small surplus of men relative to the overall Israeli or German gender ratio is negligible. Given their young age profile, it comes as no surprise that a significant number entered Germany as singles (see table 3.1). Approximately two-thirds immigrated to Germany as singles; another one-fifth were already married; and some 13 percent were of indefinite marital status at point of immigration. That is, they were either married or separated/divorced at the time of our research, but we did not know when they acquired this status. In any case, the high rate of singles is typical of voluntary migration and reflects the ease with which independent people relocate. The proportion of singles at point of immigration was two and a half times greater than that among the Israeli Jewish population at large. Although the importance of family formation is weaker in Germany than in Israel, it was even weaker among Israelis who were married when they settled in Germany than among the overall German population. The differences between the immigrants and both the sending and receiving populations should be attributed mainly to the Israelis' very young age composition.

Table 3.1. Sociodemographic Characteristics of Israeli Immigrants upon Arrival in Germany, Israeli Jews at Large, and German Population (Percentages)

	Israelis in Germany	Total Israeli Jewish Adults[a]	German Population
Age at Immigration			2011 census
Total	100.0	100.0	100.0
18–24	20.8	13.9	9.7
25–29	35.1	10.2	7.3
30–34	24.7	10.1	
35–39	11.1	9.7	14.2
40+	8.3	56.1	68.9
Gender			2011 census
Total	100.0	100.0	100.0
Male	51.0	48.7	49.3
Female	47.1	53.1	50.7
Other	1.9	—	
Marital Status			2011 census
Total	100.0	100.0	100.0
Single	65.8	24.6	40.0
Married	20.6	66.9	45.8
Married—date unknown + formerly married	13.6	8.5	14.2
Place of Residence			
Total	100.0	100.0	—
Jerusalem	13.9	11.1	—
North and Haifa	14.0	20.2	—
Tel Aviv and Center	63.6	48.8	—
South	3.3	14.2	—
West Bank	5.2	5.8	—
Education			2017 data, microcensus, age 20+
Total	100.0	100.0	100.0
No Diploma	14.4	25.4	4.3

continued on next page

Table 3.1. Continued.

	Israelis in Germany	Total Israeli Jewish Adults[a]	German Population
Education (continued)			
Matriculation	18.5	26.8	17.1
Post-secondary	7.6	15.5	59.9
BA	30.6	21.1	16.0
MA+	29.0	11.1	2.7
Employment Status[b]			
Total	100.0	100.0	100.0
Did not work	8.2	5.2	3.4
Worked	91.8	94.8	96.6
Occupation			2017 microcensus data
Total	100.0	100.0	100.0
Professional	43.2	37.7	29.0
Management	7.7	12.0	23.0
Technical	11.0	7.7	24.0
Arts	5.1	2.0	3.4
Sales, clerical, services	18.2	23.7	13.7
Blue-collar	14.8	16.9	6.9

[a]Central Bureau of Statistics: *Statistical Abstract of Israel, 2015*. For marital status and education—2013 Israeli Pew survey. For occupation—*Statistical Abstract of Israel, 2014*.
[b]For Israeli Jewish adults at large: main working-age group (25–54).

The immigrants came from different parts of Israel. By geographic distribution, people from Tel Aviv were overrepresented among them and those from surrounding cities and peripheral towns in the north and south, less so (see table 3.1).[1] The proportion of immigrants from Jerusalem largely resembles their share in the total Israeli Jewish population. Approximately 5 percent of Israelis in Germany lived in the West Bank before emigrating—a proportion similar to their share among the Israeli Jewish population. We suggest that these people (or their parents) did not settle in the West Bank for ideological or religious motives; instead, they took advantage of the cheap housing and other economic incentives offered there.[2]

The Israelis who moved to Germany are highly educated. Six out of ten landed in their new country with a bachelor's or higher degree in hand, twice the rate of that among the total Israeli Jewish population (see table 3.1), and 29 percent had advanced degrees (master's or PhD), compared to only 11 percent of peers who stayed in Israel. Very few (14 percent) reached Germany without a high school diploma, whereas this level of education characterizes one-quarter of Israeli Jews at large. The immigrants' educational attainments are even more salient when one considers that only some one-fifth of Germans are university graduates.

The proportion of immigrants who had not worked before leaving Israel somewhat exceeds that among the total Israeli Jewish population (see table 3.1) and surpasses the overall German jobless rate by a factor of nearly three. Nevertheless, more than 90 percent of the emigrants had been breadwinners in their country of origin. Among them, four of ten (43 percent) had held white-collar jobs in fields such as teaching and research and development (compared to 38 percent of all Israeli Jews), 18 percent had held sales/clerical/service jobs (vs. 24 percent of their peers in Israel), and 11 percent had held technical posts (compared to 8 percent of Israeli Jews). The proportion of those who had made their living in the arts was two and a half times greater than their share among Jews in Israel—5 percent and 2 percent, respectively. True to their educational advantage, Israeli immigrants are more heavily concentrated in professional jobs than are their German hosts.

Overall, the Israeli emigrants to Germany are a select group of young men and women: highly educated, disproportionally originating in the center of the country, and having practiced professional occupations in Israel. They do not mirror the average population of origin; instead, they constitute what may be described as highly qualified if not ultra-qualified migrants, resulting in their mythification in both Israel and Germany. In Israel, they are sometimes presented under the cloud of being "ultra–Tel Avivians," that is, people who take the Tel Aviv lifestyle to an extreme. This lifestyle is characterized by secularism if not hedonism, strong historical connections to the founding Ashkenazi power elite, and location in economic center of the country. In Germany, this mythification is manifested in defining them by their whiteness and thus, intuitively, treating them as Europeans, and in stressing their high level of education, thus confirming stereotypes of clever Jews and transferring them from the Levantine "silo," as Israelis, to the Jewish one. They are, Ofri Ilany remarked, "somebody else's fantasy" (Lapidot and Ilany, 2015: 6)—Israelis who benefit from popular perceptions among the German population (Kranz, 2018c) that do not hold for Israel as a country at large (Hagemann and Nathanson, 2015). But, a perception which is supported by an above average presence of academics, artists, and experts who in turn come to Germany based on institutionalized structures in the shape of scholarships and grants.

Chronology of Migration

Time of Arrival and Veterancy

Immigration of native-born Israeli Jews to Germany is a rather new phenomenon. Only a tiny proportion of the Israelis who reside in Germany today arrived there before the fall of the Berlin Wall and the reunification of Germany (see figure 3.1).[3] A somewhat larger number settled in Germany during the 1990s—twice the rate as in the previous decade (2 percent and 4 percent, respectively), but small nevertheless. The substantial shift occurred in the 2000s: the proportion of immigrants among the total Israeli population in Germany ramped gradually from 9 percent who arrived in the first quintile of that decade to 15 percent in the following five years. More than two-thirds of the Israelis who resided in Germany in 2015 had immigrated in the preceding five years.

The reasons for these changes are generational and reflect evolving attitudes toward Germany. The first "Israelis" to reach Germany (mostly West Germany) were Jews of German origin (*yekkes*) and German-speaking Jews from Eastern Europe. While both groups are lingo-culturally German, the

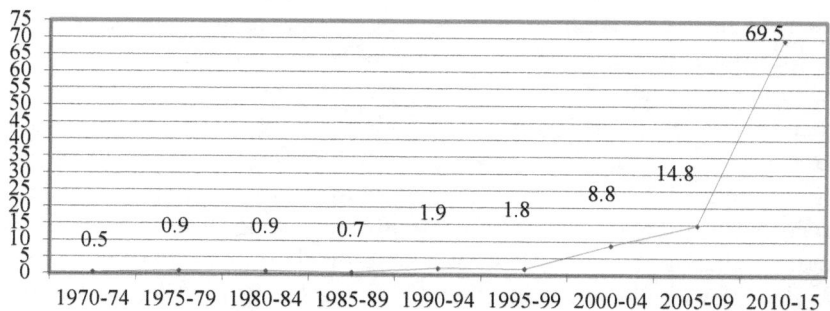

Figure 3.1. Distribution of Israelis in Germany by Year of Immigration (Percentages).

former group had access to German citizenship under section 116 of the Basic Law, whereas the latter did not qualify for this treatment and had to undergo naturalization (Panagiotidis, 2012; 2019). Concurrently, members of both groups "vanished" statistically because they were not necessarily registered as Israeli citizens: if they naturalized they had to renounce Israeli citizenship in most cases, and the Mikrozensus analyzed familial background only since 2005. Notably, the Mikrozensus is a statistical tool that allows insights into the socioeconomic structures of the resident population of Germany, it is regulated by the *Mikrozensusgesetz* (Microcensus Law, MZG), which is a dynamic law, just as citizenship law, evidencing that Germany reacts to the permanence of migration and other societal changes across legal, social, and societal realms.

The improving ability to "track" Israelis should not deflect from the unknown amount being out of reach. In some cases, dual Israel-German citizens were registered as Germans and no trace of Israeli citizenship existed, and vice versa. Ronald Webster (1995) elaborates on these cases historically, because they give insights on the identity politics of this early remigrant group, which felt German, was German, but was also traumatized and in denial of its permanent presence in Germany. In the present, Israelis who hold dual or triple or even quadruple citizenships might be registered under any "alias." This makes counting Israelis unduly hard: the Mikrozensus ran a special evaluation concerning how many Israelis—that is, single Israeli citizens, German Israeli citizens, and individuals with a statistical migration background Israel—reside in Germany. The numbers per state were so low that the total could only be disclosed to ensure data protection: 25,000 (personal email to Dani Kranz, December 1, 2016). Figures below 5,000 cannot be released in order to ensure anonymity, and will show as zero. We put the figure even lower than the Mikrozensus, at 20,000 for the whole of the country, as the Mikrozensus contains anybody with a background "Israel," for example, also individuals who are not citizens, who were born in Germany but have one parent who was born in Israel. Our estimate is based on discussions with the Mikrozensus experts, Destatis, and also local statisticians, who drove our attention to issues of reliability. For example, if an individual holds EU citizenship and registers with it, he or she will be asked if they hold any other citizenship. The answer is voluntary, as the head statistician of the statistical offices in Berlin-Brandenburg explained (personal email to Dani Kranz, November 25, 2016). She herself doubted the reliability of the data "second citizenship," which should be interpreted as a trend, in her opinion. In other states and communes data are collected, though differently, making for interesting insights into how statistics are constructed (Cohen and Susser, 2009), but leading us to be very cautious on the overestimated numbers we found in the media in German, Hebrew, English, and other languages: Israelis in Germany carry a strong emotional currency for various stakeholders and they conduct ideological labor (Bodemann, 1996), but their actual, factual numerical amount is rather small, not to say tiny. The sole somewhat reliable figures are on those who hold Israeli citizenship only, or those who hold dual German/Israeli citizenship, as giving information on a second or third citizenship is not voluntary for German citizens. Whether they will surrender this information is debatable, as well as if the information could even be entered: typically, German forms allow for the registration of two citizenships only. However small the numbers that can be traced might be, the way of Israelis to Germany was and is complex. The arrival of Israelis consists of a mixture of single acts of individuals, of families returning from exile, and of those who are curiosity about the new Germany; but the migration, and the changing image of Germany, also owes something to public and private endeavors of those who sought to contact Israeli Jews.

Private citizens among the second generation (non-Jewish Germans born after the war) initiated contacts with Israelis that culminated in visitation programs for former residents (Nikou, 2020). Following these efforts, individuals in state institutions began to initiate academic exchange programs (Hestermann, 2016) that produced rapprochement on a scientific level. These developments were supported by the validation of Israeli passports for travel to Germany in 1956; until then, Israel had forbidden their use by imposing an "Except for Germany" ("*prat le'germania*") provision (see photo 1). The establishment of official diplomatic relations in 1965 set off an increase in soft-diplomacy investments in (West) Germany, prompting second-generation Israelis—offspring of *yekkes* and others—to visit Germany mainly for higher education. The situation in East Germany was markedly different: the country never had diplomatic relations with Israel, and its other ties were strained at best.

Private travel to Germany remained rare throughout the second half of the twentieth century. Some of the aforementioned second-generation Israelis stayed in Germany, because they found jobs that were too attractive to turn down (Kranz, 2009); others met Germans on location and established families. One second-generation migrant of Hungarian parentage described this outcome by quipping, "Life happened." Permanent migration to Germany, she elaborated, had never been her aim, but she had met her husband during her degree studies, married, had children, and divorced. By the time of her interview, however, she had grandchildren in Germany and leaving

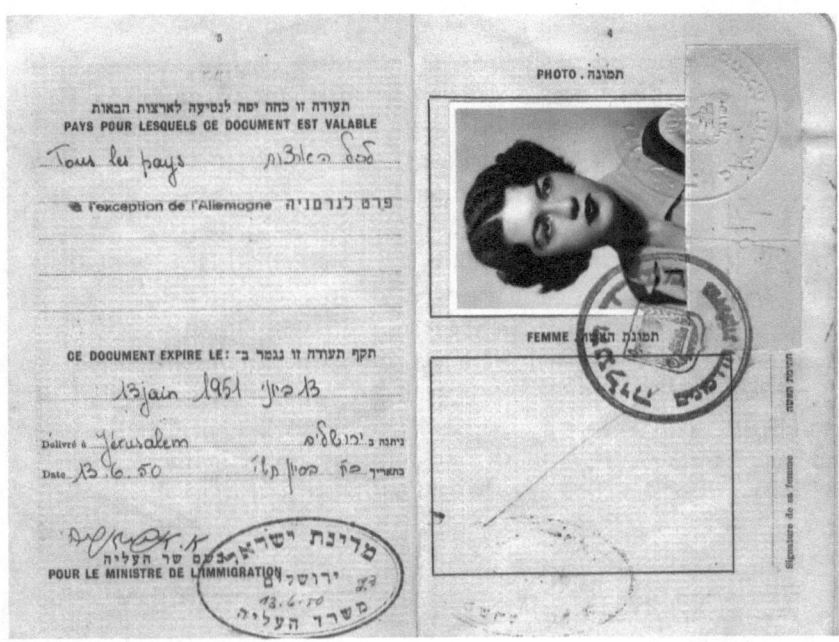

Photo 1. Israeli Passport with Stamp Prohibiting Travel to Germany. Source: Asher and Ira Koch Album, The Shoshana and Asher Halevy Photo Archive, Yad Ben Zvi (Jerusalem), ybz.0167.918.

had become a nonoption for her. Another migrant had reached Germany to pursue a specific applied degree that was not available in Israel. As a native speaker of German and the holder of German citizenship, he saw no issue in going to Germany, although he had not planned to remain in the country for good. Like the previously quoted Israeli migrant, he stayed on because his children live there. Other Israelis completed their degrees and left Germany. However, the number of emigrants of this kind who returned to Israel cannot be determined; nor can one ascertain what other countries they moved to. These data sets can be traced only qualitatively, and even then only to some extent, by following up individuals, social networks, and alumni or similar associations, if they exist.

The situation changed remarkably when the third generation of Israelis came of age. Further removed from the Holocaust and exposed to a different Germany by way of the changing bilateral relationship, soft-diplomacy efforts, and foreign travel, these Israelis were curious about Germany. This curiosity was also abetted by growing numbers German non-Jews who visited Israel and encounters between Israelis and Germans abroad in the course of travel or study, causing contacts, including intermarriage, to increase (Kranz, 2018b). Likewise, third-generation Israelis have been naturalizing as EU citizens in record numbers since the 1990s for both pragmatic and ideological reasons: one was not only Israeli but Israeli plus, an EU passport earned its holder a specific status (Harpaz, 2012). Descendants of *yekkes* were particularly apt to exercise their entitlement to citizenship (Kranz, 2015c; 2016b). While this initially induced an internal conflict as a result—the Israeli set of statuses and privileges combined with rejection of the Israeli mainstream discourse (Harpaz, 2012; Kranz, 2016b)—these passports were also gateways to Europe and useful facilitators of emigration to other destinations. Yet, while Germany became increasing popular as an emigration destination, the actual number of Israelis of all generations who actually live there remains small and should not be blown out of proportion, despite the growing number of migrants of the third generation: the increase of dual German/Israeli citizens in Germany should not be attributed to descendants naturalizing in Israel but to children born in Germany to third-generation Israelis, and local Germans.[4] The highly educated, secular, young people, some of them sojourners, others transmigrants, fit in with other migrants to Germany, and to Berlin specifically, who come from the Global North. Using the mobility that their intersecting privileges afford them, they may end up settling in Germany permanently, plans to the contrary notwithstanding.

The length of an immigrant's stay in the new country—his or her veterancy—is a function of his or her time of arrival. We sorted the most recent Israeli immigrants into short arrival cohorts and lumped earlier immigrants into wider ones (see figure 3.2). Approximately half of the Israelis

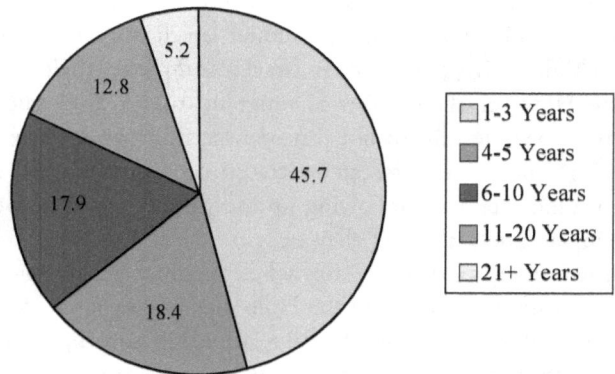

Figure 3.2. Israeli Immigrants' Veterancy in Germany (Percentages).

had been in Germany for up to three years, slightly less than one-fifth for four or five years, a similar proportion six to ten years, and about one in ten eleven to twenty years. Only 5 percent had been living in Germany for more than two decades.

Time and Reasons for Emigration

There is a relation between time of emigration and reasons for leaving Israel. Generally speaking, earlier migrants found it more difficult than later ones to point to a specific reason. This may be due to the fading of memories over time, but migration is a dynamic process and initial motivations for staying in the new country may not have remained paramount. It might also be the case that the aspect of migration in the biography is smoothed in and over, so that it fits with the overall life-story when it is told in retrospect (Sarbin, 1986). This effect is particularly pronounced among Israelis who moved to Germany as part of a couple but remained in Germany even after their relationship foundered and despite not having children. Namely, they had developed a sense of home there. By contrast, those who left in recent years indicated more clearly one or several well-defined factors that had played a role in their decision to emigrate. Not only did they better remember the circumstances under which they had left Israel; the list of reasons that they were shown may have fit better with contemporary social, economic, cultural, and political considerations and less so with reasons for emigration two or more decades ago.

We identified five major factors that distinguish between recent and early emigrants. A large percentage of those who moved in the past decade emphasized the political and security conditions in Israel, lack of opportunities for professional development, inability to progress economically, options for acquiring higher education, and the involvement of the religious establishment in everyday life as paramount considerations for their decision to emigrate. For example, as many as 46 percent of Israelis who settled in Germany between 2012 and 2015 indicated that they were somewhat or heavily affected by the political and security situation in Israel, whereas this was true for half the share—23 percent—of counterparts who arrived in Germany before 1995 (see table 3.2). Similarly, seven out of every ten Israelis who moved to Germany in the past few years were pushed, among other things, by perceived obstructions to their economic development, as opposed to four out of every ten among those who emigrated more than two decades ago. Despite the fine reputation of Israeli universities, about half of the most recent emigrants felt limited by educational opportunities in Israel

Table 3.2. Time of Emigration, by Reasons for Leaving Israel (Somewhat/Very Central)

Time of Emigration	Political/ Security	Professional Development	Economic Development	Educational Opportunities	Religious Establishment	Family/ Friends	Other
2012–15	46.0	61.3	70.1	47.0	52.4	11.5	28.0
2010–11	41.9	53.1	66.3	35.7	52.0	10.4	28.6
2005–09	42.8	58.2	61.3	38.8	37.7	11.3	31.0
1995–04	33.3	49.2	46.1	43.1	32.3	4.6	33.9
–1994	23.1	40.0	42.3	32.0	28.0	12.0	36.3

versus about one-third among those Israelis who lived in Germany for the longest duration. Degree programs are increasingly specialized and some of them, especially in areas such as the arts and music, are not widely available in Israel. Likewise, the larger number of academic institutions in Germany increases the chances of admission and of receiving a scholarship. Recent immigrants to Germany were almost twice as likely as the most veteran ones (52 percent and 28 percent, respectively) to specify the involvement of the religious establishment as a factor of some or great centrality in their decision to leave their native country. Still, it should be emphasized that the largest variations between the most recent immigrants and the earliest immigrants regarding their reasons for emigration concerned the political/security situation in Israel and the religious establishment's involvement in Israeli daily life. Accompanying family or friends played a rather similar role among all emigrants, regardless of when they left Israel. Recent emigrants were more strongly affected by one or several of the reasons specified above; earlier ones were pushed from Israel by other considerations as well.

Given these dynamics and coupling them with memory issues, we found one salient pattern in the personal interviews: the volume of German programs aimed at Israelis induced many more Israelis to migrate to Germany. The recent arrivals often took up a specific opportunity that presented itself, whereas long-established migrants had sought out such programs deliberately. The reasons for leaving Israel followed this pattern: more recent emigrants left Israel and pursued specific paths due to an active interest in personal development. Thus, one recent arrival explained, "I heard about this program and I took it up. I can't survive on the money I'd make [as an artist] in Israel, but here I manage." The more veteran the migrants were, the more inclined they were to describe their migration as "One thing led to another. I did my degree, I made friends, I married, I had children. I'm still here."

TIME AND REASONS FOR CHOOSING GERMANY

The reasons for choosing Germany as the destination country also vary by time of migration (see table 3.3). The more recent the migrants were, the more likely they were attracted by German culture, opportunities for economic and professional advancement, search for new challenges, and, to some extent—albeit not consistently—educational programs available at destination. In contrast, while about half of the veteran immigrants moved to Germany in the footsteps of a partner, this was true for only one-fourth to one-third of the more recent arrivals. Overall, family considerations have lost some of their prominence in the decision to move to Germany. Newer immigrants were more inclined to trace their decision to reasons other than those specified to them, that is, they were motivated by a wider range of reasons than were earlier arrivals. Still, in all migration cohorts, the reasons for choosing Germany are better defined by the specific options available to respondents than reasons for leaving Israel (as indicated by the lower percentages in the "Other" column of table 3.3 than those in table 3.2). While generational shifts—from family to individual migration—hide behind these figures as newer arrivals stress individual reasons, these data again bear witness to Germany's having become a desirable destination for immigrants in pursuit of a specific lifestyle. Older arrivals were more likely to follow a partner/spouse; younger ones came for individual goals ranging from education to professional pursuits to specific habits and way of life. The last-mentioned element was evinced with special emphasis by Israelis who felt that they enjoyed greater personal freedom in Germany or had been marginal in Israel. Single women who did not want children stressed this matter, as did Israelis who felt out of sync with the Zionist discourse or mainstream society (Amit, 2017; Merkur, 2019).

Determinants of Time of Migration

The time of settlement in Germany is influenced not only by push and pull factors but also by considerations that embody attributes such as age, gender, and education, to name only a few. Some of these factors are interrelated. To assess the net role of each in the timing of arrival in Germany, we used multivariate analysis.

The paramount determinant of the time Israelis moved to Germany is education (see table 3.4). Israelis who hold a matriculation certificate or an academic degree are more closely associated with later migration than are earlier migrants, who tend not to have completed high school (the reference group). Further, each wave was more educated than its predecessor, as manifested in rising values of the coefficients commensurate with educational attainment. For example, relative to Israelis with no matriculation (reference group), who on average immigrated in 2002 (constant), those with post-secondary education immigrated about 4 years later (in 2006), and those with bachelor's degree did so 6.6 years later. Israelis who reached Germany with advanced academic degrees in hand are a rather new group, many having arrived in Germany only since 2009. This phenomenon might also be supported by opportunities afforded to the skilled and highly skilled,

Table 3.3. Time of Immigration, by Reasons for Choosing Germany (Somewhat/Very Central)

Time of Immigration	Education	German Culture	Professional/ Economic	Family Origin	German Partner	Seeking Challenge	Other
2012–15	47.7	59.4	69.8	23.2	26.5	56.0	12.2
2010–11	38.8	45.9	54.1	16,2	31.6	58.2	7.2
2005–09	40.9	43.8	59.2	13.2	35.7	45.9	10.7
1995–04	50.0	46.0	49.3	21.9	46.2	54.0	1.8
–1994	26.9	34.6	50.0	38.4	26.2	42.3	4.4

Table 3.4. Determinants of Time of Migration

Variables	Unstandardized Coefficient (B)
Sociodemographic Characteristics[a]	
Age at immigration	
18–24	−1.604
25–29	−2.454[i]
30–34	−1.536
35–39	0.609
Gender	
Female	−0.381
Other	3.144
Education at immigration	
Matriculation	4.658*
Post-secondary	4.110*
BA	6.641*
MA+	6.895*
Area of residence in Israel	
North and Haifa	0.130
Tel Aviv and Center	−0.775
South	−1.633
West Bank	4.529
Occupation in Israel	
Professional	2.838
Managerial	1.819
Technical	3.503[i]
Sales and services	3.323*
Arts	5.748[i]
Blue-collar	2.680
Reasons for Emigration from Israel[b]	
Political/security	−0.741[i]
Professional development	−0.298
Economic development	1.704*
Education	−0.976[i]
Religious establishment	0.510
Family/friends	0.337
Other	−0.369
Reasons for Choosing Germany[b]	
Education	1.155*
German culture	0.890*
Professional/economic	−0.964*

Variables	Unstandardized coefficient (B)
Reasons for Choosing Germany[b] (continued)	
Family origin	−1.017*
German partner	−0.615*
Seeking challenge	−0.101
Other	0.670
Constant	*2002.4*
Explanatory Power	*17.9%*

*Significant at least at the 0.05 level; *i* Significant at $p < 0.10$.

[a]Reference categories: age at immigration—40+; gender—male; education—no diploma; area of residence—Jerusalem; occupation—did not work.

[b]Each variable is ordered as follows: not at all, a little, somewhat, very.

and run through the federal government program Make It in Germany. Compared to the costs of living, incomes in Germany are higher, as one software developer outlined, and, he mused, "I did not belong to the poor in Israel either."

Those who worked in Israel immigrated more recently than those who did not. This is especially noticeable among people employed in sales and service as well as technical jobs, who, on average, arrived in Germany three years later than those who did not work at all. The average year of arrival among artists was 2008, six years later than their unemployed peers. The reasons for this belatedness are complex, as we discovered in our ethnographic fieldwork. They relate to the rising cost of living in Israel, which has made art a harder and harder way of earning a living—in fact, beyond the reach of all but a few. Concurrently, artists are often tied to local networks of other artists and specific buyers, making migration riskier for them than for individuals whose professions more easily fit into the commercial sector. This also means, however, that artists tow other artists in their wake, as one of our respondents explained: "There's a whole network of Israeli artists in Berlin."

Ceteris paribus, reasons for leaving Israel also play an independent role in the timing of migration. Especially significant is the lack of opportunity for economic advancement, which correlates positively with later migration. Typically, these migrants had already acquired social, cultural, and educational capital that they wished to grow by migrating. As one interviewee—an MBA who holds a "blue card" (a vocation-specific European Union work permit)—explained, "Germany is part of my pursuit of a global career." All other things being equal, early immigrants were strongly attracted by opportunities for professional advancement and familial considerations; more recent immigrants were drawn to Germany mainly by its educational opportunities and culture. The last two parameters hold true for the youngest bracket of migrants: often attracted by the lower expense of earning a degree in Germany and lured by the local culture, they sought out Germany due to a mixture of pragmatism and lifestyle. They were also the most individualistic in their decision: "It was a chance I could not pass up."

Characteristics such as age, gender, and place of residence in Israel were not significant for the timing of migration. Overall, the sociodemographic variables, reasons for leaving Israel, and reasons for choosing Germany as the new country explained nearly one-fifth of the time span of migration among Israelis in Germany. The remaining explanation belongs to individual and contextual factors in Israel and Germany that are not indexed by our data.

Berlin or Elsewhere?

Gateway Cities and Internal Migration

Slightly more than half (53 percent) of the Israeli immigrants first settled in Berlin (see table 3.5, right-hand column). The second most-preferred place, albeit far behind Berlin, is Munich, which 7 percent chose as their gateway city. Thereafter, in descending order, are Cologne (5 percent), Hamburg (4 percent), and Frankfurt (3.5 percent). That still leaves more than one-fifth (23 percent) of Israeli immigrants to have settled in smaller and less central cities (e.g., Hanover, Leipzig, Freiburg, Göttingen, Heidelberg, and Saarbrücken). These Israelis typically chose their destination for a specific job or a local partner or spouse; few opted to live in remote areas as a matter of lifestyle. In one conspicuous exception, a male immigrant moved to a remote arborous area because he likes hiking and literally living in the woods. Another ruminated: "I'd really like to move to Monschau [a small town in Aachen District, near the Belgian border]. It's so quiet; [. . .] I feel so calm [there]."

The spatial distribution of Israelis in Germany today (see table 3.5, bottom row; and figure 3.3) attests to the growing attractiveness of large cities over other places, mirroring general trends in Germany as a whole. Thus, the number of Israelis who currently live in Berlin, Munich, Cologne,

Table 3.5. Geographic Distribution and Internal Mobility of Israelis in Germany (Percentages)

Place of settlement	Berlin	Munich	Cologne	Hamburg	Frankfurt	Dusseldorf	Stuttgart	Other	Total at Arrival
Berlin	<u>95.2</u>	0.3	0	0.7	0.3	0	0	3.4	**53.3**
Munich	5.0	<u>87.5</u>	2.5	0	5.0	0	0	0	**7.3**
Cologne	7.7	0	<u>88.5</u>	0	0	3.8	0	0	**4.8**
Hamburg	4.5	0	0	<u>86.4</u>	0	0	0	9.1	**4.0**
Frankfurt	21.1	0	0	0	<u>63.2</u>	5.3	0	10.5	**3.5**
Dusseldorf	14.3	0	7.1	0	0	<u>78.6</u>	0	0	**2.6**
Stuttgart	9.1	9.1	0	0	9.1	0	<u>72.7</u>	0	**2.0**
Other	12.2	7.3	1.6	5.7	0.8	0.8	0	<u>71.5</u>	**22.5**
Total 2015	**55.7**	**8.4**	**4.9**	**5.1**	**3.1**	**2.6**	**1.5**	**18.7**	**100.0**

and Hamburg is on the rise. In contrast, Frankfurt has lost some of its appeal to Israelis.

The changes in geographical distribution from time of arrival to the present hide internal migrations in different and sometimes, perhaps, opposite directions (see table 3.5). Berlin has the strongest holding power: 95 percent of Israelis who first settled there still live there (see table 3.5, diagonal). Residential stability, that is, people who did not move to another city, is also rather strong in Cologne (89 percent), Munich (88 percent), and Hamburg (86 percent). However, less than two-thirds (63 percent) of Israelis who settled in Frankfurt still live there. Similarly, Stuttgart and "other" cities fall short on retentive power. The internal mobility that we found relates to specific characteristics of the cities in question. Thus, while Frankfurt is the financial center of the country and home to a number of large global financial and law firms, the city is seen as less desirable from a lifestyle perspective, an issue that it shares with Stuttgart. The automobile industry and medium-size high-tech companies dominate the economy of the Stuttgart area, but even Israelis who have skill sets appropriate to that vicinity relocate to other cities and areas where they can find appropriate work and also pursue the lifestyle that they prefer. As one Israeli put it, "Stuttgart is just so boring. It is nice. But boring." Salaries are likely to be higher than in Berlin but, for many Israelis, Berlin resembles Tel Aviv in cultural opportunities, places of entertainment, exhibitions, and style of interpersonal communication (Amit, 2013). Thus, Israelis move to Berlin from different cities, for different reasons, and at different stages in life, mirroring the country's general Berlin-centric domestic migration pattern. In 1977, for example, Anat Ziv migrated from Krefeld, where she taught graphic design, to Berlin to study psychology (Golan, 2015b). In 1995, Amir Kuzinsky left Frankfurt in favor of Berlin when he changed his field of study (Sapir, 2014c). In 2001, when her German husband retired from his work in Düsseldorf, Dorit Levita-Harta relocated to Berlin (Saberdlov, 2013).

As noted, there was also intensive relocation from large cities to "other" cities in the country, also reflecting the broad demographic trends of the country (depopulation and ageing of the countryside, rejuvenation and growth of cities). This trend is so pronounced that discussions of how to revive the countryside and make sure the rural population has adequate infrastructure have become a political issue. Doctors, for example, are incentivized to practice in the countryside. Conversely, the scarcity of affordable housing, rising rent levels, and pressure on infrastructure in major cities have become matters of political urgency at the opposite pole.

The end distribution of these internal flows is reflected in increasing concentration. The share of Israeli immigrants who chose Berlin, Munich, Cologne, or Hamburg as their first place of settlement in Germany climbed from 69 percent upon arrival to 74 percent today. Generally speaking, the spatial distribution of Israelis attests to concentration in a few cities along with some presence in many parts of the German landscape (see map). The cities offer more than job opportunities; the immigrants' ongoing residence there also provides evidence that their social life supports their stay. That is, they make friends not only among other Israelis but also among nonimmigrants. Overall, they described their relations with others—Germans and other migrants—as positive and commonly manifested in friendship. Some referred to these social developments as "sinking roots" and "becoming at home." These issues are key to our understanding of their sojourn, because each additional domestic migration means severing ties, losing social contacts, and starting from scratch again. Berlin, with its growing Israeli population, evidences this trend in the expression "Every Israeli knows at least one other in Berlin," meaning that moving to Berlin carries lesser social risks because it is easy to establish contacts with other Israelis as a starting point toward rootedness. At the same time, Israelis in Berlin are spread across different parts of the city and mix with the many nationalities that make up the city's population of approximately four million (Amit, 2013).

Geography and Sociodemographic Characteristics

For the sake of convenience and given the small number of Israelis in some areas, we distinguish from here on among Berlin, other major cities,[5] and other places (see table 3.6). Inclination of Israelis to settle in each of these areas varies by their time of arrival in Germany, their sociodemographic characteristics, and their social and economic attainments. Berlin attracts mainly Israelis who arrived in Germany in the past ten years. Until then, fewer than half of the Israeli immigrants chose Berlin as their place of settlement. This was all the more striking among Israelis who arrived in Germany before 1995: fewer than one in ten initially settled in Berlin and most avoided all the major cities. This was a function of Berlin's specific geopolitical location. The city had been partitioned until 1990, and the

Map 1. Map of Germany with Major Concentrations of Israelis.

Table 3.6. Places of Settlement by Time of Arrival and Sociodemographic Characteristics (Percentages)

	Berlin	Other Major Cities	Other Places	Total
Total	53.3	24.2	22.5	100.0
Time of Arrival				
2013–15	59.6	21.6	18.8	100.0
2011–12	57.0	25.0	18.0	100.0
2006–10	54.0	24.0	22.0	100.0
1996–05	44.1	26.5	29.4	100.0
<1995	7.7	38.4	53.8	100.0
Age at Immigration				
18–24	55.4	22.8	21.8	100.0
25–29	58.0	23.3	18.7	100.0
30–34	45.7	22.4	31.9	100.0
35–39	59.7	27.4	12.9	100.0
40+	47.8	30.5	21.7	100.0
Gender				
Male	54.3	22.5	23.2	100.0
Female	59.1	22.4	18.5	100.0
Education in Israel				
No diploma	46.0	16.0	38.0	100.0
Matriculation	55.8	24.1	20.1	100.0
Post-secondary	44.1	35.3	20.6	100.0
BA	60.6	22.9	16.5	100.0
MA+	45.6	28.2	26.2	100.0
Occupation in Israel				
Professional	63.2	21.5	15.3	100.0
Managerial	47.1	29.4	23.5	100.0
Technical	54.0	30.0	16.0	100.0
Arts	45.5	36.3	18.2	100.0
Sales, clerical, services	59.5	25.0	15.5	100.0
Blue-collar	49.1	24.5	26.4	100.0

Western sector, part of West Germany, had barely been viable. It had been supported by redistribution of federal funds for ideological rather than economic reasons associated with the Cold War geopolitical landscape. This made West Berlin, although an urban enclave surrounded by East Germany, an inexpensive place to live. Furthermore, men who moved there were exempted from military service as residents of a frontier city. Consequently, West Berlin attracted a specific population from West Germany (Cohen and Kranz, 2017), but was rather irrelevant economically. The distribution of economic and financial power in Germany continues to follow these west/east lines, with the former West Germany being the economic powerhouse, home to the wealthy elites and the power elites alike.

Among all Israelis in Germany, Berlin is disproportionally attractive to the young. Relative to the overall percentage of Israelis who settled in Berlin, the rate is higher among those who were eighteen to twenty-four years old upon arrival in Germany, even more conspicuously so in the next age bracket (25–29), and also characteristic of Israelis in their late thirties. Interestingly, almost one-third of Israelis aged thirty to thirty-four settled in areas away from Berlin and the other major cities. This may be associated with their being married and having young children, thus preferring to reside in detached houses in small villages where housing is more affordable and infrastructures such as childcare and healthcare are less stressed. The oldest Israelis, those over age forty at arrival, had a rather strong preference for other major cities, probably under the influence of their early settlement in Germany. The trend among young Israelis matches that among domestic migrants and other international migrants: because Berlin is a poor city, it is relatively cheap to live in, meaning that one can get by with jobs that would not allow this in other cities. This has changed since the major years of the arrival of Israelis, and living expenses in Berlin have skyrocketed. Generally, this interpretation should be taken with caution: even a relatively inexpensive city verges on the unaffordable if one is constantly strapped for cash. This also begs the question of what will happen once these Israeli migrants—and their German and international peers—outgrow their current phase in life. That is, will a trend of transience such as that evidenced in other cities, for example, London, manifest in Berlin as well? While London is extremely expensive, it still attracts young migrants in pursuit of economic and educational opportunities but loses many of them over time (London Assembly, 2017). Furthermore, the Berlin issue begs the question of where the Israelis will move once they leave: Will it be elsewhere in Germany, a third country, or back to Israel? (See also the section "Future Migration" below.)

Women have a stronger preference for Berlin than do men, who are more heavily concentrated in other cities. The relationship between place of settlement and education (at time of arrival) is somewhat inconsistent, indicating that Israelis may move to a place where they know somebody, either other Israelis or local Germans. Substantial variations exist in the geographic distribution of adjacent education groups (along with similarities between education groups that are far apart). Israelis at both educational extremes—those who lack matriculation certificates and those with advanced degrees—were less attracted to Berlin and had the highest rates of settlement in "other" cities. The underlying reason is similar for both groups: scarcity of well-paying jobs in Berlin, irrespective of level of education. Israelis who have a postsecondary education and those with advanced degrees are highly concentrated in other major cities, where they enjoy the presence of academic and research institutions and attractive high-tech companies. Some highly educated people who work in large cities prefer small-town or even rural lifestyles, those of areas that may also host heavy and service industries that employ the poorly schooled.

Israelis who arrived with nothing but a matriculation certificate or a bachelor's degree were the most inclined to settle in Berlin. Those in the matriculation-only group, insofar as they moved to Germany for educational reasons, may have chosen Berlin due its profusion of academic institutions. Those armed with academic degrees hoped that they would find work in Berlin that matched their qualifications—an outcome that, as underscored in the interviews and the fieldwork, was not always attained. Berlin seems to offer much when seen from a distance, but no few Israelis learned the hard way that even an inexpensive city is not that inexpensive if one cannot find sufficient work. Successful start-up entrepreneurs and IT specialists were the exceptions to this rule. Enjoying Berlin's still comparably low cost of living and its huge labor force that maintained strong connections to Israel, they have managed to capitalize on their transnational ties (Salloum, 2014). They also benefit from specific economic programs of the State of Berlin-Brandenburg that aim to attract business to Berlin (and Brandenburg), allowing practitioners of allied professions such as law and accountancy to find adequate work in Berlin if they come with appropriate qualifications and can familiarize themselves with German law/accounting quickly enough to obtain dual qualifications. Indeed, German law firms in Berlin have begun to set up "Israel desks" to cater to this specific bracket. However, while an expensive city, Munich is a very strong competitor to Berlin in start-ups and high tech, and the offices of the Bavarian prime minister (*Staatskanzlei*) include a specific department that deals solely with two mechanisms of Bavarian/Israeli cooperation: the Bavarian Israeli Partnership Accelerator (*BIPA*), and *EXIST* Startup Germany. Both have proven to be so successful that they are being implemented in multiple Germans cities.

Indeed, a large proportion of professionals (63 percent), some lacking advanced academic education, settled in Berlin. Another group that expresses a preference for Berlin is Israelis who work in sales and services. They benefit from their ability to speak English and Hebrew. As a major tourist destination, Berlin needs English-speaking personnel; proficiency in Hebrew is also a definitely favored skill, given the city's immense popularity among Israeli visitors. Furthermore, the Berlin area is home to call centers that consider foreign languages a desirable skill set. These service positions, however, pay poorly and are often limited to a specific stage in life. Consistent with the data on education, it was found that a high proportion of immigrants in blue-collar occupations, who presumably lack academic education, live in other places. Israeli immigrants in managerial positions, technical jobs, and the arts also tend to settle in other major cities relative to the share of these cities among all Israeli immigrants in Germany.

The Israelis' dispersion among these cities resonates with their qualifications. Thus, while Berlin attracts all sorts of Israelis, mainly for lifestyle reasons, the other cities are home to high-tech, IT, and other companies that operate in fields in which the migrants have expertise. Cologne, for example, is home to Ford Germany, and the adjacent Leverkusen hosts the chemical conglomerate Bayer, making the latter city interesting for engineers and life-science specialists. Another highly specialized company, Electronic Arts, attracts Israelis and other migrants with the appropriate, specialized qualifications, which are sought after in Germany. Düsseldorf, home to communication companies such as Vodafone, attracts engineers who had previously worked for Israeli high-tech conglomerates such as Amdocs and Elbit. Munich hosts various consulting and IT companies; Hamburg has an assortment of IT and design firms. The specialized and highly skilled Israelis who find employment with them earn substantial incomes that offset these cities' high cost of living.

Reasons for Moving to Germany and Place of Settlement

We also ask whether and to what extent the factors that pulled Israelis to Germany channeled them to specific cities and areas. To answer, we linked place of settlement to reasons for moving to Germany. The results are the percentages of respondents who rated each given reason as "somewhat" or "very" central (see table 3.7). Above-average percentages attest that the chosen place of settlement can best fulfill their expectations from Germany, namely, the reason for which they moved to the country.

Israelis who settled in Berlin disproportionally sought educational opportunities, German culture, professional and economic advancement, and

Table 3.7. Places of Settlement by Reasons for Choosing Germany (Somewhat/Very Central)

	Education	German Culture	Professional/ Economic	Family Origin	German Partner	Seeking Challenge	Other
Total	**43.7**	**50.8**	**61.2**	**20.3**	**32.2**	**53.3**	**9.3**
Berlin	48.8	60.9	67.0	20.9	27.6	61.0	10.1
Munich	26.4	42.1	65.8	20.6	34.2	64.8	4.3
Cologne	29.2	37.5	54.2	8.4	33.0	54.1	9.5
Hamburg	42.9	47.6	77.3	4.8	59.1	38.0	14.3
Frankfurt	41.4	52.9	76.4	17.6	33.3	47.1	0
Düsseldorf	50.0	28.5	71.4	14.2	50.0	50.0	10.0
Stuttgart	33.3	50.0	55.6	12.5	50.0	55.5	0
Other	40.1	34.5	26.5	25.8	33.9	34.5	6.6

a challenge. These responses corresponded to the immigrants' relative youth and the specific lifestyle they wished to pursue. Düsseldorf also attracted many Israelis who moved to Germany for higher education; the city has a university and several academies of applied sciences, as well as other educational institutions within commuting distance. Düsseldorf, Frankfurt, and Hamburg also attracted Israelis who sought professional and economic advancement by signing on with specific industries there. Notably, Düsseldorf is a state capital, meaning that specific jobs related to the needs of the state administration are common. Furthermore, Düsseldorf houses several high-tech companies and is an affluent city; thus, Israelis manage to find work there due to their previous experience in Israel. Düsseldorf also homes a very significant number of Japanese tech and high-tech companies, which manifests in the Japanese Chamber of Commerce that has nearly 600 companies as members. These companies, highly specialized themselves, add to the attraction of Düsseldorf as Israeli residents in Düsseldorf and Cologne areas—the two cities are in close spatial proximity—evidenced.

A large share of Israelis who followed a partner to Germany became residents of Stuttgart, Hamburg, Düsseldorf, and other places. A relatively large number of Israelis who moved to Germany because of family roots are dispersed among places other than the seven major Israeli communities in the country, presumably settling in the hometowns and, at times, even the villages of their German partners and spouses. As most of them have not been living there for long, it remains unclear whether they and their partners/spouses will stay there or move to another place in Germany or in some other country. Longer-established Israelis who moved to their partners' hometowns or villages show little interest in either form of relocation; according to interview data, they have sunk roots and feel at home. Arrival at the place of residence and also home ownership and formation of local friendships were stressed as markers: all individuals who emphasized these parts of the migration process were fluent in German or spoke it at a near-native level. One of these Israelis reasoned that since his wife was a teacher in their town of residence, their children had been born there, and he had found other Israelis in the area, he felt fine where they were. Moving, he indicated, would uproot the entire family, and neither he nor his wife was interested in any such outcome. Another migrant who moved to the remote area where his wife lived considered the matter settled because they bought a house there, had children there, and felt the youngsters were being raised in a good place. Children were often the game-changer in this regard: as with second-generation immigrants who happened to stay in Germany because they had children in the country, these two members of the third generation wished to remain in a specific location because of their children, their wives, and their having begun to feel at home.

Future Migration

Veterancy and Permanence

Internal migration is not the sole option of immigrants who feel the need to move on. Some may entertain doubts about their permanence in the new country and anticipate either returning home or moving to another land (Bilsborrow, 2016). This is especially true in regard to unrestricted migration among developed countries. Insofar as immigrants in the new country hold a passport that carries benefits across the European Union, they are free to move, study, work, and live in many places. This increases the likelihood of another migration. In regard to Germany, Israelis and other Global Northerners benefit from preferential treatment (Bundesagentur für Arbeit, 2017). This preferential treatment makes Germany more attractive as an emigration destination based on the economic imperatives that underpin the program, and which benefit immigrants.

Slightly more than half of the Israelis in Germany intend to stay in the country in the next five years (see table 3.8). About one-third think

Table 3.8. Expected Place of Residence Five Years On, by Veterancy in Germany (Percentages)

Veterancy in Germany	Expected Place of Residence			
	Germany	Israel	Other Country	Total
Total	57.0	11.5	31.5	100.0
1–3 years	49.4	12.4	38.2	100.0
4–5 years	56.9	13.7	29.4	100.0
6–10 years	58.2	13.3	28.5	100.0
11–20 years	77.5	5.6	16.9	100.0
21+ years	72.4	6.9	20.7	100.0

it likely that they will leave Germany in favor of another country. One in ten considers returning to Israel. Thus, the overwhelming majority seems to have decided to leave Israel permanently.

Three Israelis who live in Berlin express different stances. Uri, who works for a large German bank, does not think of returning to Israel even for a moment. He finds Germany "a wonderful country to live in. The major difference between it and Israel is that Germany puts the citizen in the middle, whereas in Israel the 'center' and the country are not synonymous" (Amit, 2013: 22). At the other extreme, Asaf Moses, who owns a start-up online clothes shopping called UPcloud and has an Israeli girlfriend, does not see his future in Germany. "When I establish my own family, I think it will happen in Israel. I've been in Berlin nine years now but still can't imagine my life here further. It's hard for me to see myself putting my children in a kindergarten here. I haven't planted roots here. [. . .] It's not bad for me here, but also not good [. . .]" (Amit, 2013: 20). Some vacillations, mainly associated with work and livelihood, were expressed by Tal Shaham-Drishiner. Whenever she and her husband visit Israel on vacation, they always ponder the idea of staying in Israel for a year or two to allow their children to catch up with Hebrew. "The idea is romantic but I don't want it. If we do it, he [her husband] and I will be in Berlin half the time for work in any case and I'll have to do more designs for advertisements, whereas what I really love is theatre and opera. If I work around the clock at the Cameri [in Tel Aviv] to make a living, I won't have time for the children. My husband won't be able to earn in Israel what he's paid here and he won't have a place to develop in" (Amit, 2013: 21).

Intending to stay in Germany is associated with veterancy in the country (see table 3.8). Fewer than half of new immigrants—those who settled in Germany in the past three years—expect to be staying there by 2020. The intention increases commensurate with veterancy and crests at three-fourths among those with eleven to twenty years in Germany (retreating slightly thereafter). We surmise that recent migrants are less integrated economically and culturally, hence somewhat uncertain about their future in the new country. As time passes, they will probably be more confident about staying on. That many newcomers (1–3 years after immigration) do not intend to stay in Germany does not imply that they will return to Israel; in fact, the opposite is true: most of those who will not stay in Germany would like to try another country.

Place of Residence and Permanency

Specific ambiguities were expressed in our interviews and fieldwork conversations. Recent young arrivals were not sure whether they wanted to stay, move on, or return to, all indicative of their specific stage in life. Others, in the course of completing their degrees, were weighing their options in terms of whether and where they wanted to obtain more education. Those who held nonpermanent academic exchange positions were certain that they would move, as one of them said, to "wherever I can find work; I'm a desperate academic." The immigrants most certain about remaining were those who had a German partner/spouse and children in the country. Even they, however, expressed ambiguity. "[. . .] But if we ever break up, I'll have nothing here without him," intoned a women whose assets in Germany comprised nearly twenty years of veterancy, fluency in the language, and three children. Another lamented, "Sometimes I'd like to be among other Israelis in order to speak my language." Although his children spoke Hebrew, what these migrants missed were cultural references that other—native—Israelis understood. His German-born and -raised children, in contrast, were literate in Hebrew but only partly literate in Israeli culture. Couples comprised of two Israelis spoke differently: while they had some ties to Germany, speaking about moving and moving again were common even after years in Germany and despite having children in the country. In most cases, "migration talk" did not take the form of actual migration during the time of our study because remigration—back to Israel, within Germany, or abroad—would trigger the same exhausting process of migration all over again. Although one cannot determine for sure whether these migrants would take this step again, our fieldwork indicated that migration talk was more common than the realization of migration.

Another issue that may impact the sojourn/return of Israelis is antisemitism. Irrespective of how the increase in antisemitism came about and whether it is recorded accurately, both of which are vigorously debated, we found that parents in particular worried about their children: "I'm not sure it's okay for [the children] to tell other kids they are Jews" (Kranz, Hotam, and Shoshana, 2019). While beyond our actual target group, it is worth noting that younger Israelis expressed opinions on these issues too, and that they were aware of Jewish/non-Jewish relations. A very vocal fifteen-year-old expressed his own ambiguities about being in Germany: "I can't imagine moving back to Israel anymore. It's so nice and quiet here, the quality of life is so much higher, and people are nice. But [. . .] you know, I haven't had any negative experiences about being a Jew—yet." Child/teenage migrants surely voice their hopes and fears to their parents, and their well-being may be the tipping point in their family's decision to remain in Germany, return to Israel, or move on again.

Our investigation of future geographic patterns by current place of residence yields substantial variations (see figure 3.3). Israelis in Frankfurt and Hamburg exhibit high rates of intending to stay in Germany. Rates resembling the total average characterize Israelis in Berlin and Munich. In contrast, a low proportion (fewer than half) of Israelis in Cologne and "other" places intend to stay in Germany for five years. Approximately one-quarter (27 percent) of the former thought it likely that they would return to Israel, many of whom came just to acquire advanced education, while the paramount intention among those in "other" places was to relocate to a new country (45 percent). This pattern attests that work might not be available at the place of education, or the place of education is unattractive as a long-term residence option.

Cities with a high proportion of Israelis who intended to stay—Hamburg, Frankfurt, and Munich—are considered rich cities, and some of the Israelis with the highest incomes lived in these places. The mixture of their substantial incomes, and the sizes of the cities support, as well as the quality of life of the locales, long-term residence plans. A survey of the *WirtschaftsWoche* (Economic Week), a widely read weekly, ranks Munich at the top city in terms of livable cities, Frankfurt is ranked fifth, Hamburg ninth. Cologne ranks twenty-seventh, Berlin comes in at thirty-eight (*WirtschaftsWoche*, 2019) in the *Städteranking* 2020 (City Ranking 2020). The ranking filters in "soft factors" like quality of life, but also educational facilities for children for example, kindergarten, property and rental prices, economic developments, and average income per capita. These factors become more important once migrants consider settling, and raising families: the cool clubs of Berlin do not do it for the migrants in

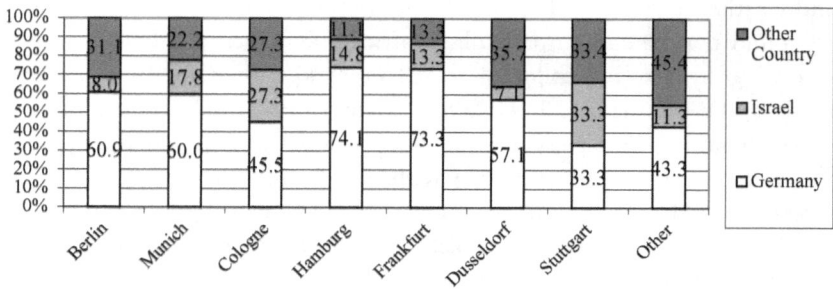

Figure 3.3. Place of Current Residence by Expected Place of Residence Five Years On (Percentages).

the long run. Both Berlin and Cologne have high rates of crime, and along the structure of their labor market may push some people away. Another factor that we found mainly in regard to Berlin was the temporal nature of migration: while Berlin attracts Israelis, this does not mean they develop ties. A specific parameter that indicates this trend toward temporality is that Israelis in Berlin displayed a weaker knowledge of the German language than their peers in other cities and that they live in an English-speaking cosmopolitan bubble (Almog, 2015; see also table 4.1, below) with some Hebrew opportunities. This structure is specific to Berlin, which homes a significant number of transient migrants; many Israelis tend to fit this pattern.

These intercity variations also are partly associated with reasons for moving to Germany: Israelis who settled in Berlin, Frankfurt, and Hamburg were strongly attracted by their desire for professional and economic advancement, and it is likely to hold them in the new country; Israelis in Hamburg were often pulled by a local partner, which also help to plant strong roots. At the same time, Hamburg offers serious work opportunities. By contrast, many of the Israelis in Cologne were not motivated by a well-defined incentive, increasing the likelihood for a repeat migration in search for a new place or returning to Israel. Some of the Israelis who settled in "Other" places were tied to a spouse who wished to return to the town in which he or she was born. But there are those who chose these "other" towns because of family origin, and it seems that nostalgia alone can't replace long-term considerations of work, culture, and friends. At this juncture, it became clear to these Israelis that being of German origin in Israel, and feeling ties to a specific ancestral place is very different from living in Germany, and having to deal with the imagined place of return. Still, some of the places, foremost Berlin, with a rather large proportion who wish to stay in Germany, have a high concentration of Israelis providing a critical mass for a vital social and cultural activities in Hebrew and feeling of being at home away from home. Yet, as mentioned before, lifestyle migrants in Berlin are characterized by transience, and weak moorings outside of the Hebrew or cosmopolitan bubble. Perhaps more than any other place, Israelis in Berlin are torn between strong hold incentives, on the one hand, and push negative factors, on the other hand, resulting in relatively high proportions of people who intend to stay and others who consider leaving the country.

Reasons for Choosing Germany and Permanency

Table 3.9 provides insights into intentions regarding future mobility among those who were attracted to Germany to a large extent by each of the following

Table 3.9. Expected Place of Residence Five Years Later, by Reasons for Moving to Germany (Percentages)

	To A Large Extent			
	Germany	Israel	Other Country	Total
Education	67.1	11.6	21.3	100.0
German culture	70.9	5.0	24.1	100.0
Professional/economic	65.9	12.4	21.7	100.0
Family origin	71.4	8.6	20.0	100.0
German partner	67.5	13.2	19.2	100.0
Seeking challenge	65.0	12.5	22.5	100.0
Other	66.7	9.1	24.2	100.0

factors: education, German culture, professional and economic opportunities, family background in Germany, German partner, challenge, and other. Obviously, if a given factor was central in the decision to move to Germany, it is likely to generate a strong intention to stay. Still, there are variations, sometimes quite substantial, in intentions as a dependency of the specific reason for settling in Germany. Israelis who moved to Germany because of local culture or family background are the most likely to stay. They typically knew what they were getting into, in contrast to many new arrivals who saw Germany as a place of adventure (see also Cohen and Kranz, 2017). Some had been attracted to Berlin by word of mouth or by hearing about other Israelis' (positive) experiences. Indeed, those who sought a challenge, but also those in search of professional and economic advancement, are the most disappointed and are relatively disinclined to stay. Often, they were ignorant in matters of Germany, Germans, and the country's structures, resulting in frustration; "I thought things would go *chik-chak* [real fast] but everything's so slow. [. . .] It takes forever to get a flat." This ill-informed Israeli had moved to Berlin because "there are loads of opportunities [there], everyone said." When asked who "everyone" was, he replied, "other Israelis." That these others may have only had limited knowledge did not occur to him; nor did he imagine that some of them may have glossed over their own—problematic—experiences. Problems that indicate lack of understanding of the local culture and structures seemed to be taboo among some recent arrivals in Germany—Berlin in particular—as part of the Berlin hype (i.e., cultural incentives); frustration was voiced only in Israel-specific forums, if at all. Israelis who moved to other locations did not explain this phenomenon. Often, they had visited their intended place of residence, had previous experience in the country, and enjoyed a range of social contacts before emigrating. In other words, they had access to the crucial resource of social networks.

Regardless of their reasons for moving to Germany, most of those who do not intend to stay expect to relocate to a new country. An especially weak intention to return to Israel was found among those who had moved to Germany mainly because of the local culture. These Israelis often had psychological roots in Germany or Eastern Europe and found Germany culturally attractive and easy to connect to. They evinced the results of strong intergenerational transmission of Germanness in terms of *"yekkishkeit,"* a specific historically infused notion of pre-Holocaust German Jewishness or a Europeanness in terms of Ashkenazi Jewish ethnicity in their families of origin (Kranz, 2016b; 2018d).

Determinants of Future Place of Residence

Veterancy in Germany, current place of residence there, and reasons for immigrating to Germany are strongly interrelated. Likewise, other family background and sociodemographic characteristics may influence an émigré's desire to stay in Germany or to leave and, in that case, whether to return to Israel or to move to a new country. To appropriately assess the independent role of each of these factors in future migration, we conducted a multivariate analysis.[6] We looked at both the determinants of returning to Israel and moving to a new country versus staying in Germany. A coefficient greater than 1 attests to a stronger likelihood of leaving Germany (returning to Israel or immigrating to another country, respectively); a coefficient lower than 1 is indicative of tendency to stay in Germany. We complemented these findings with insights from our in-depth personal interviews.

Few factors are significant for future place of residence (see table 3.10). All other things being equal, later arrival (year of immigration) is more likely to induce return to Israel than lengthy veterancy in Germany. In contrast, those who left Israel due to political and security considerations or the religious establishment's involvement in public life were less inclined to return than were those who did not consider these reasons central. Similarly, those who chose Germany for its cultural opportunities were more determined to stay than to move back to Israel. Our research partners' words and expressions also show that their thoughts about staying or returning are anchored in specific stages of life (particularly German children and family), developing a sense of home over the years, and lifestyle. Israelis who left Israel with a bitter taste were unlikely to return even though, fascinatingly, their social and cultural activities revolved around the country they so deeply spurn

(Kranz, 2020b). Israelis who rejected Zionism and Israeli politics and policy displayed this tendency with particular intensity (Amit, 2018). Some of them were engaged in creating a new Hebrew diaspora in Berlin and attempting to decolonize the Hebrew language from the Zionist discourse (Amit, 2017). Regardless of their political stance, Hebrew language constituted the border that encircled the construction of Israeliness (Merkur, 2019). Most Israelis were less extreme than those who seek to create a radical Hebrew diaspora, although their unhappiness about Israel's political landscape and social development was widespread. That these matters would suffice to make these Israelis stay abroad or return at some point is a contentious matter that came up repeatedly in our discussions, as even Israelis who had renounced Israeli citizenship and opted for German citizenship returned to Israel regularly. Others had weighed denaturalization as a symbolic act but decided to remain Israel citizens because they still had family in Israel. However, the notion of "still having family" was ambiguous, because "family" could denote one of two things: kin who remained in Israel or continuing to belong to the Israeli family in a legal sense. Thus, in some ways, all of the migrants maintained some tie to Israel despites their ambiguities, happiness in Germany, or unhappiness about Israel.

The more recently Israelis settled in Germany, the more they considered moving to another country (see table 3.10). As discussed above, these are often young and highly skilled migrants, or those still attending university and at a stage of life where they feel neither the need nor the desire to settle down or decide where to move on. A paramount determinant of intended future migration is having parents or grandparents who are Holocaust survivors; this doubles the likelihood of wanting to leave Germany in favor of another country, compared with those with no such immediate family. Our interpretation is that a family background associated with the Holocaust evokes sensitivity toward and disapproval of the member who has gone to Germany. As Harry Maor (1961) and Jacob Oppenheimer (1967) indicate in reference to the children of survivors, the wish to leave Germany was pronounced and paramount among those who had been born and (partly) raised in Israel (Panagiotidis, 2015). For current Israelis, a Holocaust background does not eliminate disapproval of returning to Israel but does have this effect on staying in Germany.

Israelis who attached much importance to the religious establishment's involvement in their decision to emigrate are ill-inclined to leave Germany. They are probably satisfied with the absence of religion as they know it in their new place of residence, because religion is often less visible in Germany than in Israel. That is, civil marriage is available, public transportation runs all

Table 3.10. Determinants of Future Place of Residence

Independent Variables	Israel/Germany Odds ratios	Other Country/Germany Odds ratios
Year of immigration	1.104*	1.124*
Reasons for Emigration from Israel		
Political/security	0.657[i]	1.068
Professional development	1.036	0.912
Economic development	0.768	0.820
Education	1.190	1.159
Religious establishment	0.480*	0.640*
Family/friends	0.726	0.927
Other	1.200	0.909
Reasons for Choosing Germany		
Education	1.041	0.830
German culture	0.697[i]	0.974
Professional/economic	1.304	0.938
Family origin	1.236	1.085
German partner	1.108	0.807[i]
Seeking challenge	1.089	0.872
Other	1.227	1.088
Sociodemographic Characteristics		
Age at immigration: 18–24	3.147	1.008
25–29	1.330	0.867
30–34	0.693	0.926
35–39	1.612	2.665
Gender: Female	0.752	0.612[i]
Other	0.254	0.211
Place of residence: Large cities	0.592	1.720
Other places	0.486	0.889
Family Reaction to Leaving Israel		
Strongly opposed	1.091	0.684
Opposed	1.057	1.338
Neutral	1.482	1.049
Supportive	0.594	1.188
Family Reaction to Choosing Germany		
Strongly opposed	1.115	0.208
Opposed	0.789	0.590
Neutral	1.802	0.741
Supportive	1.661	0.766
Parents/grandparents Holocaust Survivors		
Yes	0.850	2.220*
Explanatory Power	48.2%	

*Significant at least at the 0.05 level; *i* Significant at $p < 0.10$.

Reference categories are: Age at immigration—40+; gender—male; place of residence—Berlin; family reaction to leaving Israel/choosing Germany—strongly supportive; parents/grandparents Holocaust survivors—no.

week long, Sabbath and Yom Kippur laws do not exist, and dietary (kosher) rules do not restrict food production. At the same time, most Israelis have not been in Germany long enough to understand the power of the country's churches and its Christo-normativity, some of which became palpable only during the—discursively—constructed refugee crisis. After being welcomed by parts of the population at the height of their migration in 2015, the mainly Muslim migrants quickly became suspects in terms of not fitting into Germany's value system, triggering an upturn of the German Right in particular. Rates of both antisemitism and Islamophobia climbed measurably (Beauftragte der Bundesregierung, 2016), begging the historical—and current—question of how "genuinely" European Jews and Muslims can become (Doughan and Tzuberi, 2018). Indeed, negative attitudes toward both groups often correlate (Pew Research Center, 2018), and the main parameter of rejection of either or both of them is the "closed worldviews" outlook, which denotes the rejection of outgroups (Pew Research Center, 2018; Schwander and Manow, 2017). While some Israelis of longer veterancy picked up on these developments with the help of their proficiency in the German language and discourse, newer arrivals did not.

Israeli women are less expected to leave Germany for another country than are Israeli men. Being the mother of a child with a German partner is certainly one reason for this. Also, however, Israeli women migrants stressed that they perceived their lives in Germany as more favorable than living Israel (Cohen and Kranz, 2017). This notion needs to be seen within its biographical context: Germany being favorable to them as individuals should not be equated with its being a gender-equal society or with the idea that women there do not experience gender discrimination. According to Eurostat, women in Germany earn 21 percent less than their male peers and the gap is constant. That women become mothers is less expected than in Israel. However, that highly qualified German women do not have children is not only based on a different ideology; for a significant number of women, combining a career with motherhood seemed impossible, as the sociologist Jutta Almendinger, herself the president of the *Wissenschaftszentrum Berlin* (*WZB*, Berlin Social Science Center), argued in numerous publications throughout her career (Allmendinger, 1994; Allmendinger and Haarbrücker, 2017; Allmendinger and Kübler, 2020). It should be noted that Almendinger is a member of various consulting boards for the German government on the issue, yet she does not tire of outlining that it remains an uphill battle.

Although only a few factors had significant effects, they managed to explain about half (48 percent) of variation among Israelis concerning their plans to stay in Germany, return to Israel, or move to a new country.

In sum, Israelis have been relocating to Germany in small numbers throughout the years. At the beginning of this century, however, a watershed was crossed: the overwhelming majority of Israelis who live in Germany today moved there since then. Most of them are young men and women who emigrated after acquiring academic education in Israel and amassing some work experience in professional jobs. Whether compared with the characteristics of the total Jewish population at origin or with that of the German host population, these Israeli migrants stand out positively in many particular ways. Although their most preferred city is Berlin, substantial numbers settled in other large cities as well as smaller towns across the German landscape. Not all of them see Germany as their permanent home for the foreseeable future; many intend to relocate to a new country, but only few give thought to returning to Israel. These settlement patterns do not operate in a vacuum; rather, they are associated with the émigrés' reasons for leaving Israel, the factors that attracted them specifically to Germany, their family background in World War II Europe, and their sociodemographic characteristics.

Chapter 4

Social Integration

The Multifacetedness of Integration

Irrespective of the considerations for migration—push factors associated with place of origin, pull factors at destination, or just seeking a challenge—newcomers wish to successfully integrate into their host environment. Immigrants crave well-being, safety, and opportunities for themselves and for their actual or potential children. They may experience integration in different ways and rhythms, depending on their motives for immigrating; demographic characteristics such as age, gender, educational attainment, and occupational qualifications; time of settlement and the economic conditions in the new locality; the host population's willingness to accept them; their status (skilled, labor, or illegal), and so on. The social and economic heterogeneity of immigrants, including the replenishment of their population through the arrival of additional immigrants, paves the way to other trajectories of integration, including segmented assimilation into specific high/low strata and the creation of ethnic niches (Alba and Nee, 1997; 2003; Glick and Park, 2016; Hirschman, Kasinitz, and DeWind, 1999; Portes and Zhou, 1993; van Tubergen and Kalmijn, 2005; Waters and Jimenez, 2005).

Adaptation to a new country is multifaceted. Its dimensions are strongly interrelated (a "cumulative process"), yielding an array of possible intersections. Cultural assimilation—often including the acquisition of the local language, among other things—is one of the first reactions of immigrants to the host society. This type of change may take place absent other types of assimilation. Structural assimilation into the core society's social and economic class, in contrast, enhances informal interactions and also, eventually, intimate relationships that may evolve into marital assimilation ("amalgamation"). So suggest Alba and Nee (2003), Gordon (1964), Hirschman (1983), Waldinger (2001), and Glick and Park (2016). Others, however, propose that in multicultural countries, socioeconomic assimilation is not necessarily accompanied by intermarriage or that intermarriage hinges on specific local core parameters that support or inhibit it. Such parameters may be structural, such as lack of the option of civil marriage (Burton, 2015), or social, for example, negative stereotyping (Weißmann and Maddox, 2016). For some groups, upward social and economic mobility increases concentration at the upper limits of the structural ladder; this, in turn, enhances intragroup interactions, turns religious and ethnic peers into partners in a set of social, cultural and political styles, and maintains group cohesion including endogamy (Goldscheider, 2004; Muttarak and Heath, 2010; Portes, 1995; Portes and Zhou, 1993; Rumbaut, 1997). Still, some ponder the causality of this process, suggesting that it is intermarriage that abets economic rewards and not the other way around (Furtado and Song, 2015).

Even if language is not imperative for other dimensions of integration, it diminishes social distance and strengthens interethnic acquaintance, hence fostering amalgamation. Likewise, some proficiency in the local language may often be a prerequisite for immigrants to gain legal status, including citizenship. Marrying a native-born may also help immigrants to obtain residency status in the destination country or citizenship (Castaneda, 2008). This, in turn, is likely to be positively associated with income and accumulation of wealth and property (Extra, Spotti, and van Averment, 2009; Glick and Park, 2016; Kringelbach, 2013; Parisi, 2014; Stevens and Swicegood, 1987; Terdy and Spener, 1990).

Against this background, Israelis' social integration in Germany is explored in the current chapter. The discussion focuses on levels of integration, how they change with veterancy, and the role of the precipitants of immigration, settlement characteristics, and demographic and socioeconomic attainment in the integration processes. Our concern is with four dimensions of integration: proficiency in German, marriage composition, citizenship, and homeownership. Notably, since all members of our targeted population share one origin country (Israel) and settled in one destination country (Germany), they were exposed to similar contextual and structural conditions of immigrant-integration policy (although there may be some variations among German states or cities in the welcoming of immigrants and in sources and forms of community amenities and government assistance) (Glick and Park, 2016). According to the Migration Integration Policy Index (MIPEX), which takes into account components such as immigrants' labor-market mobility, long-term residence, access to naturalization, and antidiscrimination, Germany ranks tenth among thirty-eight European and other Western countries for its policies on inclusion and has improved its score in the past few years (MIPEX, 2015). However, German society, and with it German politics, have been displaying trends of polarization. Thus, the national elections in September 2017 underlined nationalistic tropes and culminated in an unprecedented rightward swing, and a European Union election in May 2019 emphasized resistance to liberal social trends and gave powerful evidence of generational conflicts. Similarly, intergroup relations in German society have been impacted and sentiments toward migrants, including Israelis, have risen to prominence in the social discourse. In regard to Israelis, in particular the issue of Israel specific antisemitism has been hotly debated since the German parliament passed the so-called anti-BDS (Boycott, Divestment and Sanctions movement against Israel) resolution in May 2019. This resolution defines BDS as antisemitic, and strips it of access to any public funding.

German-Language Proficiency

Linguistic adjustment, the process through which immigrants become proficient in the language of their new country, is a paramount aspect of integration into the host state's majority. Three major mechanisms determine proficiency in the dominant local vernacular: *exposure* to the language, *efficiency* in learning it, and *economic incentives* that encourage the acquisition of linguistic skills. Each of these mechanisms is comprised of several components that, while not matched with a specific mechanism on a one-to-one basis, are often linked to two or even all three mechanisms (Carliner, 2000; Chiswick and Miller, 1995; Grenier, 1982; Kulkarni and Hu, 2014; Lopez, 1999; Rebhun, 2015; van Tubergen and Kalmijn, 2005).

Exposure is related to opportunities to learn the new language through characteristics such as veterancy in the destination country, motive(s) for migration (push-pull), intention to settle permanently, spouse's nativity (and, in turn, mother tongue), and the presence of children who bring the new language home from school. Efficiency denotes the process that converts exposure to the destination language into language proficiency, parsed by affinity characteristics such as age at immigration and education.[1] Economic incentives view language as a form of human capital that enhances productivity in the labor market and in consumption. Since language skills also boost the independence of the migrant, they act differently on immigrants as a function of their education, which, in turn, is positively associated with opportunities in the labor market; of young age at immigration, which reflects lengthier benefiting from the social and economic returns of the investment in acquiring a new language; and, based on the latter logic, of the intention of staying in the current country, moving to another country, or returning to the origin country. Economic incentives are also likely to vary by gender, as immigrant men need strong proficiency in the new language more than women do in order to find work (Beenstock, 1996; Chiswick and Miller, 1995; 2007; Chiswick and Repetto, 2000; Stevens, 1999); that is, men often remain the higher-grossing member of a couple, even within the EU (Eurostat, 2017).

Language is composed of three major elements: speaking, reading, and writing. While each is affected by the others, speaking and understanding a new language are acquired first and are expected to make the other two easier to learn. Speaking is critical in interpersonal communication; it allows immigrants to amass information about their new abode and improves their prospects of economic attainment. Hence, it is a paramount linguistic tool of adjustment to the host society.

For Israeli Jews in Germany, however, German carries an emotional charge (Katz, 2011). Many associate German, in general, and certain words, in particular, with the Nazi era and the Holocaust, evoking negative associations. German is often presented by Israeli immigrants as a language that, at least upon arrival but also after many years in Germany, constitutes a burden that needs to be suffered (Amit, 2013; Sweid, 2016). It may be a "blow in the diaphragm" (Yair, 2015: 60). Consciously or unconsciously, it relates to an injured place (Yair, 2015: 63; Katz, 2011). The Israeli ear is sensitive to German; for Israelis, it is "full of radioactive words that also in daily routine we—not them, only we—are exposed to the ongoing discomfiting flow of poisoned material into our arteries" (Oz-Salzberger, 2001: 157). Examples of words that may be especially grating to Israelis are *raus* (get out), *Arbeit* (work), *frei* (free), *schnell* (fast), and *Achtung* (danger). To this day, fans of the Hertha Berlin football club shout the victory word *Sieg*, originally used in Nazi political rallies, in the Olympic stadium that the Nazis built (Oz-Salzberger, 2001: 158). While the German language has not changed to the scorched ears of non-native-speaking Israeli, who perceives it as the supreme cultural component of German society and continuity (Yair, 2015: 61), this perception changes markedly with time (Katz, 2011). As the Israeli émigrés gradually pick up the nuances of the language, they realize that native speakers of German no longer use specific Nazi-tainted words such as *undeutsch* (non-German), and they contextualize words such as *Arbeit* and *Achtung*. Indeed, if Israelis use these words carelessly around German native speakers, they fall on differently scorched German ears.

We cannot determine whether and how much this sensitivity inhibits Israeli immigrants' progress in learning German. Guy Katz (2011), in his assessment of German/Israeli business relations, found that the effect lapses quickly. Katz's participants had a common goal that our participants did not share with the same clarity. In some cases, however, we found Israelis who were eager to learn German rapidly and fluently in order to understand the extensive German discourse about the past as well as that related to present-day Jews and Israel. Indeed, most of our respondents have at least some command of German. Approximately one-fifth self-assessed their proficiency in German as "very good," one-fourth "good," and another one-fourth mediocre; the others have either weak knowledge of German (23.7 percent) or none at all (5.7 percent) (see figure 4.1).

Linguistic proficiency improves with veterancy (see table 4.1). The proportion of respondents who indicated weak command of German gradually diminishes from 37 percent of those who immigrated in the past three years to fewer than one-fourth of those with four or five years of veterancy, to

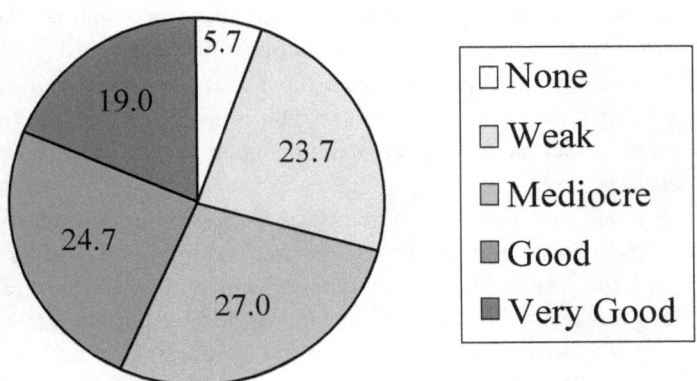

Figure 4.1. German-Language Proficiency among Israelis in Germany (Percentages).

Table 4.1. German Language Proficiency by "Exposure" Factors (Percentages)

	None	Weak	Mediocre	Good	Very Good
Veterancy					
0–3 years	11.9	37.0	32.8	11.9	6.4
4–5 years	0	23.9	31.5	34.8	9.8
6–10 years	1.2	10.5	24.4	43.0	20.9
11–20 years	0	1.5	13.2	27.9	57.4
21+ years	0	0	0	31.8	68.2
Place of Residence					
Berlin	7.5	23.5	30.2	24.6	14.2
Other large cities	3.9	21.7	22.5	26.4	25.6
Other places	1.3	27.6	27.6	27.6	15.8
Employment Status					
Employed	5.6	20.1	29.1	26.3	19.0
Self-employed	5.7	20.5	25.4	27.0	21.3
Student	3.4	19.1	25.8	33.7	18.0
Unemployed/retired/other	7.6	35.5	27.2	13.6	16.1
Children					
No	5.4	25.6	30.7	23.1	15.2
Yes	7.8	16.2	20.8	27.9	27.3

one-tenth in the next category of veterancy (6–10 years), and to nearly zero among those who have spent more than ten years in the country. The rate of Israelis who have mediocre proficiency in German also declines commensurate with veterancy. Concurrently, the proportion of Israeli émigrés who speak German very well increases from 6.4 percent of recent arrivals to a peak of 68.2 percent among the most veteran immigrants. After more than twenty years in Germany, all Israelis exhibit good or very good command of the local language.

It is likely that recent immigrants learn German more quickly than veteran peers who arrived in the 2000s. Back then, less Germans spoke English and the Israeli immigrants, rather fluent in English, were able to find jobs quite easily. Today, in contrast, the local labor market expects people with advanced career aspirations to be comfortable in both German and English; individuals of these kinds who stumble in German are especially unlikely to survive in the country (Amit, 2013). Daniel Norman, who arrived in Germany in 2014, expressed this view in an interview with

Social Integration | 105

Spitz when he was asked about his learning German: "[. . .] I continue to study every day. It's a process that never ends. [. . .] At the same time, I realize that more people here speak English. [. . .] Simply, this [Berlin] is an international city" (Sapir, 2014a: 16). Berlin and other urban areas, however, are outliers in this respect: they are home to large numbers of

Photo 2. Cover Page of *Spitz Magazine*, no. 2 September 2012. Illustrator: Avital Yomdin. "So What You Will Live On? They told you that you don't need lots of money to get by in Berlin and that if you have German citizenship the Job Center will help you. It's all true. But very soon you'll discover that even in the coolest city on earth you still have to work. So how do you make a living in Berlin without fluent German? Here's how."

migrants and have international bubbles that accommodate Germans who work or act internationally and are fluent in English and/or other languages. This is less often the case in remote areas.

A place of residence is not only a physical space but also a social and cultural environment. As we have seen in the previous chapter, Israelis tend to settle disproportionally in cities and various areas across the German map. Places with high concentrations of Israelis provide more opportunities for personal interaction and participation in organized activities in Hebrew. Where concentrations of Israelis are smaller, the émigrés' informal social networks are likely to be composed mainly of local people, resulting in intensive exposure to the German language. Indeed, in Berlin, which boasts the largest concentration of Israelis—far ahead of other areas—the share of Israelis who speak German well or very well is lower (38.8 percent) than in other large cities (52 percent) and other places (43.4 percent). At the other end of proficiency in German, the proportion of Israelis in Berlin who cannot speak German at all is twice as high (7.5 percent) as among Israelis in other large cities (3.9 percent), and six times more than Israelis in other places (1.3 percent) (see table 4.1).

This data set also reveals the higher transience of Israelis who settle in Berlin. While Israelis in other cities are more likely to settle in Germany for the long term, Berlin Israelis tend to be younger and more ambivalent about remaining, causing them to take less interest in the social and economic returns that might be theirs if they master the local language. Furthermore, amplifying the disinterest factor, one can get by in Berlin and other major cities with English due to the city's substantial foreign cosmopolitan population and social media groups that cater specifically to internationals. This is not the case for smaller cities or villages. At the same time, reflecting the size of its Israeli population, Berlin also has the largest number of Israelis who hold EU citizenship and accordingly, do not need German language skills in order to obtain residence as only non-EU citizens are required to attend language and integration courses.

People who work interact with colleagues, customers, or clients, requiring use of the local language. These encounters are often more intensive for employees than for the self-employed, apart from self-employed who have client-focused businesses or provide a customer-related service. Students are also heavily exposed to the new language and are expected to be proficient in it. Taking together the two highest levels of speaking, students are the most proficient in German among the Israeli émigré groups. At the other end, only a tiny proportion of Israelis who do not work or are retired (or have some other employment status) speak German well or very well in this regard. Somewhat surprising is the disadvantage of employed immigrants as against their self-employed counterparts, albeit the differences are small (see table 4.1). In our qualitative fieldwork, we found that the most skilled and highly skilled Israelis spoke German very well or well and that some—despite non-German and non-Yiddish linguistic backgrounds—spoke German at a native level. One of the latter explained, "I came to Germany as part of a delegation and it was my aim to take something home with me: I decided to really learn German." Twelve years after his arrival, he is still in Germany. Although the German language was not the only skill he had acquired during that time, he remains—understandably—proud of his accomplishment. Another Israeli who came to Germany at the end of the 1990s understands German fully but finds German grammatical structures frustrating; therefore, his diction retains case and syntax errors and a noticeable Hebrew accent. While both of these respondents have similarly high levels of education (PhD and MSc, respectively), the respondent who speaks German flawlessly is not only married to a German native speaker but, while not ruling out a return to Israel, is unequivocally content with being in Germany. His MSc-decorated fellow countryman, in contrast, remains acutely ambivalent about being in Germany and torn about where he wants to be. He is also less exposed to Germans in his leisure time and remains on the hunt for a German-Jewish spouse. His case indicates that language acquisition and proficiency also relates to psychosocial factors of content and belonging, which we could trace only through ethnographic research due to their highly idiosyncratic contours. Overall, as Hanna Yagar proposes (2012), the best advice for someone who wants to earn a living in Germany is to learn German and to do so as quickly as possible.

Having children, who are presumably enrolled in a local school, amplifies parents' exposure to the new language. In fact, children are important agents of socialization, helping their entire family make the cultural adjustment. Israelis who have one child or more are almost twice as likely to have very good command of German as childless peers (27.3 percent and 15.2 percent, respectively) (see table 4.1). This stresses the importance of emotional and psychological anchoring points that favor acquisition of the language and the desire to—literally—understand the significant other. "I want to be able to help [my son] with his homework," one father explained. As it turned out during our conversation, the father wanted to participate in his son's life, in which the vernacular (German) was dominant. His wife, also an Israeli of non-German background, followed the same logic: she too, has stepped up her investment in learning German because she wishes to participate as a parent.

At the same time, Israelis with children of kindergarten and school age recounted that while educational settings expose them to the German language and improve their own language skills, they contrast strongly with their own experiences of interaction with teachers in Israel. "I told [the teacher] several times she could call me Ilana [an alias], but she insists on using my last name." Although the respondent spoke German well, the crucial distinction in the use of names, which codes the level of formality of social situations in Germany, did not translate into this Israeli's social praxes, indicating that understanding social practice and linguistic skills may diverge.

Proficiency in the destination language is associated with age at immigration. Young people learn new languages faster than do elders (Long, 1990). Likewise, youth at immigration means that migrants will have longer to enjoy the social and economic benefits of investing in linguistic human capital (Chiswick, Lee, and Miller, 2004). It may also be assumed that young immigrants establish social contacts with natives more smoothly than do older immigrants and accordingly enjoy intensive exposure to the new language. Research on social contacts according to stages in life bears this out (Munch, McPherson, and Smith-Lovin, 1997). By and large, Israelis in Germany act on this reasoning. Four of every ten who immigrated at ages eighteen to twenty-four speak German very well, as do about one in four who immigrated in their late twenties. Very few of those who immigrated at age thirty-five-plus speak German very well.[2] At the other end of the language continuum, the proportion of migrants with no or weak command of German increases slightly with age at migration. In this respect, older Israeli émigrés may live on pensions instead of labor income, a situation that seems to diminish their wish to strengthen their German language skills. For example, while only one of ten Israelis who moved to Germany at age twenty-four or younger assessed their ability to speak German as weak, three or four times as many among those who immigrated at age thirty-five-plus did. For those who could not speak German at all, the differences between the youngest and oldest cohorts were 5.1 percent and 9.3 percent, respectively (see table 4.2).

General education is helpful in learning a new language efficiently. If education (postsecondary in our case) is acquired in the new country, hence in the local language, it further abets the strengthening of linguistic capabilities. Remember that approximately half of our respondents specified the acquisition of education as an important consideration in their decision to move to Germany; furthermore, only some universities offer specific courses and degrees in English. Likewise, education expands opportunities in the labor market. Since the types of jobs suited to highly educated people are nonmanual (Chiswick and Miller, 2001), the better schooled a migrant is, the more he or she gains in earnings by being proficient in the destination language (Grin, 1990; Chiswick and Miller, 1995). Our insights into the relation between education and German-language proficiency are somewhat ambiguous: Israelis with advanced academic credentials are the ones most likely to speak German well or very well (49.4 percent). Isolating the highest level ("very good") only, however, we find Israelis who lack matriculation ranking first. Likewise, Israelis with postsecondary education have better German skills (good/very good) than do their counterparts who hold bachelor's degrees (see table 4.2). We speculate that Israeli migrants with specific educational attainments also differ in other demographic and socioeconomic aspects, including migration characteristics, which may act as stronger determinants of language capacity.

Our qualitative fieldwork was able to elucidate only some of these speculations. The paramount issue that came up was that Israelis who lacked matriculation certificates did have some other kind of training that required them to speak German in the specific positions that they held. In one case, an IT specialist revealed that he had no formal education, not even having

Table 4.2. German-Language Proficiency by "Efficiency" Factors (Percentages)

	Not At All	Weak	Mediocre	Good	Very Good
Age at Immigration					
18–24	5.1	10.2	20.4	25.5	38.8
25–29	2.1	19.8	27.8	26.2	24.1
30–34	7.6	30.3	28.6	24.4	9.2
35–39	12.1	37.9	27.6	19.0	3.4
40+	9.3	34.9	32.6	23.3	0
Education					
No diploma	3.4	27.6	22.4	17.2	29.3
Matriculation	10.4	16.7	33.3	25.0	14.6
Post-secondary	0	29.3	22.0	34.1	14.6
BA	6.3	25.0	31.3	23.1	14.4
MA+	4.6	24.3	21.7	25.7	23.7

finished high school; he had learned his job by doing and by having joined an Israeli high-tech company at the lowest level, gradually working his way up. Another Israeli was a well-established photographer. Having finished high school, he had learned his trade the same way. Both of these (male) migrants had German-passport-holding wives and entered Germany as tied spousal migrants. For one of them, the spouse was a native German speaker, as were their two children, affecting his language proficiency for the better. In the other case, the migrant's wife held a German passport due to her eligibility as the grandchild of German Jews, but spoke no German. Yet her spouse, by dint of his work, learned the language, albeit much less fluently than did the husband of the native-German-speaking wife.

Reasons for migrating to Germany dovetail with the workings of social and economic incentives. Factors that strongly pull Israelis to Germany may also encourage them to learn the local language in order to fulfill their well-defined expectations of the new country. The psychological factor of attraction to German culture also affects the language uptake. Other factors that are less central in moving to Germany may not trigger a craving for fluency in the new language. Among respondents who specified a given reason as very central in their decision to move to Germany, figure 4.2 shows the ratio between the proportion whose proficiency in German is "good"/"very good" and the proportion among all Israeli migrants who exhibit these levels of proficiency. A value higher than one attests to a better command of German as a specific reason for migration than the average

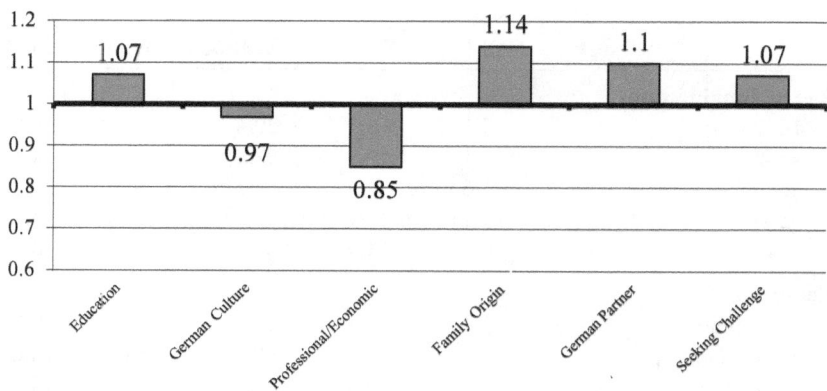

Figure 4.2. German Language Proficiency ("Good" and "Very Good") by Reasons for Immigration to Germany (Ratios).

among all Israelis in the country; a value smaller than one reflects weaker proficiency. Israelis who were strongly attracted to Germany by its educational opportunities, who had a family background in the country or a German partner, or who sought a challenge are better trained in German than are the others. They invested in acquiring German for a combination of pragmatic and emotional reasons. Unsurprisingly, this was especially salient among Israelis who had an immediate family member of German origin. They had either been exposed to the German language at home but not learned it actively or had experienced a pronounced transmission of Germanness within their family constellations, making the active acquisition of German complementary to their preexisting German identities. In contrast, those who moved to Germany for the local culture or for economic and professional advancement were weaker in the language. Since German literally did not come natively, acquiring it carried less emotional and identity currency. In fact, moving to Germany because of a German partner was an important determinant of language proficiency. Even if these intimate relations were not anchored officially (i.e., in marriage) or later broke down, they were indicative of current and/or past intensity of use of German and, in turn, strong command of the language.

The investment in learning a new language is more profitable for immigrants who intend to stay in Germany for the long run than for those who intend either to move elsewhere or to return to their home country. Notably, in a cross-sectional study such as ours, we cannot always distinguish between cause and effect, namely, whether the intention to stay enhances learning of the local language or failure to acquire linguistic competency pushes people out. Either way, the data in table 4.3 clearly show

Table 4.3. German Language Proficiency by "Economic Incentive" Factors (Percentages)

	None	Weak	Mediocre	Good	Very Good
Future Migration					
Germany	3.1	19.6	26.2	30.1	21.0
Israel	8.6	34.5	25.9	17.2	13.8
Elsewhere	9.9	26.1	31.0	18.3	14.8
Gender					
Male	4.7	23.7	31.0	25.9	14.7
Female	6.8	25.6	23.3	24.7	19.6

that Israelis who intend to stay in Germany over the next five years exhibit much higher levels of language proficiency than those who consider leaving the country. For example, slightly over one-fifth of Israelis who expect to stay in Germany speak German very well and another 30.1 percent speak it well; the respective figures for those who think they will return to Israel are 13.8 percent and 17.2 percent, and among those who consider moving to another country 14.8 percent and 18.3 percent. Israelis who plan to return home have very poor German: 43.1 percent speak it poorly or not at all, as opposed to 36 percent of those who intend to move to another country and only 22.7 percent of the more permanent settlers. Perhaps those who expressed an intention to return to Israel viewed their move to Germany from the beginning as a kind of adventure or had another reason that lacked strong motivation and, hence, were not strongly driven to master the language. Our qualitative data suggest that these short-term sojourners felt that English suffices to get by, also giving indication that they had no vested interested in joining the labor market for prolonged periods of time. Return migration may also provide evidence for difficulties in learning German and foreign languages more generally.

Typically, men are more likely than women to migrate for economic reasons and, hence, to join the labor force, abetting stronger competence in the new language (Massey et al., 1993). However, women's growing participation in the labor force in Western societies means that immigrant women are affected as well, making it probable that gender gaps in language proficiency are narrowing. In the case of our target population of Israeli immigrants in Germany, the overwhelming majority is young and unmarried, increasing the likelihood among both men and women of enrolling in higher education or finding work. Notably, too, we found no significant gender differences among the respondents in reasons for emigrating generally and settling in Germany particularly (see chapter 2); this may further blur gender differences in motivation to learn the host language. Thus, a higher proportion of Israeli women than their male counterparts speak "very good" German (19.6 percent and 14.7 percent, respectively—see the bottom of table 4.3), but slightly more women than men do not speak German at all or have weak proficiency. Overall, immigrant women are disproportionally concentrated at the strongest and weakest ends of the linguistic continuum, while immigrant men are more dispersed, with a salient proportion admitting to a mediocre command of German.

Ethnographic fieldwork yields insights on this oddity: Israeli women migrants appeared in some ways as a binary. Highly skilled women were often migration drivers if married. Married or single, they migrated for self-fulfillment. Single highly skilled Israeli women immigrants stressed in particular that Germany offered them a preferable lifestyle (Cohen and Kranz, 2017). At the opposite end of the spectrum, Israeli women immigrants who were less fluent, were married, and had children were tied to spouses; busy raising children and running a household, they were less able to learn German. These women highlighted the burden of migration more often than did those who were initiators of migration; they also regularly pondered returning to Israel.

To ease the vagueness that emerged in some of the descriptive observations, we performed a multivariate analysis (see table 4.4). The results point to three major determinants of German-language proficiency, each associated with a different mechanism of exposure, efficiency, and economic incentives. For the first mechanism, veterancy is positively associated with speaking the new language. In comparison with the most recent arrivals—those who immigrated in the past three years (the reference group)—longer veterancy corresponds to higher levels of fluency that ramp gradually to a peak among Israelis who have been in Germany for more than two decades (as evident by the size of the coefficients). In the second mechanism, the significant determinant of proficiency in German is age at immigration. This is especially true for the two youngest cohorts and the positive effect is stronger among those who came at age eighteen to twenty-four years old than among the following age group. These immigrants were most often single, still studying or holding odd jobs, and able to forge multiple social contacts in their new surroundings due to less pressure on their time. Immigrants who reached Germany in their thirties do not differ significantly from those who were forty or older when they settled there, indicating that age and stage in life impact language acquisition.

All other things being equal, two pull factors strengthen immigrants' motivation to learn the new language: having a German partner, and wishing to acquire education in Germany. Moving to Germany for professional and economic advancement, in contrast, slows the pace of acquisition. We surmise that people who have the latter motive are involved in international business and therefore use English in the main; some may even work in Germany–Israel services, in which case they also have opportunities to speak Hebrew.[3]

Although few variables played a significant role in this model, they were able to explain more than half of the variation in Israeli immigrants' ability to speak German.

Table 4.4. Determinants of German-Language Proficiency[1]

		Logic Coefficient
Exposure Variables		
Veterancy in Germany:	4–5 years	1.311*
	6–10	2.220*
	11–20	3.550*
	21+	4.166*
Place of residence:	Other large cities	0.041
	Other places	0.189
Employment status:	Employed	−0.077
	Self-employed	0.084
	Student	0.160
Children: Yes		0.066
Efficiency Variables		
Age at immigration:	18–24	2.084*
	25–29	1.236*
	30–34	0.569
	35–39	0.267
Education:	Matriculation	0.021
	Post-secondary	−0.358
	BA	0.377
	MA+	0.302
Economic Incentive Variables ("Very Central")		
Reasons for choosing Germany:		
	Education	0.457[i]
	German culture	0.449
	Professional/economic dev.	−0.757*
	Family origin	0.227
	German partner	0.712*
	Seeking challenge	−0.283
Future migration:	Germany	0.469
	Elsewhere	0.147
Gender:	Female	0.068
	Other	−1.962
Explanatory Power		*51.9%*

[1] Ordered logit coefficients
*Significant at least at the 0.05 level; i Significant at $p < 0.10$.

Reference categories are veterancy—0–3 years; place of residence—Berlin; employment status—unemployed/retired/other; children—no; age at immigration—40+; education—no diploma; economic incentive variables—not at all/a little/somewhat central; future migration—Israel; gender—male.

Intermarriage

In their study on migration and social integration in the United States, the sociologists Richard Alba and Victor Nee (2003) define intermarriage as the litmus test of assimilation. Intermarriage connects people from different national, religious, ethnic, or racial backgrounds at the most intimate and ostensibly equal levels. Accordingly, the volume of mixed marriage attests to the extent of elasticity and blurring of group boundaries. The present-day flow of international migration, accompanied by growing emphasis in major destination countries on pluralism and individualism, is encouraging the "internationalization of intimacy" (Rodriguez-Garcia, 2015) (see also Alba, 2020). Still, intermarriage rates vary by the extent of the host society's acceptance of specific groups and the migrants' desire to mix with the native population. Notably, immigrants' intermarriage is likely to involve two dimensions: with people of a different nativity (native and foreign-born) and, because immigrants do not always share the dominant religion of the host society, with the crossing of religious lines.

Germany shows several specific patterns of intermarriage that create an intersection of the social and legal spheres. Religion is socially often defined as belonging to the private sphere and not to be discussed despite Germany being a Christo-normative society. Further, in Germany as in all European societies, Christianity is seen as the "norm" from which all other religious deviate (Anidjar, 2003; 2015). Although religion is deemed private, deviations from the Christian norm trigger ongoing conflicts (Doughan and Tzuberi, 2018). This is manifested most saliently in the 2012 circumcision debate that affected both Jews and Muslims (Dekel, Forchtner, and Efe, 2019), in ongoing regular discord and litigation ostensibly about Muslim headscarves,[4] and unequal production of knowledge about Jews and about Muslims (Doughan and Tzuberi, 2018). The upturn in antisemitic incidents, both in verbal form (Schwarz-Friesel, 2018) and in physical violence (RIAS, 2018), coexists with escalating Islamophobia (Beauftragte der Bundesregierung, 2016); the two often march in tandem (Pew Research Center, 2018). Judaism counts as a religion and not an ethnicity under German law; the same goes for Christianity. The religious institutions of either are public bodies under public law (*Körperschaft des öffentlichen Rechts*), state-recognized and state-protected. These features set these two religions apart from other religions in the country, indicating the higher level of integration of Jews (relative to any religious group that does not benefit from this legal status) into the socio-legal texture. The oddity of this relationship ramifies into the area of intermarriage: intermarriages between Jews and non-Jews rarely raise eyebrows with non-Jews in Germany (Rapaport, 1997), but marriages between Muslims and non-Muslims startle (Kranz, 2018c; Weißmann and Maddox, 2016).

Yet even as religion is deemed private, it carries public currency. Official data collection in Germany replicates this paradoxical structure: data on binational intermarriages are gathered within a sociodemographic framework by way of its connection to the legal realm ("family reunification"), whereas data on interreligious marriages between German citizens are collected randomly. Thus, for example, statistics for the State of North-Rhine exist for marriages of Jews for 1977 to 2013 (personal email to Dani Kranz, January 30, 2019). The Jews behind these figures, however, were self-identified Jews. Jews who do not disclose their Jewishness or belong to no Jewish community are statistically out of reach. What is more, this statistic does not contain data on citizenship, just as the national statistic of *Destatis* lacks data on religion. If a German citizen marries a foreign national, only his or her citizenship is recorded. In other words, a marriage between a German Jew and an Israeli Jew would be deemed an intermarriage in the German national statistics but not in the statistics of the State of North Rhine–Westphalia, while a marriage between a German Jew and a German Muslim might enter the intermarriage statistics at the state level, where Muslims are categorized as "other religions," but not on the national level, as both partners are German citizens. Thus, the statistics for this state reveal that historically more Jewish men married non-Jewish women, which replicates what sociologist Lynn Rapaport (1997) found for her second-generation respondents who were members of the Jewish community in Frankfurt. With the third generation it changes: slightly more Jewish women marry non-Jewish men. Be that as it may, intermarriage, which is contentious among Jews in Germany, has been common, and it remains common. By that token, Israeli Jews do not act differently from the "local Jews."

This peculiar legal structure is relevant for our analysis due to the sizable number of Israeli émigrés who hold EU citizenship. Even though they may be partnered with a German citizen, they will not appear in the statistics on "family reunification" visas. Other Israelis will not appear in the statistics as participants in "Israeli/German" intermarriages because one partner holds French citizenship and the other holds German citizenship, or because both spouses hold passports of other EU countries and neither is a German citizen. We found all these variations in our fieldwork, as well as dual Israeli/Swiss citizens who had German nonmarried partners. The statistical situation is even more complicated when Israeli migrants have minor children with a German citizen; then the Israelis' residency rights are legally secured via parenthood and are independent of marital ties unless they hold EU, European Economic Area, or Swiss citizenship.

Here we focus on marriages between Israeli Jews and non-Jews as documented in our survey. About four of every ten of Israelis in Germany (42.7 percent) are currently married. Another one in five (16.8 percent) lives with a partner. In Germany, as in Western Europe, more generally, the latter style of living may include having children together; hence, it is a substitute for official marriage. The remaining Israelis in Germany are either single (33.3 percent) or formerly married (5.1 percent). Nearly half (45.9 percent) of married Israelis have a non-Jewish spouse (see figure 4.3). Among those who are not married but live with a partner, the rate is even higher (three quarters). We cannot determine whether the latter avoided marriage due to religious differences, or for other reasons simply preferred not to anchor their intimate relations in a formal contract, or deemed marriage unnecessary due to EU citizenship or parentage of German minor children, whose existence secured their residency rights.

We now parse differences in marital patterns by family background, immigration factors, and sociodemographic characteristics. We focus only on Israelis who reported that they are married, to the exclusion of those who live with a partner due to uncertainty about the strength and long-range commitment of these ties. We found strong relations between families' reaction to moving to Germany and marital patterns. Israelis whose immediate family opposed their move to Germany tended less to marry outside the Jewish faith (see table 4.5). More specifically, fewer than one in three of

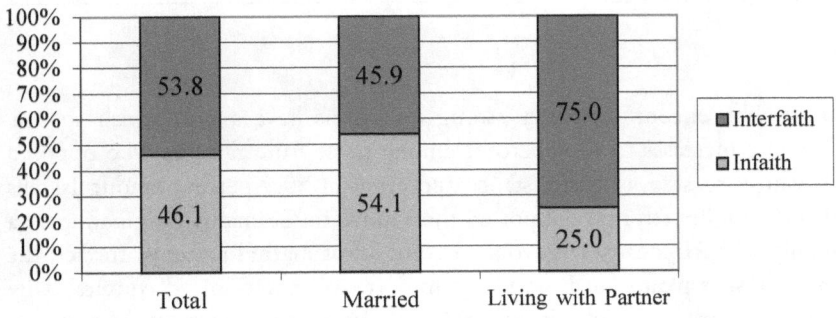

Figure 4.3. Marriage Composition among Israelis in Germany (Percentage).

Table 4.5. Marriage Composition by Family Background and Reasons for Migration (Percentages)

	Total	Jewish Spouse	Non-Jewish Spouse
Reaction of Family to Moving to Germany			
Strongly opposed	100.0	69.0	31.0
Opposed	100.0	55.6	44.4
Neutral	100.0	55.6	44.4
Supportive	100.0	50.0	50.0
Very supportive	100.0	49.1	50.9
Family Background			
Not Holocaust survivors	100.0	52.3	47.7
Holocaust survivors	100.0	53.0	47.0
Reasons for Emigration from Israel ("Very Central")			
Political/security	100.0	50.0	50.0
Professional development	100.0	56.1	43.9
Economic development	100.0	57.9	42.1
Education	100.0	50.0	50.0
Religious establishment	100.0	49.2	50.8
Family/friends	100.0	50.0	50.0
Reason for Choosing Germany ("Very Central")			
Education	100.0	54.5	45.5
German culture	100.0	49.0	51.0
Professional/economic development	100.0	66.0	34.0
Family origin	100.0	51.3	48.7
German partner	100.0	26.2	73.8
Seeking challenge	100.0	50.0	50.0

those who encountered very strong objections have a non-Jewish spouse. The rate increases to 44.4 percent among those from families who opposed or who expressed a neutral stance and crests at 50.9 percent among Israelis whose families strongly supported their move to Germany. Originating in a family with Holocaust survivors does not affect marital patterns. In fact, the Holocaust is plainly of little if any importance in the mixed couples' daily lives; they try to avoid talking about this issue and manage to be together without having this historical elephant in their home. If they associate it with anything, they do not judge their German spouses by what their grandparents may or may not have done some seventy years ago (Onger, 2013). This pattern is very different to what is known about the existing intermarriages (Rapaport, 1997; Speier, 1988) and interpartnerships (Schaum, 2020) of locally born and raised Jews.

Israelis who specified a given reason as significant ("very central") in their decision to emigrate are often characterized by above-average intermarriage rates. Similarly, if they were strongly pulled to Germany for a certain reason, they manifest their wish to integrate deeply into the general local environment by having a strong tendency to marry non-Jews. Predictably, the intermarriage rate is especially salient among those who had a German partner before migrating. Israelis who left their country for economic reasons or chose Germany in search of professional and economic opportunities are outliers in that they have below-average rates of intermarriage; still, four out of every ten and one-third of them, respectively, have non-Jewish spouses.

Our qualitative data reveal that Israelis who entered Germany as singles had not filtered in the marriage issue. As young people often bent on educational accomplishments or pursuit of careers, they placed marriage and children on the back burner: "This is all really far removed from me," one respondent said. Concurrently, since the vast majority of Israelis in Germany are secular and Israeliness dominates Jewishness, they overlook the Jewish components of their Israeli identities, which may surface as they amass veterancy and gather strength when they become parents. This leads to potentially unexpected consequences for the migrants themselves, but more so for their partners/spouses, who had encountered them as secular, nonobservant Israelis and now confront a puzzling change.

Early age at immigration is positively associated with intermarriage (see table 4.6). It stands to reason that those who immigrated in their twenties were still single at that time and could have met their spouse in the new country. By contrast, some of their peers who immigrated at later stages of the life cycle had married in Israel before emigrating and, hence, showed lower rates of intermarriage. Early immigrants are more prone to intermarriage than are more recent arrivals (see table 4.6). The intermarriage rate is almost three times higher among Israelis with more than twenty years' veterancy compared to those who immigrated in the past three years; the intermarriage rate of the latter is significantly lower than that among all Israelis in Germany. We propose two nonmutually exclusive explanations for

Table 4.6. Marriage Composition by Migration and Settlement Factors (Percentages)

	Total	Jewish Spouse	Non-Jewish Spouse
Age at Immigration			
18–24	100.0	36.7	63.3
25–29	100.0	41.7	58.3
30–34	100.0	55.8	44.2
35–39	100.0	80.0	20.0
40+	100.0	63.9	36.1
Veterancy in Germany			
0–3 years	100.0	76.0	24.0
4–5 years	100.0	52.8	47.2
6–10 years	100.0	42.9	57.1
11–20 years	100.0	32.7	67.3
21+ years	100.0	29.4	70.6
Place of Residence			
Belin	100.0	55.8	44.2
Other large cities	100.0	50.6	49.4
Other places	100.0	59.0	41.0
Future Immigration			
Germany	100.0	40.4	59.6
Israel	100.0	84.4	15.6
Other country	100.0	64.6	35.4

these differences: (1) as seen in the previous chapter, early immigrants are more likely than more recent ones to have been attracted to Germany by a local partner; (2) over time, the pool of Israelis in Germany has grown and so, accordingly, have opportunities to date and establish intimate relations within the Israeli-Jewish community. The former point is confirmed by qualitative data, whereas Israelis who had non-Jewish spouses and partners in Germany had often maintained close if not intimate contact with non-Jews in Israel before emigrating.

There are no substantial differences in intermarriage by place of residence. In all three area categories (Berlin, other major cities, other locations), the proportion largely resembles that of the national scene among Israelis in Germany. We speculate that the rate for Berlin reflects a trade-off of a concentration of Israelis (and local Jews) and hence the availability of a larger Jewish marriage market, on the one hand, and a highly secular orientation among Israelis there, as many of them had lived in Tel Aviv before emigrating, on the other hand. These are "extreme Tel Avivians," as one Israeli observer described them; secularism as well as indifference to Jewish law is part of their identity, which one may term a specific "zeitgeisty" brand of secularism. Intermarriage rates are slightly lower in small places that have fewer Israelis and also, presumably, small Jewish communities (see table 4.6). These findings contrast with our assumption of an inverse relation between community size (small) and rates of intermarriage (high). This may attest to the social and cultural nature of Berlin and other large cities as pluralistic and permissive places. These features lead to the blurring of religious and ethnic boundaries and emphasize freedom of choice including that of partnership; they also bear witness to the different makeup of the Israeli resident population in Germany. Concurrently, Berlin knows the *Neutralitätsgesetz* (neutrality law), which flows from the Prussian-Protestant ideology of confining religion to the private sphere. This invisibility of religious outer accoutrements supports the perception among Israeli Jews that Germany and its large cities—including of course Berlin—are secular, an issue that social scientists strongly challenge (cf. Amir-Moazami, 2018). In other words, the mainstream Christian religion in Germany is invisible at first glance, while minority faiths come across as hypervisible due to specific symbols related to them. This does not mean that Christian religion is absent in Germany; instead, an undercurrent of specific Christian-infused secularism dominates perceptions of "appropriate" religious visibility in the public sphere.

More in line with expectations is the relation between future migration and marital patterns. Israelis who sank deep roots in Germany had the highest rates of intermarriage (59.6 percent). They often had children with their non-Jewish spouses and made their home in Germany. Thus, one respondent attested, "But this *is* home!" indicating he found the very question—Where do you feel at home?—strange. Another respondent noted that whereas he managed to find work in Germany and learn German, his wife would not do as well as those in Israel and he saw no reason to uproot his family. A third participant, torn about where he wished to live, indicated that his (very serious) girlfriend had a profession tied to Germany, making him wonder whether "In ten years, I'll be one of those Israelis: married to a non-Jew, kids, I guess it's a done deal." By implication, while he had not planned to immigrate permanently, the combination of love for his girlfriend, his own career progress, and parental supportiveness would inadvertently make his emigration permanent. Among Israelis who intend to return to their home country, in contrast, fewer than one in five has a non-Jewish spouse, indicating that they may see their stay in Germany as a mere sojourn and may have brought their aversion to intermarriage with them. Israelis who expect to move to another country in the next five years fall somewhere in-between (see table 4.6). Some of them have non-Jewish spouses who do not hold German citizenship; they may return to their home country and bring their Israeli wife or husband along.

Israeli women are slightly more inclined to marry outside the Jewish faith than are their male counterparts (see table 4.7). In contrast to Israel, Israeli women in Germany—as we found in our fieldwork—were highly aware that their marriage and potential motherhood with a non-Jew would not endanger their children's Jewish descent under rabbinical law. At the same time, we found that Israeli women were attracted to non-Israeli men on the basis of their negative perception of Israeli men. Whether individual Israeli men live up to these women's derogatory stereotypes, and to what extent, lies in the eye of the beholder, although machismo is indeed part of

Table 4.7. Marriage Composition by Sociodemographic Characteristics (Percentages)

	Total	Jewish Spouse	Non-Jewish Spouse
Gender			
Male	100.0	59.1	40.9
Female	100.0	53.7	46.3
Education			
No diploma	100.0	33.3	66.7
Matriculation	100.0	54.2	45.8
Post-secondary	100.0	58.3	41.7
BA	100.0	61.2	38.8
MA+	100.0	53.0	47.0
Occupation			
Professional and arts	100.0	41.9	58.1
Management	100.0	41.2	58.8
Technical	100.0	68.2	31.8
Sales/service/blue-collar	100.0	50.0	50.0

Israeli culture. Marrying a non-Israeli is certainly a mechanism that would distance an Israeli from his or her native country, be the reason what it may. Research into German/Israeli intermarriage/partnership indicates that fantasy about the other plays a significant role for some Israelis and Germans (Rau, 2016). It is strongly debatable, however, that this exoticism and the fantasy about the "other," who is only human at the end of the day, can lend substance to any relationship, because long-term stable and happy marriages, including intermarriages, rest on homophilous values.

Cultural differences between Israelis and their German spouses are likely to generate disagreements and tensions. Regardless of which spouse is Israeli and which is German, differences revolve around matters such as organizing things, managing time, tolerance, professional ambition, and spending money. Lack of fluency in German also often abets spousal misunderstandings. For some Israelis, cultural differences were found to be serious obstacles in maintaining intimate relationships that otherwise might have evolved into marriage (Onger, 2013). It can be hypothesized that in some cases cultural differences substantiated interpersonal differences, leading to marital breakdown—a well-established pattern among intermarriages, in which the divorce rate is higher (Kalmijn, de Graaf, and Janssen, 2005).

The relation between education and marriage patterns is somewhat inconsistent. Still, Israelis who did not finish high school tend more to marry out than those who hold academic degrees (bachelor's or advanced). Immigrants who are at a human-capital disadvantage (e.g., short on education) may view a local spouse as a springboard to social and economic mobility (Kalmijn, 1998). Alternatively, on the negative side, they may not be seen as marriage material by coethnics, who do not find them exotic because they can spot other Israelis rather easily.

Much in harmony with the high intermarriage rates among those lacking high school matriculation and the low rates among people who have matriculation but no more than that, those in the lowest occupational category approximate the national average in their intermarriage rate (see table 4.7).[5] What appears puzzling in the quantitative data is the very high proportion of Israelis in professions and the arts who intermarry—six out of ten—even though the rate among degree-holders was similar to or even slightly below the average. Artists, we found, pursue a specific lifestyle and have specific attitudes that support interpartnership/intermarriage. Artists often construe their vocation as transgressive and challenging to the status quo. Intermarriage/interpartnership ties into both qualities and with nonnormative self-fulfillment. One performing artist put her relationship and her emigration from Israel into an intergenerational perspective and linked it with intermarriage: "I have the relationship with a non-Jewish man that my grandmother (who was displaced from Greece) could not realize . . . and I left Israel, where my grandmother did not want to be."

Although we were able to discern this pattern, which in some cases was additionally supported by the attraction to the "other," we have no data on the longevity of these relationships. Some degree-holding Israelis hold professional jobs, which are characterized by high rates of intermarriage because the sides encounter each other in a setting dominated by a non-Jewish majority. One may argue that their marriages to non-Jews were predicated on chance, windows of opportunity, and also marriage squeeze, as non-Jews outnumbered Jews among eligible partners. Others, with similar levels of education, found their way to managerial and perhaps technical positions in which intermarriage is less prevalent, indicating that a specific career trajectory may result in "professional endogamy." Importantly, data not shown here suggest that the differences in intermarriage rates among professional, managerial, and technical workers do not stem from wage employment versus self-employment. The mere fact of being self-employed offers no clues about an individual's personal investment in a specific line of work; mostly it illuminates his or her actual or potential preference or a legal requirement.

By performing a refined multivariate analysis of the associations among background variables, immigration factors, and sociodemographic characteristics and marriage composition, we were able to verify key observations of the descriptive findings. No major reasons for leaving Israel are significantly associated with marrying out of the Jewish faith (see table 4.8). Two factors, however, did increase the likelihood of intermarriage, albeit not very powerfully (i.e., significantly): the political/security situation in Israel and limitations on professional mobility. These push factors should be viewed as rebuffing any desire of returning to Israel and, in turn, deep acculturation into the new country, including amalgamation. In a metaphorical sense, the Israeli migrant sets up a safe and stable new home in the new country, indicating a relation between feeling physically and professionally safe and place-making. Many Israelis who moved to Germany in the wake of their German partners eventually married them, as evidenced in the positive and significant relation of this conduct with intermarriage. Choosing Germany because of its professional and economic opportunities is negatively associated with intermarriage.

Israelis in Germany who intend to stay are more likely than others to have a non-Jewish spouse, indicating that intermarriage and presumed

Table 4.8. Determinants of Marriage Composition[1]

		Exp(B)
Background Variables		
Family reaction:	Opposed	0.216
	Neutral	0.407
	Supported	0.578
	Strongly supportive	1.185
Parents/grandparents Holocaust survivors:		
	Yes	1.223
Reasons for emigration from Israel:		
	Political/security	1.223
	Professional development	1.46
	Economic development	0.855
	Education	0.975
	Religious establishment	0.745
	Family and friends	0.962
Reasons for choosing Germany:		
	Education	0.973
	German culture	1.451
	Professional/economic	0.581*
	Family origin	1.042
	German partner	1.938*
	Seeking challenge	1.067
Migration and Settlement Variables		
Age at immigration:	18–24	2.087
	25–29	2.418
	30–34	1.508
	35–39	0.406
Veterancy in Germany:	4–5	1.589
	6–10	2.643
	11–20	0.972
	21+	2.579
Place of residence:	Other large cities	1.370
	Other places	0.635
Future migration:	Germany	7.173*
	Elsewhere	3.898
Socio-demographic Characteristics		
Gender:	Female	1.204
	Other	1.000
Education:	Matriculation	0.148[i]
	Post-secondary	0.778
	BA	0.705
	MA+	0.992

continued on next page

Table 4.8. Continued.

		Exp(B)
Socio-demographic Characteristics (continued)		
Occupation:	Professional and arts	3.417[i]
	Management	2.566
	Technical	1.053
	Sales/service/blue-collar	1.755
Explanatory Power		51.6%

[1] Logistic regression.
*Significant at least at the 0.05 level; [i] Significant at $p < 0.10$.
Reference categories: family reaction—strongly opposed; parent/grandparents Holocaust survivors—no; age at immigration—40+; veterancy—0–3 years; place of residence—Berlin; future migration—Israel; gender—male; education—no diploma; occupation–doesn't work.

permanence of emigration intersect. At the same time, the pool of eligible Jewish partners/spouses is small in Germany: approximately 125,000 Jews live in the country (DellaPergola, 2018), among a total population of more than 80 million. Thus, it is rare for someone to come across an eligible Jewish partner/spouse, even if one has contact with other Jews and a social network that encourages such linkages. If so, marriage patterns are affected not only by individual Jews' attitudes toward exogamy/endogamy but also by the paucity of Jews in Germany.

Among the sociodemographic characteristics, Israelis with high school matriculation are less inclined to intermarry than peers who lack this diploma. Israelis in professional jobs and in the arts are the group most likely to marry non-Jews. This ties into their personal investment in their jobs, where they meet their partners, and with the likelihood that shared professional interests outweigh Jewishness as a parameter of homophily. All other correlations, whether evidencing the strengthening or the weakening of the tendency to intermingle, are insignificant. Overall, the model was able to allude to a rather high level of explanation (51.6 percent) of variation among Israelis in Germany in marrying within or outside the Jewish faith.

Citizenship

Perhaps no characteristic connects individuals to their country of residence more than citizenship. This official status is the most comprehensive expression of national belonging. It attests to the individual's legally recognized entitlement to membership in the local polity and, in turn, to the state's protection. As such, citizenship is anchored in mutual rights and obligations between the state and its citizens and should verify permanency in the country (Castles and Davidson, 2000; Bilsborrow, 2016; Brown and Bean, 2016).

Immigrants may acquire citizenship by sharing a religious or ethnic origin with the majority population (Yakobson and Rubinstein, 2008) in places where the citizenship model is biased toward *jus sanguinis* (law of blood), although ethnic citizenship is typically subject to challenges (Weiss and Levy, 2002). Even where it is the main characteristic of citizenship law, it is not applied evenly, and is influenced by interpretation (Panagiotidis, 2019). Granting of citizenship may vary among immigrants from different countries of origin (Plotke, 1999). Likewise, some countries may require immigrants to fulfill certain conditions such as basic proficiency in the dominant language, minimum veterancy, or having a first-order family member who is a citizen (Chiswick and Wenz, 2006; Espenshade and Huber, 1999; Extra, Spotti, and van Averment, 2009). In any case, the likelihood of obtaining citizenship rises in tandem with veterancy in the new country (Plotke, 1999).

Countries may condition the naturalization of newcomers on the renunciation of any other citizenship they may hold, although exemptions exist in most cases because some countries do not allow citizens to relinquish their citizenship and, in other cases, origin citizenship may be unclear due to war and displacement or unavailability of documents. Concurrently, globalization and diasporism create increasing opportunities for flexible or postnational citizenship, in which the individual maintains a civic attachment to two or more countries (Bloemraad, Korteweg, and Yurdakul, 2008; Brettell, 2016; Faist, Gerdes, and Rieple, 2004). Finally, an individual who holds dual or multiple citizenships may see citizenship as a strategic asset (Harpaz, 2019; Ong, 1999).

Depending on the legal framework, Chauvin and Garcés-Mascareñas (2012) suggest that "The distinction between citizen and noncitizen is not dichotomous one, but rests on a continuous and reversible gradation . . ." (242). Indeed, increased population movements have thrust noncitizens' rights into a high-intensity legal dynamic. Thus, present-day citizenship is more than a political status or a juridical contract; it embraces many social and cultural components. (For an in-depth discussion of this view, see Brettell, 2016.) Notably, a single family may accommodate members who hold different statuses, for example, citizens, noncitizens, and undocumented children (Glick and Park, 2016; Gomberg-Munoz, 2017).

However crucial citizenship is, for some immigrants legal residency may be even more important, insofar as it determines civic, social, and economic rights (Brubaker, 1989, in Brown and Bean, 2016). Still, citizenship is an important resource and differences in this status may affect patterns of adjustment in the new country (Glick and Park, 2016).

Only about one-fourth of Israelis in Germany hold German citizenship (see table 4.9), presumably, at least partly because most Israelis who

Table 4.9. German Citizenship by Migration Characteristics (Percentages)

	Total	German Citizenship	No German Citizenship
Total	100.0	26.7	73.3
Veterancy			
1–3 years	100.0	23.8	76.2
4–5 years	100.0	16.2	83.8
6–10 years	100.0	22.9	77.1
11–20 years	100.0	43.7	56.3
21+ years	100.0	62.1	37.9
Reasons for Emigration from Israel ("Very Central")			
Political/security	100.0	24.3	75.7
Professional development	100.0	27.7	72.3
Economic development	100.0	23.9	76.1
Education	100.0	28.9	71.1
Religious establishment	100.0	28.8	71.2
Family/friends	100.0	30.4	69.6
Reason for Choosing Germany ("Very Central")			
Education	100.0	29.8	70.2
German culture	100.0	31.2	68.8
Professional/economic development	100.0	26.3	73.7
Family origin	100.0	59.4	40.6
German partner	100.0	16.1	83.9
Seeking challenge	100.0	30.1	69.9
Age at Immigration			
18–24	100.0	33.9	66.1
25–29	100.0	22.9	77.1
30–34	100.0	28.8	71.2
35–39	100.0	19.4	80.6
40+	100.0	29.5	70.5
Future Immigration			
Germany	100.0	28.5	71.5
Israel	100.0	22.6	77.4
Other	100.0	26.8	73.2

migrated to Germany did so in the past few years. Germany just agreed in November 2019 to permit naturalization of Israeli citizens as Germans without the previous requirement to renounce Israeli citizenship or to apply for a specific permission to maintain it. The latter was granted or declined on discretion. Israelis who descend from German citizens and satisfy the requirements of the Basic Law and the German Citizenship Law do not fall within these restrictions and could always maintain their Israeli citizenship. For all others, citizenship is strongly linked to veterancy: while there are no significant variations among those whose stay in Germany is short, that is, less than ten years (typical of approximately one-fifth of those have citizenship), 43.7 percent of Israelis who have lived in Germany for eleven to twenty years have local citizenship and the rate rises to 62.1 percent among the most veteran Israelis in Germany—those who have stayed more than two decades (see table 4.9).

Indicative of the specific vagaries of German naturalization is the requirement that noncitizens maintain residency for a specific amount of time before applying. Since the Federal Republic was founded in 1949, its citizenship law has been amended several times, and amending directives of how to apply it have been changed as many times. The underlying statute that defines who is German and establishes a baseline for regulations is the Basic Law (*Grundgesetz*, abbreviated as *GG*). Section 116 of the GG outlines who is German and who can obtain citizenship by way of descent. Some individuals may run afoul of its changing definitions in terms of time frames granted for naturalization under specific, directive regulated, stipulation. For example, children of German-citizen women would be Germans only from the beginning of 1975, except for the offspring of unmarried German citizen mothers. Prior to 1975, German citizenship was staunchly patrilineal. German citizen mothers could naturalize their children who were born before 1975 with German embassies and consulates until the end of 1977: since that date, this window of opportunity closed, and these nonnaturalized children of German mothers could only naturalize if they satisfy specific conditions set by the German state, making them unequal to children of German fathers. This status was only changed in 2019, when the children of German mothers who had fled Germany under the Nazis became eligible, while children of German emigrant—as opposed to refugee—mothers remain excluded. These directives in turn were only turned into law in 2021, which means that access to German citizenship of these individuals does not carry any discretion anymore.

Israelis who renaturalized experienced these dynamics within their own family. One migrant, born to a German/Israeli citizen mother and an Israeli-citizen father in Israel in 1977, refers to Germany as a "fatherland," attesting to an emotional tie that he further explained: "I feel I fit in better here than in Israel." Thus, while enjoying the specific benefits of citizenship, he also maintains a positive relationship with Germany and Germanness. His sister, born before 1975, sees her Germanness denied to date, and she feels uneasy about applying for citizenship even under the new legislation. She does not relate to Germany as a fatherland. She finds her noncitizenship infuriating, and relates it directly to the events of the 1930s and 1940s as well as prevailing gender inequalities. If she will apply for German citizenship remains to be seen. This family history ties in with our quantitative finding that Israelis who emigrate in large part for familial or socioeconomic reasons have a slightly higher rate of naturalization than the average among all Israelis in Germany (see table 4.9); some of these Israelis may be of German extraction.

Concurrently, moving to Germany because of a German partner diminishes the likelihood of naturalization. This can be explained by the fact that German citizenship also grants important rights to the recipient's Israeli partner. As one Israeli recounted, "My wife and my children are Germans; I'm on safe ground." That his legal status is inferior to that of his (native German) wife and his children did not bother him; "The German authorities have always treated me fairly," he reasoned. Likewise, a disproportionately high number of Israelis who were attracted to Germany because of its culture, or who viewed living in Germany as a challenge, have German citizenship (see table 4.9). For these Israelis, the arduous and lengthy process of obtaining citizenship resembled the final act in mastering a task.

We found no linear relation between age at immigration and citizenship. In contrast, Israelis who intend to stay in Germany in the foreseeable future have slightly higher rates of citizenship than those who expect to move away, with especially salient differences vis-à-vis return migrants (see table 4.9).

The first part of table 4.10 attests to a clear connection between citizenship and proficiency in German. The proportion of Israeli immigrants that hold German citizenship increases commensurate with better command of the local language, which bases itself on two specific parameters: one must have language skills to naturalize if one uses residence as an inroad, and the more language skills one has the more one understands the local discourse and the costs/benefits of naturalizing versus remaining a noncitizen. While only one in ten Israelis who speak no German have local citizenship—*jus sanguinis* German citizens—this is true for four of ten among counterparts who are very fluent in German. Israelis in cohabitation (living with a partner) are somewhat less likely to hold German citizenship. Bear in mind that most of their partners are not Jewish. Thus, consistent with the decision to move to Germany following a partner, the fact that few of them are Jewish Germans is associated with a below-average citizenship rate. More than one-third of formerly married Israelis have German citizenship, possibly reflecting older age and hence longer veterancy in the country (see table 4.10). The naturalization pattern of formerly married Israelis is indicative of the right to German naturalization: some of these Israelis had been citizens owing to their own German descent, others naturalized while married, and yet others benefited from the option for non-co-ethnic permanent migrants to naturalize. While this path to naturalization is narrow, it does exist and does not entail kinship with German citizens.

Citizenship is associated with several sociodemographic characteristics. Above-average citizenship rates were found among Israelis with high school and post-secondary education, students, employees, and holders of managerial and

Table 4.10. German Citizenship by Linguistic and Familial Characteristics (Percentages)

	Total	German Citizenship	No German Citizenship
German Language Proficiency			
None	100.0	10.0	90.0
Weak	100.0	19.5	80.5
Mediocre	100.0	23.7	76.3
Good	100.0	30.1	69.9
Very good	100.0	41.0	59.0
Marital Status			
Single	100.0	27.5	72.5
Partner	100.0	20.9	79.1
Jewish spouse	100.0	26.9	73.1
Non-Jewish spouse	100.0	28.2	71.8
Formerly married	100.0	37.0	63.0

blue-collar jobs (see table 4.11). It stands to reason that some interrelations would exist among these sociodemographic characteristics: people with high school matriculation but no degree may well be enrolled in post-secondary studies and hold temporary part-time jobs in services and sales. Similarly, immigrants who in overwhelming majority are young and new to the country and hold managerial jobs are likely to be employees rather than proprietors of their own business, a model that often requires a substantial financial investment. These clusters of sociodemographic characteristics seem to ease the way to naturalization. Alternatively, people in these sociodemographic strata are more in need of citizenship and therefore rush to acquire it. In this regard, it should be noted that people wishing to establish their own business may receive governmental support without being German citizens. A well-publicized case is that of Asaf Moses, owner of the start-up company UPcloud, which uses information about customers' size and weight to create physical profiles with which they may be fit with clothing. The

Table 4.11. German Citizenship by Sociodemographic Characteristics (Percentages)

	Total	German Citizenship	No German Citizenship
Education			
No diploma	100.0	29.2	70.8
Matriculation	100.0	30.2	69.8
Post-secondary	100.0	35.0	65.0
BA	100.0	24.0	76.0
MA+	100.0	24.4	75.6
Employment Status			
Employed	100.0	28.1	71.9
Self-employed	100.0	21.3	78.7
Student	100.0	30.0	70.0
Unemployed/retired/other	100.0	28.2	71.8
Occupation			
Professional and arts	100.0	23.6	76.4
Managerial	100.0	34.3	65.7
Technical	100.0	26.2	73.8
Sales/service/blue-collar	100.0	34.0	66.0

EUR 100,000 seed money for this initiative was put up by the German government, which did not condition its support on the applicant's being a German citizen. Asaf did have to meet other criteria including having a business plan, a team of workers with academic degrees, and mentorship of a university professor (Amit, 2013).

All other things being equal (see table 4.12), more than ten years' veterancy increases the likelihood of having German citizenship. Israelis

Table 4.12. Determinants of German Citizenship[1]

		Exp(B)
Migration Factors		
Veterancy:	4–5 years	0.648
	6–10 years	1.384
	11–20 years	6.105*
	21+ years	8.070*
Reasons for emigration from Israel:		
	Political/security	0.798
	Professional development	1.063
	Economic development	0.824
	Education	0.826
	Religious establishment	1.349[i]
	Family and friends	0.951
Reasons for choosing Germany:		
	Education	1.133
	German culture	0.914
	Professional/economic development	1.074
	Family origin	2.471*
	German partner	0.677*
	Seeking challenge	1.310*
Age at immigration:	18–24	0.414
	25–29	0.364
	30–34	1.073
	35–39	0.697
Future migration:	Germany	0.538
	Elsewhere	0.828
Linguistic and Familial Variables		
German language proficiency:		
	Weak	11.034*
	Mediocre	9.680*
	Good	16.503*
	Very good	17.024*

continued on next page

Table 4.12. Continued.

		Exp(B)
Linguistic and Familial Variables (continued)		
Marital status:	Single	1.227
	Married: Jewish spouse	0.961
	Married: Non-Jewish spouse	0.843
	Partner	0.940
Socio-demographic Characteristics		
Education:	Matriculation	1.081
	Post-secondary	0.901
	BA	0.797
	MA+	0.519
Employment status:	Employed	1.058
	Self-employed	0.760
	Student	2.658*
Occupation:	Professional and arts	0.811
	Managerial	1.421
	Technical	1.029
	Sales/clerical/service/blue-collar	1.244
Explanatory Power		*42.9%*

[1] Logistic regression.
*Significant at least at the 0.05 level; *i* Significant at $p < 0.10$.

Reference categories are veterancy—0–3 years; age at immigration—40+; future migration—Israel; German-language proficiency—none; marital status—formerly married; education—no diploma; employment status—unemployed; occupation—unemployed.

who emigrated largely due to reservations about the religious establishment or were drawn to Germany by family background or just for a challenge are positively associated with holding the new country's citizenship. Among the linguistic and sociodemographic characteristics, better command of the local language and being a student create a positive relation with German citizenship. In contrast, choosing Germany as the destination country due to having a German partner (leading to spousal benefits) inhibits local citizenship. This model explains slightly less than half (42.1 percent) of the total variation in Israelis' civic status in Germany.

Homeownership

Immigrants' consumption and property-purchase behaviors are indicative of the allocation of financial resources through labor-market participation and familiarity with the host culture. Among various forms of wealth accumulation and material well-being, homeownership is probably the single strongest indicator of immigrants' successful absorption. The substantial financial investment that it entails makes it major evidence of commitment to and permanency in the host society (Alba and Logan, 1992).

Homeownership necessitates contacts with individuals of higher status and different ethnic backgrounds (Myers, 2005) and more generally, may strengthen immigrants' social identity and acceptance by the mainstream population (Balakrishnam and Wu, 1992). Furthermore, since a family's housing has important implications for succession, it reflects disparities between immigrants and the native population and among different immigrant groups. It also serves as an indicator of potential intergenerational socioeconomic inequality (Hamnett, Harmer, and Williams, 1991; Saunders, 1990). The permanence involved in purchasing a home is likely to foster an improvement in residential conditions and acquisition of other household goods that combine to facilitate a comprehensive assessment of housing success.

More generally, housing characteristics are helpful in establishing a person's class, economic activity, and political preferences; it may also influence social relations (Mitchell, 1971; Slater, 1997; United Nations, 1989). People's willingness to make housing decisions increases with better understanding of the local market, the perceived impact of the general economy on their households, and the security of their employment ("consumer confidence") (Garner, 1991; McCray, Weber, and Claypool, 1986; Zagorski and McDonnell, 1995). Therefore, in the case of immigrants, housing is an important indication of multifaceted social and economic integration as well as the success of policies aimed at meeting immigrants' expectations and the host society's goals.

The determinants of differences in homeownership among immigrant and ethnic groups fall into three major groupings: human capital and financial resources such as education, employment, and language proficiency; immigration factors, that is, reasons for migration and age at immigration; and macro conditions in the housing market, reflected, among other things, in time of arrival and place of settlement (e.g., Borjas, 2002; Constant, Roberts, and Zimmermann, 2007; Haan, 2005; Morris and Winter, 1978). That the population under discussion here arrived from a single country (Israel) suggests that all of its members share the cultural norms of their home country's housing patterns; similarly, they seek to adjust to one destination country (Germany) and make housing arrangements that approximate the local norms (Rebhun, 2009), which are stratified along the lines of their preferred lifestyle if they can afford it. This pattern—Israelis wishing to buy property if they can get the wherewithal together—can be found in any location. Munich is a case in point: Israelis in Munich who had "made it" bought properties in central areas such as Maxvorstadt. Others, who meanwhile married and had children, moved into properties of their own in more peripheral areas, mirroring the patterns of native Germans. Yet as home rental and purchases prices surged in metropolitan areas, Israelis who had enough funds due to family fortunes or sufficient disposable income often bought property as an investment or to avoid rising rents; in so doing, they were helped by low interest rates. One Israeli migrant to Berlin recounted (in German) that, "Even though I hold Swiss citizenship, I had to learn German in Germany. . . . My dad didn't pass on the language. I really feel I got somewhere after five years and now I've bought myself a flat." Thus he signaled his intention of remaining in Germany—Berlin—even after his relationship with a German (non-Jewish) woman foundered. Another Israeli, naturalized as a German citizen while maintaining Israeli citizenship, owns three flats in another German city; he explained (in German) that "Property is an investment. A very safe investment." He had been in Germany for slightly more than a decade at the time of the interview. While he was married with children, his wife was Jewish although neither German-Jewish nor Israeli.

Only about one-fifth of Israelis in Germany own a home (see table 4.13). This relative dearth should come as no surprise, given that most of Israelis in Germany settled there only in the past few years and many are young. Also, homeownership in Germany has increased only recently, as rents had been stable and owning property held few incentives. The recent strong upturn in rent has generated acute pressure on the rental market and created difficulties in obtaining a flat in some cases. Political attempts to hold rent in check, for example, *Mietpreisbremse* (the rental "price break"), have had little impact in major metropolitan areas. Matters related to rent increases and lack of affordable properties for average-income families have become a political issue that remains as unresolved as it is pressing. In particular, younger people and young families on average incomes move to areas outside of the city, and at the very edge of the conurbation areas, making for long commutes, and putting an additional stress on motorways, as public transportation tends to be limited to the confines of the cities themselves. Although housing rent and purchase prices in rural areas are more affordable, these areas typically lack jobs, meaning that working-age nonimmigrants also migrate to the cities, and the conurbation areas. The

Table 4.13. Homeownership by Human-Capital Characteristics (Percentages)

	Own	Rent
Total	**18.1**	**81.9**
Education		
No diploma	20.0	80.0
Matriculation	10.2	89.8
Post-secondary	12.8	87.2
BA	16.2	83.8
MA+	22.9	77.1
Employment Status		
Employed	19.3	80.7
Self-employed	15.6	84.4
Student	11.6	88.4
Unemployed/retired/other	12.0	88.0
Occupation		
Professional and arts	19.4	80.6
Managerial	30.6	69.4
Technical	19.1	80.9
Sales/clerical/service/blue-collar	14.4	85.6
German Language Proficiency		
None	0.0	100.0
Weak	5.0	95.0
Mediocre	8.3	91.7
Good	25.0	75.0
Very good	30.0	70.0
German Citizenship		
Yes	19.7	80.3
No	13.6	86.4
Marital Status		
Single	8.0	92.0
Partner	15.2	84.8
Jewish spouse	17.2	82.8
Non-Jewish spouse	25.2	74.8
Formerly married	24.1	75.9

two population movements—domestic and international—impact all German cities and metropolitan areas but appear most pronounced in Berlin, which once had been characterized as a "cheap city."

This has made buying an apartment more worthwhile, especially given the low level and tax deductibility of mortgage interest. Indeed, real-estate companies started promoting Israelis' purchase of apartments in Berlin by advertising in the magazine *Spitz* (see issues 4 and 5, 2013). The differences in homeownership by human capital are small but may be salient at times. Rather high and similar rates of homeownership characterize Israelis at the two ends of the educational ladder: 20 percent among those with no matriculation and 22.9 percent among those with advanced academic degrees. These two groups, we recall, also have the highest proportions of people with very good command of German. Israelis with matriculation certificates attain only half this rate. Israelis in Germany who work for others are more inclined to own a home than are the self-employed (19.3 percent and 15.6 percent, respectively); this is partially associated with taxes but presumably also reflect some reluctant of banks to give mortgage to the self-employed. The differences between students and the unemployed are even larger. This stratification also shows that many self-employed Israelis do not earn particularly well; some of them commit to self-employment in pursuit of a lifetime project of some kind and not with the prospect of earning "big money" (Cohen and Kranz, 2017). Yet given the changing conditions of home rental and the rising cost of living, it remains to be seen how these lifestyle migrants will fare in regard to housing issues and whether their migration may be impacted by the matter in the long run. Parenthetically, Israelis in managerial jobs are characterized by a high proportion of homeowners.

Two other components of human capital that are associated with and produced by migration and integration are local-language proficiency and citizenship. Language is positively and tightly linked to homeownership rates: from 0 among Israeli émigrés who speak no German to 5 percent of those with weak proficiency, around 8 percent of respondents with mediocre fluency, surging to one-quarter of Israelis who speak German well and 30 percent if they speak it very well. Israelis who hold German citizenship are more likely than others to own a dwelling (see table 4.13). They tend to work in higher paying jobs that allow them to accumulate and save to buy property; they also have stronger social networks with local Germans and thus know more about where one can buy property, which areas are up-and-coming, and what developments are at issue.

As for marital status, the two groups of Israelis with the highest rates of homeownership are those with non-Jewish spouses and the formerly married (see table 4.13). That the latter, after becoming widowed or divorced, continue to live in Germany attests to their strong wish to stay there, a circumstance anchored by owning a dwelling. It stands to reason that many of these Israelis have children and, in some cases, grandchildren in the country. Alternatively, homeownership is one factor, among others, that holds these people in Germany instead of moving elsewhere, entailing multiple arrangements that they would now have to make without the help of a partner. Likewise, people of this status are old on average, making it difficult for them to relocate. More easily understood is the tendency of the intermarried, many of whom have non-Jewish spouses who are German citizens, to have a house of their own—good evidence of their intention to settle permanently in the new country. Furthermore, the German side of the family may have supported their acquisition of property by providing funds or local contacts. We noted the rather high rate of Israelis who live with a partner who own a house (somewhat lower than the average for all Israelis in Germany but closer to married than to single Israelis); in Germany, as in Europe more generally, this type of cohabitation often substitutes for official marriages. In Germany specifically, provisions of family law that guide joint property hardly advantage the married, often making marriage an add-on. If an Israeli migrant has EU citizenship, an independent visa, or minor children with German/EU citizenship, this add-on may be romantic but not legally necessary.

How do immigration factors relate to homeownership? To answer, we first look at those immigrants who mentioned a specific reason as "very central" in their leaving Israel or choosing to settle in Germany. Two push factors stand out for increasing the likelihood of purchasing a house in the new country: political/security circumstances in Israel and reservations about the involvement of the religious establishment in Israeli civic life (see table 4.14). We propose that Israelis who were strongly affected by these factors see their move to Germany as more permanent (see table 3.10), because their reasons for emigration carry strong emotional currency. Predictably, homeownership rates are higher than average among Israelis who decided to settle in Germany because of a background associated with the country or a German partner; such incentives enhance the permanency of settlement. In some of these cases, too, ownership is arranged through the mediation of another family member who lives in Germany.

Table 4.14. Homeownership by Immigration Factors (Percentages)

	Own	Rent
Reasons for Emigration from Israel ("Very Central")		
Political/security	21.1	78.9
Professional development	11.8	88.2
Economic development	11.0	89.0
Education	14.1	85.9
Religious establishment	18.3	81.7
Family/friends	8.3	91.7
Reasons for Choosing Germany ("Very Central")		
Education	16.5	83.5
German culture	11.4	88.6
Professional/economic development	14.7	85.3
Family origin	20.3	79.7
German partner	24.2	75.8
Seeking challenge	15.1	84.9
Age at Immigration		
18–24	20.4	79.6
25–29	20.1	79.9
30–34	18.3	81.7
35–39	10.0	90.0
40+	4.9	95.1
Future Migration		
Germany	20.6	79.4
Israel	7.0	93.0
Other country	8.6	91.4

Normally, the propensity of homeownership rises with age as older people are at a stable stage of life, including marriage and children, a permanent job, and fixed income. Since most Israelis in Germany reached the country in the past few years, differences in age at immigration are a good proxy of variation in actual age. Our observations suggest that Israelis in Germany behave somewhat counterintuitively, their rate of homeownership rising commensurate with younger age (see table 4.14). We have seen that Israelis who immigrated early in life have several assets that those who made the move at a somewhat older age lack, such as better proficiency in German and a higher rate of intermarriage, which may strengthen their tendency to buy a dwelling.

Israelis who are inclined to remain in Germany are more than twice as likely to own a dwelling than are peers who anticipate moving to another country or returning to Israel (see table 4.14). Although our data do not allow us explore this, we assume that the intention to stay in Germany determines the purchase of a dwelling and not the other way around. In any case, those who indicated that they plan to stay in Germany and also own a dwelling should be expected more strongly to carry out these intentions than those who live in rented accommodations.

Homeownership was also defined as an indicator of having "made it" by Israelis who came to study, obtained a well-paying professional post, and stayed on. In some cases, Israelis with business and management background aspired to own multiple dwellings. One respondent said that he wished to own "one house for each of my [four] children," something he considered impossible in Israel. Another Israeli did not associate his several properties with his children; instead, he saw buying real estate as a logical investment amid rapidly rising home prices and escalating urbanization. At the same time, having come to Germany to study and receiving no resources from his family, he took pleasure and joy in the property that he had bought for himself and his family: "I can see the tops of the Alps from our new flat." It would be wrong to interpret his genuine delight as merely a boast about having worked his way up because, apart from being pleased with his residence, he described it as *"Heimat"* (home). By this token, homeownership may be a genuine expression of place-making and feeling at home in the country of immigration.

Dwelling availability and price vary over time, by type of property, and in different parts of the country, for example, large or small city, city center or suburb, and urban versus rural areas. Accordingly, the timing of settlement in the new country strongly affects immigrants' exposure to the fluctuation of conditions in the local housing market. Notably, time of immigration is also synonymous with veterancy; our survey data do not allow us to distinguish between them. With this caveat in mind, the findings in table 4.15 show clearly that most Israelis (70.8 percent) who arrived in Germany before 1995 own a home. The rate falls to slightly more than a third among those who immigrated in the following decade (1995–2004), plunges among immigrants of the past ten years, and bottoms out among arrivals in the past few years.

While these trends relate to veterancy of immigrants in Germany, they are indicative of broader trends in German society as well: the upward march of housing prices (Destatis, 2020) has put this commodity out of range for many younger people (Destatis, 2017b). Furthermore, the German labor

Table 4.15. Homeownership by Macroconditions (Percentages)

	Own	Rent
Time of Immigration (Veterancy)		
2012–2015 (0–3)	5.2	94.8
2010–2011 (4–5)	12.8	77.2
2005–2009 (6–10)	12.2	77.8
1995–2004 (11–20)	37.9	62.1
1994 > (21+)	70.8	29.2
Place of Residence		
Berlin	13.0	87.0
Other large cities	20.4	79.6
Other places	15.1	84.9

market is rapidly transitioning toward casualization and fixed-term contracts, disproportionally affecting individuals under the age of thirty-five (Destatis, 2017b). Problematically, though, this development also affects the highly educated; their propensity to work on a project basis undermines their ability to accumulate resources and buy a home. A high level of education does not necessarily correlate with above-average income and low unemployment rates should not be confused with financial stability. Many recent Israeli immigrants have degrees in the social sciences and humanities and have fallen into a trap along with other migrants and native Germans: if they obtain work in their field of expertise, they are often poorly paid, lapsing into unemployment as one PhD-boasting Israeli recounted in desperation "[. . .] my contract will end. And I had already been unemployed for nine months last years." While homeownership was completely out of range for her, she also took the big step to uproot herself and to apply abroad.

Homeownership also varies by place of residence (see table 4.15). Israelis in Berlin were the least likely to buy a dwelling, those in other large cities were the most likely, and the rate among those elsewhere was somewhere in between. Notably, rental housing in Berlin was cheap until about 2005, when an upturn in international and domestic migration made housing a scarce resource, pushing its price up while earnings did not keep pace. In Berlin, the state sold most of its housing, turning the city into a hotbed for speculators, benefiting national and international realtors, and outpricing people including Israelis. Much luxury housing in Berlin has been built or redone in the past decade but very little affordable housing, the kind that would serve low-medium incomes such as those of most Israelis, has been added. Spatial differences in tendencies to buy or rent a dwelling may result not only from area contextual conditions (macrolevel) or immigrants' individual characteristics (microlevel), but also from local social and cultural contexts (meso-level) that are not indexed, directly or indirectly, in our data.

Applying a multivariate analysis (see table 4.16), we found several human-capital characteristics that are significant in respect of living arrange-

Table 4.16. Determinants of Homeownership[1]

		Exp(B)
Human Capital Characteristics		
Education:	Matriculation	0.619
	Post-secondary	0.193[i]
	BA	0.876
	MA+	1.914
Employment status:	Employed	2.112
	Self-employed	2.868[i]
	Student	1.285
Occupation:	Professional and arts	0.760
	Management	2.025
	Technical	1.408
	Sales/service/blue-collar	0.631
German language proficiency:		
	Mediocre	1.473
	Good	1.369
	Very good	1.412
Citizenship:	Yes	1.132
Marital status:	Single	0.442
	Married: non-Jewish spouse	0.360[i]
	Partner	0.502
	Formerly married	0.324
Immigration Factors		
Reasons for emigration from Israel:		
	Political/security	1.411[i]
	Professional development	1.433
	Economic development	0.768
	Education	0.694
	Religious establishment	0.891
	Family/friends	0.859

continued on next page

Table 4.16. Continued.

		Exp(B)
Immigration Factors (continued)		
Reasons for choosing Germany:		
	Education	1.682*
	German culture	0.659*
	Professional/economic	0.959
	Family origin	1.531*
	German partner	1.375*
	Seeking challenge	1.212
Age at immigration:	18–24	2.998
	25–29	6.079*
	30–34	2.373
	35–39	9.791*
Future migration:	Germany	3.567[i]
	Elsewhere	0.767
Macro Conditions		
Veterancy:	4–5 years	4.165*
	6–10 years	4.338*
	11–20 years	9.407*
	21+ years	135.208*
Place of residence:	Other large cities	0.434[i]
	Other places	0.776
Explanatory Power		47.3%

[1]Logistic regression.
*Significant at least at the 0.05 level; [i] Significant at $p < 0.10$.
Reference categories: education—no diploma; employment status—unemployed; occupation—unemployed; German-language proficiency—none or poor; citizenship—no; marital status—married-Jewish spouse; age at immigration—40+; future migration—Israel; veterancy—0–3 years; place of residence—Berlin.

ments. Working as self-employed (versus being unemployed) increases the likelihood of owning a house. In contrast, post-secondary education, which for some means current enrollment in academic institutions, and being married to a non-Jew inhibit home buying. The positive relation between mixed marriage and homeownership, found in the descriptive analysis, was probably a dependency of other characteristics of Israelis who live in mixed unions. Among the emigration factors, leaving Israel due to the political/

security considerations or being drawn to Germany for higher education or by familial background or a local partner are associated with residing in one's own house. These intersections may be confirmed by qualitative data. The Israeli quoted above, who wanted to buy a house for each of his four children, is married to a local non-Jew, for example. Israelis who were at odds with Israel and suffered from the country's political and security situation might buy property in order to have a safe anchor in Germany; many of them, too, were married to or partnered with non-Jews. Moving to Germany because of cultural incentives deters homeownership. Immigration at ages that are not very young but not too old (past forty) is significant for homeownership. Among our proxies of macroconditions, veterancy in Germany increases the likelihood of owing a house in Germany. Israelis who climbed the real-estate ladder expressed pride in their accomplishment: "It's a really nice flat in a really nice area, isn't it?" asked one respondent, awaiting confirmation; another compared his situation to an imagined situation in Israel: "That house, in Israel? Never!" A third, in contrast, was frustrated with his lack of homeownership: "I should have bought when Berlin was still cheap!" Yet another elaborated: "My parents bought me the flat, as they would have in Israel." If so, support in acquiring property does exist, indicating that the familial assistance in securing their children's settlement abroad extends to creating facts on the ground. Multivariate analysis shows that variations in homeownership by place of residence pretty much disappear after controlling for differences among the Israelis in Germany in human capital, immigration factors, and veterancy. Overall, these characteristics were quite helpful, providing nearly half of the explanation for why some Israelis own a dwelling in Germany and others do not.

The Israeli immigrants in Germany who are at our focus are first generation in the country. Further, in overwhelming majority, they are recent arrivals, having settled there in the past two decades. These migration characteristics are largely reflected in the stage of their social integration: moderate rates of individuals with strong proficiency in German, and small proportions who have attained German citizenship and homeownership. Countering them are a sizable number of Israelis in interfaith marriage or cohabitation arrangements. Leaving Israel, choosing Germany of all places as their destination, and marrying a non-Jew may indicate that these Israelis are likely to distance themselves not only from Israel but also, including their children, from Jewish identity. Thus, what once would have been viewed as a triple burden may no longer be such for thousands of Israelis and their families.

Chapter 5

Construction of Identity

Identity and Modernity

Modernity is probably the most common term used to describe the social, cultural, and political patterns that developed in European-Christian civilization in the past two centuries (Eisenstadt, 2010). Among the major institutional and individual affinities of this new order are freedom of choice, autonomy, and multiple interests (Inkeles and Smith, 1974; Lerner, 1958). Another salient component of this era is avoidance of fixation and keeping all options open (Bauman, 1996), causing things to become blurred among other effects (Beck, 1992). Beck conceptualizes modern societies as "risk societies." The freedom of choice that they champion goes hand-in-hand with the unmooring of individuals and the shifting of responsibilities to them and away from societies. What Beck depicts as a chance for individual pursuits has become the double-edged sword of individual freedom and choice contrasted by sharpening class differences (often tied with ethno-religion) in stratified societies, as individuals are always parts of larger collectives.

The coupling of these neoliberal circumstances with the technological ease of transnational connections allows immigrants in their new countries to construct their group identity in different forms, the degrees of freedom for constructing of these group identities hinging on the receiving societies' social and legal structures. We define these forms as transnational, namely, attachment to home country; religio-ethnicity, meaning particularistic praxes and attitudes associated with group belonging; and localism of identity and general involvement in the host country. Like migration, the shaping of identity is a dynamic process that aims, among other things, to fulfill temporary needs of social, economic, and cultural absorption (situational or instrumental identification). Identification is further determined by the receiving country's policy or philosophy of integration (Carrera, 2006; Castles, de Haas and Miller, 2009; Connor, 2010; Owen, 2011; Süssmuth and Weidenfeld, 2005).

These forms of identity are not necessarily mutually exclusive. Immigrants may combine two or even all three or may express them situationally. Each form of identity is composed of elements of the private and the public spheres, and individuals choose those that they find the most suitable and meaningful, together shaping the way they seek to express their group identity(ies). This process involves the individual's definition of his or her belonging to various environments; tensions or complements among different identities; and distinctions, blurring, or shifting of intergroup boundaries (Alba and Nee, 2003).

Drawing on Berry's (1997) approach to identity but expanding it from a two-dimensional to three-dimensional scheme, that is, taking into account the aforementioned three forms of transnationality, religio-ethnicity, and localism, immigrants in their new country may construct their identity in the direction of *marginalization, integration, assimilation,* or *separation. Marginalization* suggests that immigrants have little desire for transnational and religio-ethnic practices and scanty interest in developing ties with members of the mainstream local society due to discrimination, exclusion, or other factors. The trajectory of *integration* takes a contrasting view. It postulates that structural assimilation is not functionally congruent with other types of assimilation and does not blur group identity. Rather, immigrants strengthen their religious and ethnic identity because this helps them to cope with the hardship of leaving home and settling in an unfamiliar new environment. Insofar as attachment to an ancestral country or a holy site is a major component of religio-ethnic identity and communal activity, it may help to maintain, or even enhance, transnational ties (see also, Merkur, 2019). Under such circumstances, immigrants refrain from adopting local cultural and national customs. Integration often takes place in different variants and degrees and transnationalism and religio-ethnicity and local connections may develop in different directions. Thus, commensurate with the *assimilation* path that they choose, immigrants view their adjustment to the receiving society as composed concurrently of acculturation into the local mainstream and gradual waning of transnational and religio-ethnic identification due to limited time and resources. Alternatively, from the *separation* perspective, immigrants may express preference for local connections with the receiving mainstream culture while maintaining either transnational or religio-ethnic patterns but not combining the two; this, in turn, attests to the importance that immigrants attach to particularistic identification, which one expects them to choose selectively. Due to the physical possibilities of travel and advances in communication technology, all four potential paths—marginalization, integration, assimilation, and separation—coexist and may be experienced and practiced by individuals at different times. By this token, we see Berry (1997) as a useful base from which to expand and amend migration theory more than twenty years after it was formulated, at a time when smartphone, a key instrument for communication and information, was virtually nonexistent.

The discussion that follows assesses group belonging among Jewish Israelis in Germany. While our interest lies in depicting developments in these immigrants' identity, we will pay due attention to the specifics of the receiving country because Israeli Jewish and Jewish migration to Germany are publically and politically charged on both the German and the Israeli side. As such, the issues at hand also impact the immigrants' private sphere (Cohen and Kranz, 2017). We begin by offering insights into the overall structure of identity and identification, namely, relations among various indicators, and by elaborating on the position of migration cohorts (i.e., parsed by period of arrival) in this structural array. Then we call attention to the intensity of the various forms of identities—transnational, religio-ethnic, and local—and how they evolve as immigrants gain veterancy in the new country. To complement the understanding of group identification, we apply a multivariate analysis that yields insights into the way background characteristics, migration factors, and sociodemographic variables weaken or strengthen the different forms of identification. The analysis of the quantitative evidence is accompanied by observations and analysis from our in-depth interviews and ethnographic fieldwork with our informants.

Structure of Group Identity

Social research, such as that concerned with group behaviors and attitudes, should first conceptualize and define, in substantive terms, the structure of its target population. We do this here by applying facet theory (Guttman, 1959; 1968), which portrays coherent areas and boundaries of the relevant contents of group identification. We then analyze group identification by mapping several clusters of engagement as the respondents expressed them. The analysis also explores the proximity of categories of veterancy in Germany to the various identificational components.

Identification is defined by three facets (a facet being a set used for the classification of research issues) (Levy, 1985; Shye, 1978). A suitable framework for defining the research variables, which simultaneously considers the classification of group identity and its practical manifestations, is exhibited in the mapping sentence (see figure 5.1). Facet A distinguishes between two spheres of identification: private (primarily internal) and public (primarily social). These modes are concerned with three contents (Facet B), each reflecting a different manifestation of group identification: transnationalism, religio-ethnicity, and localism. These contents relate to cognitive or instrumental expressions (Facet C). Table 5.1 shows the name of each indicator and how it relates to the mapping sentence. Codes are used for

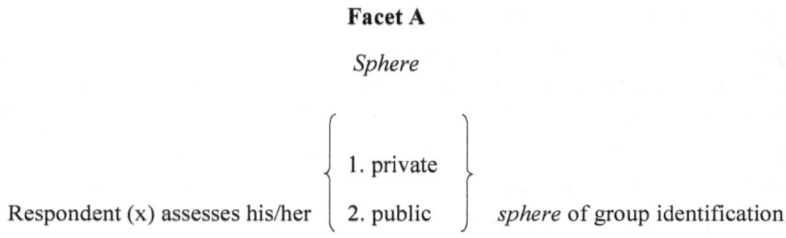

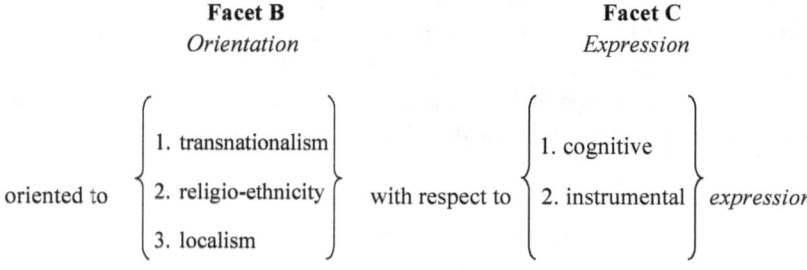

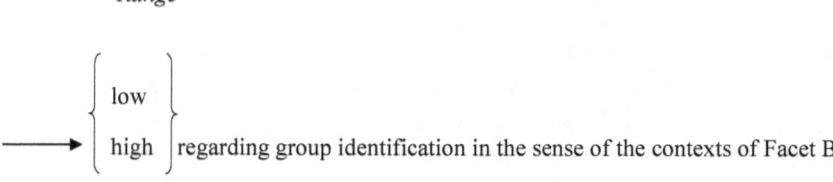

Figure 5.1. Mapping Sentence for Group Identification among Israelis in Germany.

Table 5.1. Indicators of Group Identification and Associated Facets

Indicator	Code
Define self as Israeli (DSISR)	private, transnational, cognitive (a_1,b_1,c_1)
Feel Israel home (ISRHM)	private, transnational, cognitive (a_1,b_1,c_1)
Celebrate Israel's independence (CISRIND)	public, transnational, instrumental (a_2,b_1,c_2)
Visit Israel (VISR)	public, transnational, instrumental (a_2,b_1,c_2)
Contact with family in Israel (CFAMISR)	private, transnational, instrumental (a_1,b_1,c_2)
Contact with friends in Israel (CFRISR)	private, transnational, instrumental (a_1,b_1,c_2)
Friends Israeli immigrants (FRISRIMM)	public, transnational, instrumental (a_2,b_1,c_2)
Attend events of Israelis in Germany (EVISR)	public, transnational, instrumental (a_2,b_1,c_2)
Read Israeli written and electronic press (RDISRPR)	private, transnational, instrumental (a_1,b_1,c_2)
Surf Israeli websites (ISRWEB)	private, transnational, instrumental (a_1,b_1,c_2)
Define self as Jewish (DSJEW)	private, religio-ethnic, cognitive (a_1,b_2,c_1)
Importance of being Jewish (IMPJEW)	private, religio-ethnic, cognitive (a_1,b_2,c_1)
Attend events of German Jews (EVGERJEW)	public, religio-ethnic, instrumental (a_2,b_2,c_2)
Friends German Jews (FRGERJEW)	public, religio-ethnic, instrumental (a_2,b_2,c_2)
Importance of Holocaust memory (IMPHOLCM)	private, religio-ethnic, cognitive (a_1,b_2,c_1)
Level of religiosity (RELG)	private, religio-ethnic, cognitive (a_1,b_2,c_1)
Mezuzah on doorpost (MEZUZAH)	private, religio-ethnic, instrumental (a_1,b_2,c_2)
Synagogue attendance (SYNGATT)	public, religio-ethnic, instrumental (a_2,b_2,c_2)
Friday candles/kiddush (SHABBAT)	private, religio-ethnic, instrumental (a_1,b_2,c_2)
Fast on Yom Kippur (KIPPUR)	private, religio-ethnic, instrumental (a_1,b_2,c_2)
Light Chanukah candles (CHANK)	private, religio-ethnic, instrumental (a_1,b_2,c_2)
Attend Passover seder (PASSOVER)	private, religio-ethnic, instrumental (a_1,b_2,c_2)
Define self as German (DSGER)	private, local, cognitive (a_1,b_3,c_1)
Feel Germany home (GERHM)	private, local, cognitive (a_1,b_3,c_1)
Non-Jewish German friends (FRNJGER)	public, local, instrumental (a_2,b_3,c_2)
Friends who are non-Jewish immigrants (FRNJIMM)	public, local, instrumental (a_2,b_3,c_2)
No conflict Holocaust-relations with Germany (CNFHLC)	public, local, cognitive (a_1,b_3,c_1)
Difficult to live in Germany (DFLVGER)	public, local, cognitive (a_2,b_3,c_1)

the various facets; for example, $a_1b_1c_2$ relates to the private environment of transnational identity expressed by instrumental (behavioral) patterns. The answer categories for each variable are worded in the sense of the specific attitude or behavior. Nevertheless, they should be interpreted in each case as ranging from low to high on a common concept of identification. This is specified in Range Facet R after the arrow in the mapping sentence.

To gain insights into the structure of the group-identification framework and the relations among its components, we use a Smallest Space Analysis (SSA) to process the data. SSA assesses the empirical correlational structure of variables. It produces a graphic translation of the matrix of correlation of all variables examined (Borg and Lingoes, 1987; Guttman, 1968). Each variable is represented as a point in a (Euclidean) space. The distance between a pair of points reflects the statistical similarity/dissimilarity of the points: the stronger the correlation between two variables is—relative to the size of the correlation of either variable with other variables—the closer they are in the space.

When the relative sizes of the correlation coefficients are employed, SSA explores a representation that corresponds to the circular structure (see figure 5.2). The circular space is partitioned into wedge-like regions that stem from a common origin, each corresponding to one of the domains introduced in Facet B. A clear distinction exists between identification on the private sphere and identification on the public sphere, each being in a delineating region in the lower and upper parts of the figure, respectively, marked by a broken line. Further, the facet of mode of identification modulates between the cognitive and the instrumental, modulating the relative distance from the origin.

The orientation of identification facet divides the space into three regions emanating from an origin, each region turning in a different direction. Each region includes elements that coincide with the orientation of identification defined in Facet B. Beginning in the left part of the circle and proceeding clockwise, the regions are ordered as follows: transnationalism, localism, and religio-ethnicity. The circular order suggests that two points in the two-dimensional space that are equidistant from the origin but belong to different regions have a high correlation coefficient because the regions are statistically close to each other but may differ in content.

The mode of the expression facet plays a modulating role. The distinction between cognitive and instrumental partitions figure 5.2 into two major rings around the origin. Cognitive identificational variables are found in the inner circle; instrumental identificational variables are located in the

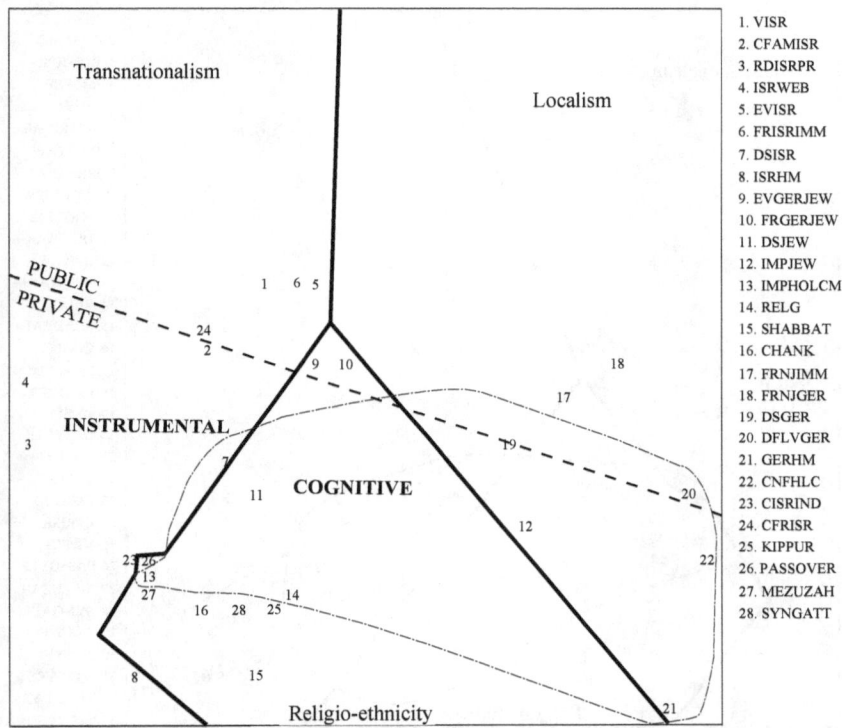

Figure 5.2. Structure of Group Identification among Israelis in Germany.

outer ring. The shape of the inner region is an ellipse stretched between the two ends of the configuration, suggesting that different regions contain items that reflect attitudes and behaviors regarding the self.

SSA allows external variables of attributes of the population, such as veterancy in the new country, to be integrated into the internal structure analysis—namely, the structure of the content—without affecting the internal structure (Cohen and Amar, 2002). The SSA diagram maps the optimal location of each external variable by superimposing it on the structure of the examined topic of the total population. The external variables appear as dummy variables. The shortest veterancy, one to three years, is located at the upper part of the configuration and is the most closely associated with transnational identity (see figure 5.3). At the bottom end is the category of twenty-one-plus years; it is located deep in the area of religio-ethnic identification. In other words, the most recent and most veteran Israeli

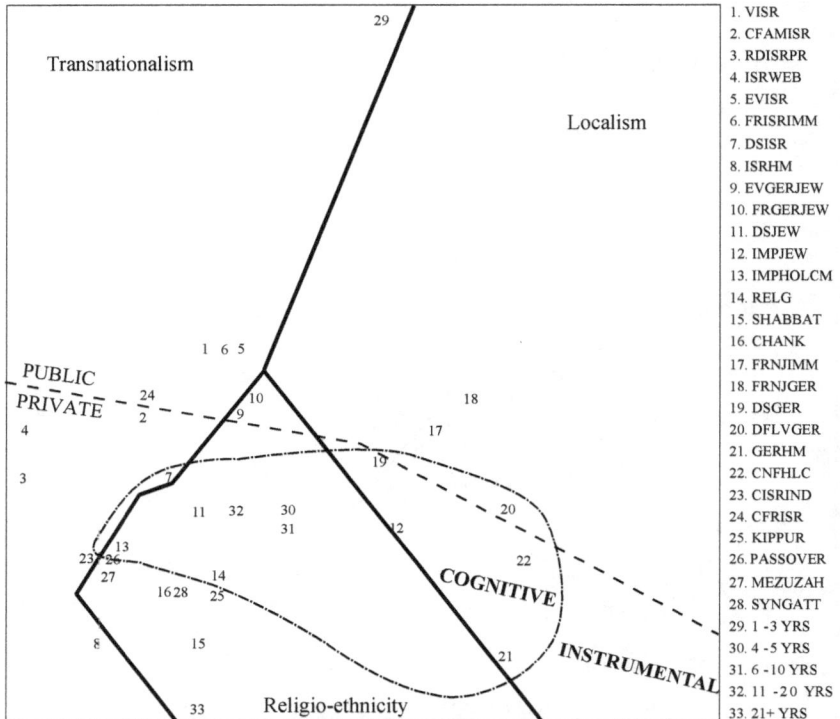

Figure 5.3. Structure of Group Identification among Israelis in Germany with Tenure as External Variables.

immigrants in Germany are positioned at the two extremes of the configuration, meaning that they conceptualize the various forms of identification in very different ways. Notably, each of these two groups is located in a different mode of Facet A, the public and the private spheres, respectively. Still, they are both on the instrumental part of the configuration. The remaining Israeli immigrants, with veterancies ranging from four to twenty years, share a common region of religio-ethnic identity; they are attached to cognitive expressions that are constructed on the private domain. These findings attest to the relevance, depth, and resilience of identification among different immigration cohorts and illustrate how the entire configuration is reconstituted through the combined performance of different waves of Israeli immigrants to Germany.[1]

Rhythm of Identity

The data in tables 5.2–5.4 show the levels of attitudes and behaviors of Israelis in Germany. Each table is concerned with a different form of identification: transnational, religio-ethnic, and local, successively. We assess the intensity of identification and whether and how it varies by veterancy in the host country and, in turn, by time of settlement.

Transnationalism

Most Israelis in Germany—more than six of every ten—no longer consider Israel to be their home (not at all/to some extent) (see table 5.2). Their

Table 5.2. Transnational Identification among Israelis in Germany, Total and by Veterancy (Percentages)

	Total	1–3	4–5	6–10	11–20	21+
Define Self as Israeli						
Total	100.0	100.0	100.0	100.0	100.0	100.0
Not at all	13.2	13.7	14.1	11.2	10.4	11.5
Small extent	6.2	8.5	4.0	2.0	4.5	15.4
Some extent	22.3	23.9	20.2	22.4	22.4	19.2
Great extent	58.3	53.8	61.6	64.3	62.7	53.8
Feel Israel is Home						
Total	100.0	100.0	100.0	100.0	100.0	100.0
Not at all	23.0	24.8	26.7	19.2	15.5	20.7
Some extent	38.3	38.8	35.6	44.4	33.8	34.5
Great extent	23.5	22.7	22.8	25.3	25.4	20.7
Very Great extent	15.3	13.6	14.9	11.1	25.4	24.1
Celebrates Israel's Independence Day						
Total	100.0	100.0	100.0	100.0	100.0	100.0
No	61.5	58.2	55.2	70.5	70.3	51.9
Yes	38.5	41.8	44.8	29.5	29.7	48.1
Visits to Israel						
Total	100.0	100.0	100.0	100.0	100.0	100.0
Every two years –	18.3	15.7	15.2	19.2	25.0	30.7
Once a year	34.1	31.1	31.3	41.4	38.2	30.8
Twice a year +	47.6	53.1	53.5	39.4	36.8	38.5

continued on next page

Table 5.2. Continued.

	Total	1–3	4–5	6–10	11–20	21+
Contact with Family in Israel						
Total	100.0	100.0	100.0	100.0	100.0	100.0
Once a month –	8.8	7.0	6.5	7.9	9.2	36.3
Once a week	43.2	37.3	51.5	55.1	40.0	27.3
Daily	48.0	55.7	42.4	37.1	50.8	36.4
Contact with Friends in Israel						
Total	100.0	100.0	100.0	100.0	100.0	100.0
None	5.0	2.6	5.4	6.7	9.7	4.3
Once a year	6.8	1.8	6.5	14.6	9.7	17.4
Once a month	29.1	26.4	25.0	32.6	37.1	26.1
Once a week	34.3	38.3	33.7	31.5	32.3	17.4
Daily	24.8	30.4	29.4	14.6	11.2	34.8
Friends Who are Israeli Immigrants						
Total	100.0	100.0	100.0	100.0	100.0	100.0
None	19.7	21.6	14.1	19.2	11.9	42.3
A few	35.8	33.6	40.4	36.4	31.3	38.5
About half	31.0	29.9	29.3	34.3	41.8	15.4
Most	13.5	14.9	16.2	10.1	14.9	3.8
Attendance at Events of Israelis in Germany						
Total	100.0	100.0	100.0	100.0	100.0	100.0
Never	38.5	41.0	34.3	40.4	30.9	38.5
Seldom	30.9	31.4	31.3	32.3	29.4	30.8
Sometimes	21.4	18.4	25.3	22.2	23.5	19.2
Often	9.3	9.2	9.1	5.1	16.2	11.5
Read Israeli Print and Electronic Media						
Total	100.0	100.0	100.0	100.0	100.0	100.0
Not at all	3.5	5.2	2.0	1.0	2.8	0
A little	21.6	28.0	20.2	14.6	9.9	29.6
A lot	32.7	29.6	37.4	38.5	29.6	25.9
Very often	42.2	37.2	40.4	45.8	57.7	44.4
Surfs Israeli Websites (Other than News)						
Total	100.0	100.0	100.0	100.0	100.0	100.0
Not at all	9.9	13.1	10.1	8.3	1.4	6.9
A little	36.6	36.9	36.4	39.6	35.7	34.5
A lot	23.3	24.2	23.2	17.7	24.3	27.6
Very often	30.1	25.8	30.3	34.4	38.6	31.0

distancing from Israel is also reflected in the high proportion of those who do not celebrate Israel's Independence Day (61.5 percent). Likewise, Israelis in Germany tend not to attend (never or only seldom) events organized by other Israelis (69.4 percent), and slightly more than half (55.5 percent) reported that none or very few of their close friends are Israeli immigrants.

The Israeli immigrants who fall into this pattern actively seek to immerse themselves in the receiving country for the purpose of settling in, or, in the case of partner migrants, they obtain access to a local German network immediately. One interviewee elaborated: "The Israeli in Berlin thing has become a monster. It is so overblown. And why would I want to hang out with other Israelis outside of Israel—just because they're Israelis?" Her interest in any kind of Israeli event was weak and in Jewish events nonexistent: her Israeliness related to Israel and her friends and family in Israel but not to other migrants. Yet while she had no interest in Israeli get-togethers, her self-definition remained Israeli. This attitude of once-an-Israeli-always-an-Israeli was commonly found in our fieldwork, irrespective of attending events, maintaining friendships with other Israelis, and so on. A respondent who opted to leave Israel for career reasons and is unsure if she will ever return offered a thoughtful and pensive answer to the question of Israel as home: "I'm an Israeli. [. . .] It's just there. It is home. It's in me." While affirming more emotionally than many of the other respondents that an Israeli is an Israeli and remains one no matter what, the meaning of being and remaining an Israeli was rarely expressed and often became an issue only after the immigrants had children and were exposed to raising them abroad. Before they became parents, many respondents essentialized Israeliness as a state of incorporated being: one is Israeli because one is not something else.

Unlike these two respondents, who had been abroad for less than a year and for two years, respectively, one Israeli with long-term veterancy (fifteen years) reported having had no interest in Israeli (or Jewish) "stuff" in his first years in Germany. His best friend, ironically another Israeli who wanted nothing to do with other Israelis or Jews, displayed the same pattern. Each found the other sufficient as a point of contact, of reference, and in speaking Hebrew. Furthermore, all four respondents travel to Israel regularly. Another interviewee, a spousal migrant, displayed the exact opposite behavior: despite speaking German like the other respondents and having access to his native German wife's social network, he was a "macher" on the Israeli scene in Berlin. Professionally, his interactions circled mainly around other Israelis, and privately, too, his principal friendships and contacts were with other Israelis. By and large, he opted to live in an Israeli bubble and visited Israel regularly. Somewhat paradoxically, however, he denied any intention of returning to Israel and wished to naturalize as a German citizen. He felt acutely that he was surrounded by "the Israelis" whom he liked and had enough of Israel by making regular visits there. Each of these five respondents, as well as the others and our fieldwork partners, defined themselves as Israelis. Even if some felt much difficulty in their relationship with the country, their Israeliness clung to them, though some yearned desperately to shed it ("I'm a self-hating Israeli," one respondent affirmed). Amir Kusinski, who has resided in Berlin for more than two decades, postulates that "If someone was raised in Israel, schooled in Israel, and served in the [Israeli] army, something very basic in his identity is Israeli" (Sapir, 2014c: 22).

In quantitative terms, eight of every ten Israelis continue to define themselves to some/great extent as Israelis (80.6 percent), maintain intensive weekly contacts with family in Israel (91.2 percent) and, less frequently, with friends in Israel (59.1 percent), and visit Israel at least once every year (81.7 percent) (see table 5.2). The 20 percent of Israelis who do not identify as Israelis may not do so out of protest, as Na'aman Hirschfeld (2014) did, when writing in *Ha'aretz* that he defined himself as "post-Israeli." Yet Israelis

Photo 3. Hebrew Library Berlin. Photo by Daniel Gottlieb.

who take extreme positions such as these, or who leave Israel for ideological motives (Amit, 2016; 2018), enter a paradoxical situation: they no longer define themselves as Israeli due to categorical rejection of what—in their view—Israel has become, while the counterdefinition reifies "their" Israel as their key point of reference. Interestingly, they follow a notion that Shlomo Sand (2014) outlined: While leaving and rejecting Israel, one remains Israeli and Israel remains the central anchor of one's identity.

Three-fourths of the Israelis in Germany keep abreast of the news in Israel and half surf other Israeli websites "a lot" or "very often." Information about Israel in Hebrew is central to their identity praxes (Cohen, 2013; Merkur, 2019) and in our fieldwork we found that the consumption of Israeli media (online, TV, newspapers) is central in their daily discourse about Israel.

The strength of Israeli identification varies commensurate with veterancy, but the differences are not uniform among the various indicators. Some respondents attest to strong identification as time passes and weaker identification among more recent immigrants, whereas in other indicators the opposite occurs, recent immigrants being more attached to Israel than their veteran peers. Moreover, neither of these two trajectories always evolves consistently; each may be characterized by fluctuations. Still, excluding the most veteran group, those with more than two decades of veterancy in Germany (because of the rather small number of cases [25]), it is found that Israelis with longer veterancy, compared with later arrivals, view Israel as their home, define themselves as Israeli, belong to informal social networks of Israeli immigrants, and express interest in Israel by reading the Israeli press and visiting Israeli websites. These variations, however, may not be necessarily associated with veterancy; they may rather reflect generational belonging. That is, veteran Israelis grew up in the formative years of Israel's nation-building enterprise with its characteristics of strong patriotism (although certain circumstances forced them to leave), social cohesion, and acute consciousness of mutual responsibility. Accordingly, they construct pleasant memories of Israel. Recent immigrants, in contrast, are more critical of Israel, especially in political and religious contexts; hence, they may display strong antagonism toward their origin country and wish to quickly distance themselves from it. It is also possible that veteran Israelis once had strong reservations about Israel, but over time, in the manner of people generally, tended to forget things or judged them in a different and more moderate way.

Concurrently, Israelis with longer veterancy in Germany diminish their contacts with family and friends in Israel as well as the frequency of their "home visits." This is to be expected, as their own families, some established with local German spouses and local friends—other Israeli migrants, local Jews, non-Jewish Germans, and others—supplant old connections. Such trends are likely to be associated with veterancy rather than being reflective of generational effects. This trend was pronounced among some recent arrivals, who had specific appreciation for the multiethnic and multireligious mix of the German resident population (Cohen and Kranz, 2017). Others among the recently landed, in contrast, actively sought out their roots and made friends with migrants from countries where their parents or grandparents had lived prior to their migration/displacement to Israel (Shemoelof, 2014).

Religio-Ethnic Identification

Only slightly more than half (53 percent) of the Israelis in Germany define themselves to some or great extent as Jews (see table 5.3). A very similar proportion (48.8 percent) indicated that being Jewish is important or very important to them. Very few somewhat or often attend events held by the local Jewish community (20.2 percent) or belong to informal social circles in which half or most members are local Jews (6.7 percent). The distance from local Jews—be they of German origin, DP, or post-Soviet Russian speakers—is pronounced. Israeli émigrés commonly stress their Israeli particularity, one that has a specific Israeli-Jewish tinge, and oppose it to the local Jewish population (Cohen and Kranz, 2017). Israelis most often engage in symbolic religious practices and family-centered activities for Jewish festivals, replicating the secular pattern of behavior that they had learned in Israel and taking their Jewish identity to places that are convenient for them (Sapir, 2012b). Local Jews, in contrast, often mix communal and family activities for the festivals. That local Jews would attend a religious service more for social than religious reasons remains strange to Israelis, who associate the synagogue and its rite almost solely with religion. Lianne Merkur replicates our find for Germany, and adds that this structure holds for Toronto—and Canada in general, too. "They [Israelis] preferred to maintain their cultural-secular Hebrew fluency and literacy rather than participate in formal religious ritual" (2019: 244).

Israeli immigrants are very secular. Apart from self-reporting a very low level of religiosity, only one in four (28.7 percent) has a mezuzah on his or her doorpost, the overwhelming majority do not visit synagogue at all or only on special occasions/the Jewish high holidays, very few regularly observe the Sabbath by lighting candles or reciting kiddush (14.8 percent),

Table 5.3. Religio-Ethnic Identification among Israelis in Germany, Total and by Veterancy (Percentages)

	Total	1–3	4–5	6–10	11–20	21+
Self-define as Jewish						
Total	100.0	100.0	100.0	100.0	100.0	100.0
Not at all	27.4	33.8	25.3	22.4	11.9	30.8
Small extent	19.6	20.5	22.2	21.4	14.9	11.5
Some extent	24.9	24.4	23.2	24.5	31.3	19.2
Great extent	28.1	21.4	29.3	31.6	41.8	38.5
Importance of Being Jewish						
Total	100.0	100.0	100.0	100.0	100.0	100.0
Not at all	23.4	30.5	17.2	20.4	14.9	23.1
A little	27.8	27.5	34.3	29.6	23.9	15.4
Important	23.3	22.3	20.2	24.5	29.9	15.4
Very important	25.5	19.7	28.3	25.5	31.3	46.2
Attendance at Events of German Jews						
Total	100.0	100.0	100.0	100.0	100.0	100.0
Never	51.5	58.8	48.5	45.5	43.3	42.3
Seldom	28.3	23.8	36.4	35.4	23.9	23.1
Sometimes	12.8	10.8	10.1	14.1	19.4	15.4
Often	7.4	6.7	5.1	5.1	13.4	19.2
Friends Who are German Jews						
Total	100.0	100.0	100.0	100.0	100.0	100.0
None	64.4	71.5	59.2	60.6	51.5	64.0
A few	28.9	23.4	34.7	33.3	36.8	20.0
About half	5.8	5.0	4.1	5.1	10.3	12.0
Most	0.9	0	2.0	1.0	1.5	4.0
Importance of Holocaust Memory						
Total	100.0	100.0	100.0	100.0	100.0	100.0
Not at all	22.4	24.8	21.8	22.2	15.5	13.8
Small extent	16.0	15.7	13.9	18.2	15.5	20.7
Some extent	25.9	25.6	26.7	25.3	26.8	31.0
Great extent	35.7	33.9	37.6	34.3	42.3	34.5
Level of Religiosity						
Total	100.0	100.0	100.0	100.0	100.0	100.0
Not religious	84.8	87.9	81.2	85.9	84.5	69.0
Slightly religious	10.8	8.8	12.9	10.1	12.7	17.2
Somewhat religious	3.7	2.5	5.0	4.0	2.8	10.3
Very religious	0.7	0.8	1.0	0	0	3.4

continued on next page

Table 5.3. Continued.

	Total	1–3	4–5	6–10	11–20	21+
Have Mezuzah on Doorpost						
Total	100.0	100.0	100.0	100.0	100.0	100.0
No	71.3	78.9	75.9	64.8	61.5	40.7
Yes	28.7	21.1	24.1	35.2	38.5	59.3
Attend Synagogue						
Total	100.0	100.0	100.0	100.0	100.0	100.0
Never	33.5	38.5	28.7	25.3	36.6	24.1
Weddings/Bar Mitzvah	44.5	42.7	48.5	56.6	33.8	37.9
High Holidays	9.9	8.8	9.9	10.1	9.9	13.8
A few times a year	7.5	6.7	9.9	4.0	12.7	6.9
Once a month+	4.6	3.3	3.0	4.0	7.0	17.2
Light Sabbath Candles/Recite Kiddush						
Total	100.0	100.0	100.0	100.0	100.0	100.0
Never	61.2	65.4	60.4	58.6	57.7	44.8
Rarely	12.1	12.5	10.9	13.1	11.3	13.8
Sometimes	11.9	9.6	12.9	14.1	12.7	17.2
Almost always/always	14.8	12.5	15.8	14.1	18.3	24.1
Fast on Yom Kippur						
Total	100.0	100.0	100.0	100.0	100.0	100.0
No	77.5	79.2	71.3	75.8	87.3	65.5
Yes	22.5	20.8	28.7	24.2	12.7	34.5
Light Hanukkah Candles						
Total	100.0	100.0	100.0	100.0	100.0	100.0
Don't light	30.3	30.3	33.7	27.3	31.0	27.6
Some nights	28.0	32.5	24.8	25.3	23.9	24.1
Most nights	19.7	18.8	16.8	23.2	21.1	20.7
All nights	21.9	18.8	24.8	24.2	23.9	27.6
Attend Passover Seder						
Total	100.0	100.0	100.0	100.0	100.0	100.0
No	32.5	32.5	40.2	27.3	33.8	25.9
Yes	67.5	67.5	59.8	72.7	66.2	74.1

and slightly less than one-quarter (22.5 percent) fast on Yom Kippur (the Day of Atonement). Particularistic Jewish behaviors that characterize a relatively large proportion—more than two-thirds—of the Israelis in Germany are lighting Hanukkah candles (on some of the eight days of the festival or more frequently) and attending a Passover *Seder*, both of which should also be seen as opportunities for family and social gatherings over a meal and occasions that may have additional, nonreligious meanings. We found specific events created by and for Israelis for these holidays such as the *Messibat Purim Yisraelit* (the Israeli *Purim Party*) in Düsseldorf in 2018, which aimed at Israelis in the region who wanted to experience an Israeli-style Purim—including typical Israeli foods not necessarily related to Purim, Israeli music, and an encounter with other secular Israeli Jews. The organizers gave special emphasis to the notion of secularism in this event and coupled it with an attempt to found a secular Jewish community as the antithesis of a religious one.

Another indicator of Jewish identity is the memory of the Holocaust, which six out of ten declared somewhat or very important to them. The Israeli migrants were severely torn about the memorial praxes of local Jews and of local Germans, two groups that they perceived as binary opposites—victims and perpetrators. They had been raised in Israel on the notion of the sabra, the strong Israeli-born and -raised Jew (Almog, 2000). This discourse was more or less reflected in the Zionist master narrative, which some Israelis reject (Amit, 2018; Merkur, 2019). Although Israelis are aware that they are (often) descendants of Jews affected by the Holocaust, replies such as "I am not a victim!" concerning their self-perception were common. Yet our ethnographic fieldwork revealed in particular that Israeli Jews were confronted by their own avoidance or rejection of their families' history in various shapes and guises when they stumbled across memorials that they had been trying to overlook. Israelis who overtly engaged with their family histories were less common, and very few actively sought to unravel their family history. More commonly, they reacted with puzzlement when the Israel-specific cultural trauma (Kidron, 2004) became personal (Kranz, 2018d; 2020b). Avi Albers Ben-Hamo also referred to attempts by Israelis in Berlin to escape from the memory of the Holocaust and "get rid of this load. [. . .] They do not want this on their back any more; they are searching for a new dialogue that is not based on the past" (Sapir, 2012c: 12–13).

Do the levels of Jewish identity remain constant, or might they vary commensurate with veterancy in Germany? If they vary, do recent immigrants have stronger or weaker levels of commitment than do their veteran immigrant peers? The most salient trend is that of strengthening of Jewish identification with veterancy in Germany, especially in feelings of belonging to the Jewish people (self-defines as Jewish and considers Jewishness important) and having connections with local Jews (attending events of local Jews and friendship with local Jews); here the particularistic features of Israeliness drop in favor of the umbrella of Jewishness. Likewise, behaviors of religious meaning such as affixing a *mezuzah* to one's doorpost, attending religious services, and Sabbath observance are slightly stronger among Israelis with long veterancy in Germany than among those more recently arrived. The other indicators either remain at a fairly stable level or fluctuate slightly across the veterancy categories but show no sign of the attenuation of Jewish identity. If and how the recent arrivals' identity will develop needs to be reassessed in due time as the number of Israelis in the country and that of Israeli-specific events multiply, offering these Israelis a very different basis for the maintenance of a more specific and particularistic Israeli (Jewish) identity than that available to earlier arrivals. Will they be able to uphold the Hebrew-language-based Israeliness that Lianne Merkur (2019) found so pronounced, and be able to develop a portable, linguistically defined Israeliness over time?

Overall, approximately half of the Israelis in Germany maintain a meaningful Jewish identity, largely expressed in self-definition and the extent of importance they attach to belonging to the Jewish collective, remembering the Holocaust, and celebrating Jewish festivals in ways that involve the gathering of family and friends over rituals and food. The rest of the Israelis have weak if any Jewish consciousness and, consequently, distance themselves from many religio-ethnic practices. Even they, however, still engage in symbolic praxes, as our findings concerning the lighting of Hanukkah candles and the importance of the *Seder* indicate. As veterancy in Germany grows, many patterns of Jewish identification gain strength while others remain stable.

Local German Identification

A third dimension of identification is identifying with the general host society. Most Israelis define themselves as not German at all (64.3 percent) or, at the most, German to a small extent (22.4 percent) (see table 5.4). This corresponds to several expressions by Israelis in Berlin, such as Liat Tal, "I'm really not a German" (Sapir 2013b: 20–21) or Amir Kusinski "Saying that in my identity I'm German? It's not so. It's exaggerated" (Sapir 2014b: 22–23). At the same time, a rather large proportion of respondents feels attached to the new place where they live, work, and perhaps raise a family, as four of every ten view Germany as a home to a very great or great extent, and another third feel that way somewhat. Given the large gap

Table 5.4. German Identification among Israelis in Germany, Total and by Veterancy (Percentages)

	Total	1–3	4–5	6–10	11–20	21+
Self-define as German						
Total	100.0	100.0	100.0	100.0	100.0	100.0
Not at all	64.3	72.8	65.3	64.3	38.8	46.2
Small extent	22.4	18.5	23.5	26.5	25.4	30.8
Some extent	10.8	7.8	9.2	7.1	26.9	19.2
Great extent	2.5	0.9	2.0	2.0	9.0	3.8
Feel Germany is Home						
Total	100.0	100.0	100.0	100.0	100.0	100.0
Not at all	22.6	25.3	21.8	16.2	21.1	20.7
Some extent	35.9	37.3	35.6	41.4	28.2	34.5
Great extent	24.1	25.3	21.8	23.2	26.8	13.8
Very great extent	17.3	12.0	20.8	19.2	23.9	31.0
Non-Jewish German Friends						
Total	100.0	100.0	100.0	100.0	100.0	100.0
None	13.7	17.8	12.1	11.1	7.5	8.0
A few	29.9	31.8	31.3	29.3	23.9	20.0
About half	40.4	38.4	40.4	44.4	46.3	32.0
Most	16.0	12.0	16.2	15.2	22.4	40.0
Friends Who are Non-Jewish Immigrants						
Total	100.0	100.0	100.0	100.0	100.0	100.0
None	25.7	26.1	23.5	22.2	26.9	36.0
A few	38.7	35.3	36.7	44.4	46.3	44.0
About half	29.6	30.3	35.7	26.3	25.4	20.0
Most	6.0	8.3	4.1	7.1	1.5	0
No Conflict bet. Holocaust and Relations with Germany						
Total	100.0	100.0	100.0	100.0	100.0	100.0
Do not agree	15.7	14.9	16.8	16.2	15.5	10.3
Agree somewhat	10.4	13.6	9.9	5.1	7.0	10.3
Agree moderately	25.0	23.6	21.8	34.3	26.8	17.2
Agree strongly	49.0	47.9	51.5	44.4	50.7	62.1
Difficult to Live in Germany						
Total	100.0	100.0	100.0	100.0	100.0	100.0
Not at all	39.6	44.9	32.3	31.6	44.8	42.3
Rarely difficult	41.7	37.2	46.5	46.9	41.8	42.3
Difficult	7.0	6.4	8.1	10.2	3.0	7.7
Very difficult	11.7	11.5	13.1	11.2	10.4	7.7

between German identity and feeling that Germany is home, we suggest that Israelis view home as a physical and not an emotional or a beloved place. More than half of the Israelis in Germany belong to informal social networks that have a salient presence of non-Jewish Germans, and more than one-third have a significant number of friends who are non-Jewish immigrants (the two uppermost categories in each variable, respectively). Most Israelis in Germany strongly or moderately agree with the statements that the Holocaust is not an obstacle to integration into the local society and culture, and that the German past poses no difficulties to living in the new country (not at all/rarely).

Israelis' patterns of interaction with local Germans are slightly different from those of German-born and -raised nonimmigrant Jews. Jews who are second- and third-generation Holocaust survivors—those born and raised in Germany as the children/grandchildren of "actual" survivors—entertain a multitude of contacts and connections with local Germans and recategorize those Germans to whom they are very close (friends, partners) as "special" Germans (Kranz, 2009; Rapaport, 1997), although they maintain some ambiguities (Frerker, 1998; Mendel, 2010; Ranan, 2014). Post-Soviet Jews also demonstrate strong connections, which increase with veterancy, with non-Jewish Germans (Schütze, 1997). However, like locally born and raised Jews who may retreat to Jewish spaces on occasion, they meet in temporally defined "Russian Jewish" spaces (Gromova, 2013), indicating that intra-Jewish subgroups exist.

Israelis are more at ease in their interaction and boundary management with German non-Jews than are locally born and raised Jews in the same age cohort. They share fewer formative parameters with them, setting them apart from locally born and raised Jews whose family histories, in turn, set them apart from other Germans (Kranz, 2015b). The distance between Israelis and local Germans decreases conflict zones due to biographical distance (Kranz, 2016a; 2019b). Furthermore, attitudes among Israeli immigrants toward Germany and Germans have been changing notably (Kranz, 2021). In particular, Israelis who are third-generation Holocaust survivors—the majority of Israeli migrants to Germany—display positive attitudes toward Germany and Germans, in contrast with those of locally raised members of the third generations, the Third Generation writ large (Kranz, 2016a; Mendel, 2010; Ranan, 2014), which reflect perpetuated trauma. Their attitudes also differ from Russian-speaking migrants in the same age cohort (Körber, 2018), who, as result of having immigrated to Germany as Jews, often reconfigure their identity narratives to fit the expectations of local

Jews and non-Jews (Becker, 2001). Israelis, who have different biographies and migration trajectories, are the most at ease in Germany, with Germans, and among Germans.

Although the course of the change is not always consistent, the most salient trend is one of strengthening or stability of local German identification with veterancy (see table 5.4). The proportion of Israelis who do not define themselves as Germans at all, for example, is declining in favor of a slightly stronger German identity; the percentage of Israelis who regard Germany as their home to a great or very great extent is rising over time; and a similar trend in the number of non-Jewish German friends is evident. As Charlotte, a German academic who wrote about Israel-German relations, suggests, Israelis who wrap themselves in their Israeliness, including intensive social contacts with other Israelis, will not survive in the new country (Amit, 2013). These quantitative findings accord with our qualitative information and the notion of being at ease with and among Germans. From the moment of their arrival in Germany, many Israelis do not feel that the Holocaust poses an obstacle to integration into the local society or that the German past places any burden on living in the country; this view does not change over time. What weakens with veterancy is the connection with non-Jewish immigrant peers. It stands to reason that after arriving in a new country, immigrants come into contact with people of similar status—foreigners—in governmental offices, residential neighborhoods, or social and cultural events aimed at newcomers. Such involvement exposes them to the experience of others and, for this reason, should facilitate their integration into the host country. Over time, their shared interests with other immigrants diminish and they seek other social circles that better suit their social and economic achievements, areas of work, and ethnic belonging. The case of the Israeli émigrés is no different.

A key parameter in this development is the Israelis' high level of education. German society remains ethnically stratified in terms of education and its corollary, career progress. Local (ethnic) Germans make the swiftest career progress, while migrants, even if highly qualified (Destatis, 2011; 2012; 2015), lag behind, particularly among those from Muslim-majority countries.[2] Like other Global Northerners, Israelis benefit from a specific perception. Factually, they have high levels of education and professional skills but, more so, "being an Israeli with a high-tech background" is a useful selling point in Germany (Knaul, 2017). Even those who lack this background are positively viewed; in our interviews with German officials, Israelis were described as diligent and hard-working migrants. They benefit from their perception as "white" in a country where whiteness connotes belonging (Wagner, 2014). In terms of Germany's social stratification and "othering," they also benefit from not being Muslims (Shooman, 2012; 2014).

We suggest that Israelis in Germany draw a line between the cognitive dimension and the instrumental dimension of local identity. They do not feel emotionally and consciously part of the German people. Yet they keenly feel—even if not always consciously—that they fit into a specific mold in German society and that they can access specific white privileges. Consciously and emotionally, their group belonging is far more attached to their Israeli and Israeli Jewish background than it is to the local Jewish population. This, however, is neither because of Germany per se nor due to the country's tragic historical connection with the Jews; rather, it seems to characterize first-generation migrants, especially if settled in the new country only recently. Still, many Israeli émigrés are strongly involved in local daily life and view Germany, as a physical, social, and cultural environment, as their new home. This sense strengthens further as their veterancy in Germany grows and is supported by their strong Israeli identity. That is, Israelis feel at ease in integrating because they are aware that they are not assimilating.

The Shaping of Identity

Group identity does not evolve in a vacuum. Rather, it is determined by different factors from both the past and present and, in the case of foreigners, also by their migration and settlement experience. Accordingly, what follows is an attempt to assess the role of background variables, immigration factors, and sociodemographic characteristics in the way Israelis in Germany shape their transnational attachment to Israel, their religio-ethnic Jewish identification, and their local German connections. To simplify the empirical investigation, we constructed three measures, each of which is composed, respectively, of the variables associated with the aforementioned three types of identities. Since each of the measures includes a different number of variables and different variables may have different numbers of values, the range of the measures is not uniform: that of transnational identity from 11 to 38, of religio-ethnic identity from 12 to 44, and of local German identity from 6 to 22.[3]

Findings from multivariate analysis (see table 5.5) show that only a few of the background, immigration, and sociodemographic characteristics are independently associated with group identity. Nevertheless, they managed to

Table 5.5. Direction (Positive/Negative) and Magnitude of the Effects of Background Variables, Immigration Factors, and Sociodemographic Characteristics on Group Identity[1]

	Transnational	Religio-Ethnic	Local German
Reasons for Emigration from Israel			
Political/security	−0.180	−1.111*	−0.166
Professional development	0.046	−0.083	−0.248
Economic development	0.225	1.008*	0.325[i]
Education	0.007	0.237	0.214
Religious establishment	−0.763*	−1.359*	0.180
Family/friends	0.462	0.13	−0.152
Reasons for Choosing Germany			
Education	0.165	−0.085	−0.017
German culture	−0.269	−0.485	0.417*
Professional/economic	−0.002	0.614	−0.020
Family origin	−0.045	0.092	0.055
German partner	0.280	0.321	0.112
Seeking challenge	0.271	−0.121	0.218[i]
Reaction of Family and Friends			
Family reaction to leaving Israel	−0.543	−0.919	0.210
Friends' reaction to leaving Israel	−0.137	−0.192	−0.111
Family reaction to choosing Germany	0.648	0.848	0.083
Friends' reaction to choosing Germany	0.000	−0.529	0.612*
Parents/grandparents Holocaust survivors: Yes	−0.070	1.184	0.883*
Age at Immigration			
18–24	2.366*	3.343*	−0.518
25–29	1.303	2.907[i]	−0.153
30–34	1.507	2.395[i]	−0.194
35–39	2.205*	1.656	−1.393*
Veterancy in Germany			
4–5	−0.072	1.367	0.497
6–10	−0.417	−0.224	0.715
11–20	−0.479	0.652	0.387
21+	0.156	−0.105	1.039
Place of Residence			
Other large cities	−0.338	0.490	0.651[i]
Other places	−1.257[i]	−0.372	0.366

continued on next page

Table 5.5. Continued.

	Transnational	Religio-Ethnic	Local German
Future Migration			
Germany	−1.863*	−2.563*	0.814ⁱ
Elsewhere	−1.697ⁱ	−2.291ⁱ	0.005
Gender			
Female	0.034	−1.509*	−0.399
Other	0.229	−4.511	1.603
Education			
Matriculation	−0.263	−0.425	0.359
Post-secondary	−0.005	0.364	1.080ⁱ
BA	0.375	0.267	0.178
MA+	1.145	1.290	−0.230
Occupation			
Professional and arts	−0.109	1.219	−0.592
Managerial	1.319	2.579	−0.026
Technical	0.724	−1.732	−0.870
Sales/clerical/services			
Blue-collar	0.330	1.065	−0.502
Marital Status and Children			
Married: Jewish spouse	0.462	1.988	−1.463*
Married: Non-Jewish spouse	−0.306	−1.997	−1.121ⁱ
Partner	−0.024	0.358	−0.618
Formerly married	−1.692	1.114	0.138
Children: Yes	0.635	2.855*	0.710
German Language Proficiency			
Weak	1.860	0.810	0.160
Mediocre	1.257	0.032	0.314
Good	0.939	1.566	0.891
Very good	1.161	3.592ⁱ	0.650
Homeownership: Yes	−0.225	−1.676	0.353
Citizenship: Yes	−0.827	0.204	0.675ⁱ
Constant	25.431	27.792	9.791
Explanatory Power	*8.3%*	*36.0%*	*32.0%*

ⁱUnstandardized coefficients (B) from ordinary least squares regression (OLS).
*Significant at least at the 0.05 level; i significant at $p < 0.10$.

Reference categories: parents/grandparents are Holocaust survivors—no; age at immigration—40+; veterancy—0–3 years; place of residence—Berlin; future migration—Israel; gender—male; education—no diploma; occupation—unemployed/retired/other; marital status—single; children—no; German language proficiency—very weak; homeownership—no; citizenship—no.

explain a high proportion of the variation in religio-ethnic identity, local-German identity and, to a much lesser extent, transnational identity. A detailed look reveals that Israeli émigrés who specified the involvement of the religious establishment in daily life in Israel as an important consideration in their decision to emigrate, who live in areas outside of Berlin and major cities in Germany, and who do not intend to return to Israel in the next several years exhibit the weakest transnational ties. Judged by the size and level of significance of the coefficients, the paramount determinant of transnational identity is future migration. Concurrently, those who left at an early age (18–24) or in their late thirties (35–39) tend more than others to maintain contacts with Israel. Individual characteristics were modest in explaining variations in transnational identity among Israelis in Germany—only 8.3 percent.

A larger number of variables were significant for religio-ethnic identity. As with transnationalism, one expects this manifestation of identity to be weaker among Israelis who indicated that the religious establishment's involvement in daily life played a strong role in their decision to leave (hence presumably explaining their broad antipathy toward particularistic Jewish patterns) and do not intend to return to Israel in the next several years. Strong reservations about the political-security situation in Israel also inhibit religio-ethnic identity. Religio-ethnic identity is weaker among Israeli women than among their male counterparts. Leaving Israel because of inability to develop economically is positively associated with religio-ethnic identity; those who emigrated on this account did not criticize Israel, possibly reflecting weak religio-ethnic or Israeli identity ab initio.

Migration at an early age and the presence of young children at home enhance Jewish identity. Obviously, these are critical stages in the lives of both parents and their offspring for the shaping of group identity. Given the important policy implications of these findings, the organized Jewish community should reach out and embrace these young families, tailor its activities to their needs, and view these Israelis as a potential source of an increase in membership and lowering the age profile of the acutely aging local Jewish community. To date, however, Israelis feel no strong attraction to the existing Jewish communal structures; instead, they set up their own structures wherever a critical mass of Israelis forms. The explanatory power of differences in religio-ethnic identification is rather high at 36 percent.

Those who are most likely to assimilate into the local German society are Israelis who were pushed out because of economic considerations (although, as we have seen, they concurrently integrate into the local Jewish community), were attracted to German culture, moved to Germany in search of a challenge, received support from close friends, have post-secondary but not academic education, and hold German citizenship. Somewhat surprisingly, Israelis from families of Holocaust survivors are positively associated with German identity. This largely coincides with the support that they received from their parents and grandparents for their decision to settle in Germany. It strongly attests to the reconciliation of these Israeli families with Germany and Germans. Israelis who were in their late thirties upon arrival in Germany, and married—whether the partner is Jewish or not—are the most likely to refrain from integrating into the general host society. This finding is of special interest because it attests that intermarriage is not necessarily synonymous with assimilation. Indeed, intermarriage among Israeli migrants in Germany somewhat weakens Israeli and Jewish identity, although the effects are not robust (i.e., statistically significant). This development is also supported by non-Jewish German spouses who, even if they do not convert, support the celebration of Jewish festivals within the family (Kranz, Hotam, and Shoshana, 2019). We did not encounter a single Israeli Jewish migrant who reported having been asked to convert; neither were antisemitism or anti-Jewish attitudes within the non-Jewish spouse's family reported. Typically, non-Jewish spouses did nothing to thwart the transmission of the Hebrew language or Jewish religion to children born of their mixed marriages; instead, they attended ceremonies with the Jewish coparent. Some were even the driving forces behind the children's Jewish and Hebrew education (ibid). These spouses tolerated their failure to understand the Israeli parent's Hebrew-language communication with the children and allowed the latter to serve them as translators. Our empirical model is able to explain approximately one-third (32 percent) of the differences in local German identification among the Israeli immigrants.

The Israelis in Germany construct their identity around three coherent major pillars associated with Israel, Judaism, and Germany. Judged by the most powerful expression of identity, self-definition, identification with Israel is the paramount component, followed by Jewish identity. Even after amassing much veterancy in the new country, Israelis do not rise to identify themselves as Germans. Such identification is also hampered by Germany's nature as an ethno-nationalistic country and by the positioning of Jews as one of several out-groups that were historically construed as non-Germans by default (Gosewinkel, 2016) and remain such for much of the German population today (Decker and Brähler, 2018). Concurrently, Israelis distinguish between group belonging and place of residence; from this perspective, many consider both Israel and Germany as their home and integrate into non-Jewish German social circles, attaining a dual belonging while not self-identifying as German. Others are trapped in a situation of nonbelonging, viewing neither of the two countries as their home. Over time, Israelis in Germany strengthen their religio-ethnic identification, especially that associated with intermittent and symbolic manifestations. The rhythm of their various identifications is affected by migration factors related to their reasons for leaving Israel, which weaken transnational and religio-ethnic identifications; reasons for choosing Germany as the destination country, which strengthen glocal German identity; and future migration, marked by the intention of staying put in the country or moving on to somewhere else but not returning to Israel, which mitigates identification both with Israel and with Jewishness. Being married also weakens German identification; while this was expected for those who participate in a homogenous marriage, Israelis married to non-Jews also distance themselves from a German identity, perhaps as a way of opposing the strong German identity of their spouse, or by seeing the exclusionary features of Germanness more clearly. In general, Israelis' group identity in Germany is split among Israeliness, Jewishness, and Germanness, with a tendency to adopt selected habits from each of the three dimensions of identity and to reject others (Lapidot and Ilany, 2015). Equally important is that Israelis in Germany are not made of one cloth. "The diversity among them is larger than the similarity and there are many groups whose common denominator is not large enough" (Alon, 2013: 14–15). Still, combining the various quantitative approaches applied here along with insights from the open-ended interviews, we find that the most salient trajectory among Israelis in Germany is stability or weakening of transnationalism in favor of Jewish identity and local-German connections and, hence, the concept of separation.

Chapter 6

Antisemitism: In the Eye of the Beholder

Context and Concept

Acceptance of minorities by the majority society, tolerance of the "other" or the "new," and intergroup relations are important requisites for immigrants' adjustment to their destination country. Immigrants may encounter hostile treatment on the part of the receiving population, or from other immigrant subgroups, either due to their religio-ethnic extraction or because the politics associated with their home country evokes international criticism. In some cases, both of these immigrant affinities, group and national belonging, may generate alienation and rejection. The distinction between the two elements, the religio-ethnic and national, is not always clear and unequivocal.

Diaspora Jews are exposed to antisemitism. In its very general definition, antisemitism is a rejection of perceived characteristics, it being clear to those who adhere to this worldview that it is directed solely at Jews (Ettinger, 1969: 159). Antisemitism treats Jews, singly and collectively, as a resented "other." This is an attitude driven by prejudice, hate, and fear (Wistrich, 2010) that sees Jews as a threat in social, economic, political, and other public arenas. Antisemitism denotes a specific worldview that sees Jews as central to all ills of humanity (Salzborn, 2018). Judaken (2018) depicts antisemitism more comprehensively as Judeophobia, adding fear and fascination to explain different modes of anti-Jewish discourse and practices. Zygmunt Bauman (1997) had referred to the phenomenon of allosemitism, in which hate of Jews and love for them exist concomitantly. In Christian-dominated Europe, anti-Judaism should not be forgotten: Christian religion knows anti-Judaism in its scripts (Anidjar, 2003). Over time, this historic form of antisemitism, resentment of Jews, has become less important than racially driven antisemitism, a phenomenon of modernity (Bauman, 1989). Depending on the region in Europe, however, anti-Judaism and antisemitism exist side by side.

Antisemitic incidents span a broad spectrum, from facial expressions or other subtle communication through demonstrations and hate propaganda, including Holocaust denial, up to severe crimes and genocide (Chanes, 1999; Judaken, 2018; Tobin, 1988). Antisemitism may be expressed in informal contacts between Jews and non-Jews, in the workplace, in residential neighborhoods, in applying to municipal or governmental services, or within the legal arena (cf. Weller and Lieberknecht, 2019) and the like. It may be manifested by individuals or by larger bodies or movements (Tobin, 1988). Notably, in Europe there are racist organizations and antireligious and anti-immigrant groups that act against minorities in general, Jews being but one of their targeted populations.

Antisemitic expressions may also be directed at the State of Israel, which is viewed as the sovereign entity of the Jewish collective (Marcus, 2015). Anti-Israel remarks of antisemitic nature and content include, among other things, objection to the Jewish people's right to self-determination, the demand that Israel meet a standard other than that of other (democratic) countries, use of antisemitic symbols and images in reference to actions carried out by Israel and/or Israelis, and likening of Israeli actions to those of the Nazi regime. However, criticism of Israel, grave as it may be, cannot be attributed to anti-Jewish bias when it invokes criteria similar to those employed in critiques of other countries, in which case, it is not regarded as antisemitism, according to the International Holocaust Rememberance Alliance (IHRA) (see also Staetsky, 2019). The IHRA definition of antisemitism was adopted by the German parliament in 2018. In 2019, the German parliament passed the anti-BDS (Boycott, Divestments, and Sanctions) resolution that draws on the IHRA resolution. This means that associations or similar who support BDS will not receive public funding. However, this does not mean that support of BDS is illegal in Germany, as had been reported: any individual, or association, can support BDS based on freedom of opinion according to the Basic Law (section 5), it just means that such an individual and association will be excluded from public funding. Neither the IHRA definition of antisemitism nor the BDS resolution are embraced by all Germans, be they Jews or non-Jews, and criticism manifested in missives across media outlets as well as ongoing petition for or against them. Yet, it is striking that petitions initiated by Jews and/or Israelis who argued against the BDS resolution received very significant attention, which evidences that "Jew" and "Israeli" carry a specific currency for the German public: it has rarely been questioned if these Israelis or Jews are area experts, understand the local discourse, or the German political landscape. Sa'ed Atshan and Katharina Galor (2020) elaborate on the issue of "criticizing Israel," arguing that Germans tend to keep quiet about their opinions because they are scared of the repercussions (Mende, 2020), as being perceived as an antisemite is the death blow to any career.

Antisemitism can be measured in three major ways. They are differentiated by the object that stands at the center of the investigation—incidents or people and, among the latter, if at issue are non-Jews' views about Jews or Jews' perceptions of the extent of local antisemitism and their self-experiencing of such hatred. Respective examples of each of these approaches are the documentation of the numbers and types of antisemitic incidents in Europe parsed by countries as carried out by the Kantor Center (2018); the ADL GLOBAL100 project of attitudes and opinions toward Jews among citizens of over 100 countries (Anti-Defamation League, 2014) or the Germany Antisemitism Assessment Study conducted by the World Jewish Congress (2019); and surveys of experiences and perceptions of antisemitism among Jews in EU member states (European Union Agency for Fundamental Rights-FRA, 2013; 2018). It is possible, of course, to consider all of the above measures simultaneously and generate an integrated three-dimensional assessment of antisemitic sentiments (JPPI, 2017).

Theoretical Considerations

Here we analyze and discuss perceptions among Israelis in Germany of the extent of antisemitism in their new country and their own experiences of antisemitic hate and discrimination. The theoretical framework within which we explore the topic is the uneven distribution of perceptions and experiences among people. That is, such matters vary by socioeconomic, identificational, and local-context (place of residence) factors. From the *integration* perspective, the more immigrants assimilate into the mainstream host society, the less alienation they are expected to experience and the more they will tend to deny the existence of prejudice against them. Close contacts with the local population are likely to mitigate preexisting religious and ethnic prejudice and intergroup tension and enhance positive feelings toward the other (Allport, 1954; Hewstone and Brown, 1986). Newer theories, however, detect a paradox in integration (El-Mafaalani, 2018): strong success and high visibility of members of the out-group—immigrants in our case—may at times amplify traditional perceptions and stereotypes by which this is known and strengthens adverse mental associations toward its members. Likewise, the more immigrants integrate into the mainstream society, the more conflicts arise because immigrants who perceive themselves as active members of the host society demand full equality and appreciation as integral parts of the society. Because Germany had experienced large-scale labor migration since the 1950s and absorbed influxes of displaced person groups, the issue is particularly pronounced in this country. In fact, however, Germany refused to define itself as an immigration country until the end of the 1990s. This conscious policy went hand in hand with legal, structural, and social marginalization of, as well as discrimination against, not only "noncitizens" but also German citizens who professed to non-Christian religions. Circumcision, of Jews and Muslims alike, has been a repeated bone of contention. Although it was laid to rest de jure in 2012, this does not mean that mainstream Germans accept circumcision for religious reasons and that resentment of Jews has vanished (Decker and Brähler, 2018). Indeed, the more Jews insist on "having the right to have rights" as Jews—to use Hannah Arendt's idiom—the more conflicted German society is in its reactions. This phenomenon is not particular to Jews; other minority groups share this experience, a key source of conflict in European countries that have moved from relative social homogeneity to diversity since World War II. Given that Ashkenazi Israelis (the majority of our research group) are perceived as white, they are shielded by their whiteness (Wagner, 2014). Even so, the dominant group may see their social convergence as a threat (Hewstone and Brown, 1986; Lowie, 1954). Differences in the perceptions and experiences of antisemitism commensurate with the integration of Israelis into German life may be reflected in structural characteristics such as veterancy, citizenship, employment, and marital status. From the social standpoint, some may claim that frequent contacts between these Israelis and nonimmigrant Germans in schools, on the job, or in residential neighborhoods may be too casual and nonintegrative to dispel or strengthen hostility (Hewstone and Brown, 1986).

The *group-identification* perspective sets out from the premise that individuals in intergroup situations "interact [not] as individuals [. . .] but as members of their groups standing in certain defined relationships to [sic] members of other groups" (Tajfel and Turner, 1986: 10). When a person has strong feelings about a distinct group, she/he will view the social environment through the prism of a social categorization that perceptually distinguishes him or her from other groups (Turner, 1991). Consciousness of group membership strengthens emotional attachment and particular behaviors, hence social identification. Since group membership is authentic and figures importantly in a person's self-esteem, a person will attempt to enhance the status of his or her group by emphasizing social differences vis-à-vis other groups, including perceptions and attitudes toward "them." Thus, one expects to find a positive association between Israeli and Jewish identification and the perceived extent of antisemitism and the experiencing of antisemitism, and the opposite of strong local-German identification.

A third perspective is that of the *environment.* Attitudes and behaviors are cumulatively affected over time by incentives from the surrounding population and by macroconditions (Harvey, 1969). In stratified societies, such a conflict reflects social, economic, and political power as well as social prestige (Oberschall, 1973). Disadvantageous economic conditions, a population composed of multiethnic and immigrant groups, and the numerical salience of, and in turn competition from, the group in question are likely to amplify negative manifestations (LeVine and Campbell, 1972; Rebhun, 2014; Welch et al., 2001). Accordingly, one should expect to find an association between place of residence and distinct levels of perceptions and experiencing of antisemitism.

Antisemitism is reported mainly in multiethnic surroundings, that is, the major cities in Germany. Berlin stood out for its statistics on reported incidents (RIAS 2018) but, as we will show, our respondents reported differently. The general statistic should be treated with caution because Berlin has the country's largest Jewish community and its most significant Israeli population. Namely, in a bitter twist of irony, in Berlin there are simply more Jews around, particularly visible Jews, those who wear traditional attire such as the *yarmulke* (kippa). While Jews in other cities sustained less antisemitic violence in terms of statistical comparison, the worst act of antisemitism in recent times in Germany happened in one "other" city, Halle, on Yom Kippur, October 9, 2019, when a right-wing German extremist attempted to shoot his way into the local synagogue. While his attempt to assault the worshipers failed, he shot dead two other innocent bystanders and expressed hatred for foreigners (*Ausländer*) and for Jews, indicating the existence in his mind of an intersectionality of racism that dwells on hatred of everything perceived of as non-German. Israelis perceived these trends clearly and wondered whether and when they would be recognizable or how to avoid being visible as Israelis and Jews. Their particular worry concerned their children and the possibility of their having experienced marginalization, discrimination, and violence in school (Kranz, Hotam, and Shoshana, 2019). Some parents acted preemptively and moved their children to Jewish schools, if they had the option. That is, Jewish schools exist only in the major metropolitan areas, which in turn indicated the largest amount of antisemitic incidents. Israelis living in rural areas did not report these issues in regard to themselves or their children, if they had any.

Antisemitism in Contemporary Germany

As early as 1949, John J. McCloy, the US High Commissioner for Germany, conveyed to the first postwar government of the Federal Republic of Germany—West Germany—that how it treated its remaining Jews and interrelated with the State of Israel would be decisive in determining the country's readmission to the league of civilized nations (Geller, 2005). While antisemitic attitudes remained stable among the West German population and antisemitic violence took place, antisemitism acquired a strong social and public stigma. Officially, Germans favored Jews (i.e., were philosemitic) and the State of Israel (were philo-Zionist) (O'Dochairtaigh, 2007; 2016). As the historian Frank Stern (1991) put it bitterly: philosemitism is the love for an enemy one is forced to love. No such "policy of forced love" existed in the German Democratic Republic (East Germany), but the claim that one was not antisemitic. The East German government, true to the doctrine of the Communist Bloc, was not supportive of Israel. Despite these differences in foreign policy, antisemitism was seen as undesirable in both Germanies officially, yet, it persisted.

In what poses a problem here is no way to determine how directly these different attitudes of non-Jews toward Jews translated into different rates of antisemitism in East and West Germany. Only in 2017 did systematic reportage of antisemitic incidents become possible when RIAS (Recherche- und Informationsstelle Antisemitismus) launched its online tool, https://www.report-antisemitism.de/. Previously, antisemitic hate crimes, if reported to the police at all, were lumped together with other forms of "political violence." The perpetrators were defined as motivated by right-wing attitudes by default, unless victims stipulated their motives clearly.

To complicate matters, the first wave of antisemitic incidents in West Germany (in 1959) was well documented, whereas violence against Jewish institutions and Jews in East Germany was not documented at all. Needless to say, East German Jews affirm the existence of both structural and physical violence against them (field notes, "DDR Juden" conference, December 15–16, 2016). Measuring post-reunification antisemitic attitudes is also problematic because the East and the West German populations have intermingled and there has been very significant migration of East Germans to the West. Consequently, all statistics relating to the matter should be treated with caution.

Antisemitic violence in the wake of the reunification has found expression in attacks on Jewish institutions as in Düsseldorf (2000), against an Orthodox rabbi in Berlin (2012), but also against post-Soviet Russian Jewish immigrants in form of a bombing at a railroad station in Düsseldorf (2000) that they commonly used to get to their German language course. The perpetrator of the last-mentioned incident has never been found, let alone brought to trial and sentenced. These incidents were well covered. Much less reported, however, is trite but brutal everyday antisemitism. According to a report meant to inculcate understanding of antisemitism in schools, various antisemitic tropes are common (Bernstein, 2018), including *Jew* as an epithet (*Du Jude!*—You Jew!) and Israel-related antisemitism was found to be increasingly prevalent (ibid, 2018) (see photo 4). A discrimination

Photo 4. Interior View of the Burnt-out Israeli-Owned Bar "Morgen wird Besser" (Tomorrow Will Be Better) in Berlin, August 2020. Photo by Danny Freymark.

consultant based in the Jewish community of Düsseldorf, who receives regular reports on incidents in schools, finds persons of Arab Middle Eastern descent overrepresented among the perpetrators (interview, August 8, 2019). The Berlin Jewish community's commissioner for antisemitism confirmed this observation in part. Schools, he stated, are "hotbeds," but most incidents reported to him take place in well-established German-, that is, nonmigrant-, dominated areas (interview, August 7, 2019).

In a nutshell, while migration has brought new antisemitism to Germany (Arnold and König, 2016), the new form coexists with the established but differently coded German antisemitism or the zeitgeist-bound transcultural versions of antisemitism that combine the different forms (Kranz, 2018c). Local variations exist. To understand these long-term developments, in-depth research is needed. Such research is lacking at the present time of writing; to date, investigations offer only quantitative or qualitative snapshots in the form of one-off surveys or interviews or by focus on the antisemitism of a specific group or age cohort.

The federal government does recognize antisemitism as a grave problem. The first report of antisemitism in Germany was issued in 2011, and the second followed in 2017. Each was compiled by a commission of experts; ironically the first such commission had no Jewish member underlining the general problem of knowledge production about Jews, and Jewish life-worlds. To date, academic knowledge production about Jews is geared at the past, philology, and religion, while very little is known about the living Jews, and their life-worlds (see Kranz 2019b, for a summary). The 2017 report coincided with increasing reportage of violent attacks, significant migration of individuals from mainly Muslim countries who were suspected of harboring antisemitic attitudes, and growing impatience among the Jewish population, which complained about the upturn in antisemitic incidents. This led to the establishment of high commissioner for Jewish life in Germany and in the fight against antisemitism (*Beauftragter der Bundesregierung für jüdisches Leben in Deutschland und den Kampf gegen Antisemitismus*) at the federal level and in (most) German states. At the present writing, the work of these respective commissioners is too preliminary to allow the outcomes to be evaluated. Be this it as it may, Jews and their protection are an official raison d'être of the Federal Republic. It is through this lens that the heated discussions about antisemitism—and also about Israel—that take place in Germany, and the fears of imported antisemitism should be seen against the background of German history and concerns triggered by the migration that occurred in the summer of 2015 (Kranz, 2018c).

Levels of Perceptions and Experiencing of Antisemitism

Prejudice against and expressions of hate toward the "other," in our case Jews, can take place in various environments. Here we focus on Israelis' perceptions of the extent of antisemitism in Germany as expressed in local media, public spaces such as workplaces and schools, and online. About one-quarter of Israelis in Germany consider antisemitism a fairly big or very big problem in the German media and the public sphere; almost four out of every ten Israelis share this conviction in regard to the internet (see figure 6.1). A recent report, *Antisemitismus 2.0 und die Netzkultur des Hasses* (Antisemitism 2.0 and the Online Culture of Hate) by the linguist Monika Schwarz-Friesel (2018), supports our observations.

Notably, according to the 2012 survey of the European Union Agency for Fundamental Rights, 61 percent of Jews in Germany regard antisemitism as a fairly big or a big problem in the country. Among the different manifestations of antisemitism, for example, in public places, political life, or graffiti, online antisemitism ranked the highest (72 percent) (European Union Agency for Fundamental Rights, 2013). Six years later, in 2018, a similar survey found that 85 percent of Jews in Germany see antisemitism as a fairly big or a very big problem in the country, and 89 percent found it especially problematic (fairly/big) on the internet (European Union Agency

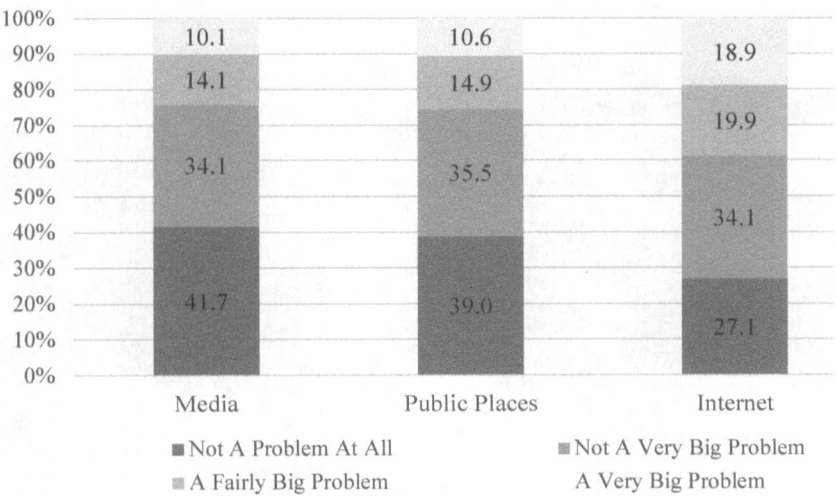

Figure 6.1. Perceived Extent of Antisemitism among Jews in Germay (Percentages).

for Fundamental Rights, 2018). In the 2018 survey, some 60 percent of Jews had the impression that antisemitism had increased a lot in the preceding five years. Overall, therefore, in the eyes of those who are targeted by the phenomenon, antisemitism in Germany has been on the rise in the past decade.

We found differences between the Israelis and local German-speaking Jews in their assessments of antisemitism in Germany. These differences, we propose, should be attributed to weaker proficiency in German among the former. Accordingly, Israelis are less likely than their German Jewish peers to understand a certain expression or words and presumably read fewer local newspapers and surf less German websites. Likewise, as recent migrants whose informal social networks are heavily composed of other Israelis, they have fewer opportunities to be exposed to antisemitism. We also suggest that since the Israelis did not experience antisemitism in their origin country, they are less sensitive to, and less likely to interpret, verbal or facial expressions as antisemitic in content or intention.

Israelis' self-experiencing of antisemitism is low but extant even when the reference period is short—the year preceding the survey. About 13 percent of Israelis in Germany reported having been verbally insulted or harassed because of their Jewishness, and another 1.7 percent experienced physical attack (see figure 6.2). According to the FRA surveys, 21 percent of Jews in Germany self-experienced antisemitism (verbal and/or physical) in 2012 and 29 percent

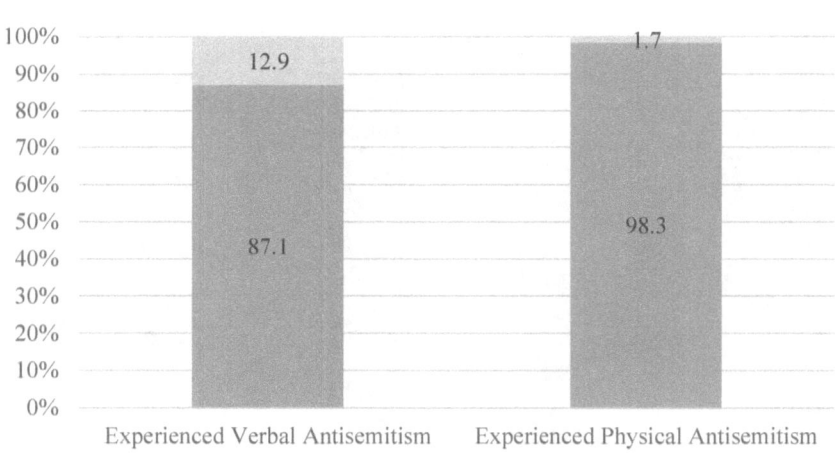

Figure 6.2. Verbal and Physical Experiences of Antisemitism among Israelis in Germany (Percentages).

had such experiences by the time of the second survey, 2018 (European Union Agency for Fundamental Rights, 2018). As with perceptions, we attribute the higher rates of experiences among local Jews than among the Israeli immigrants to the deeper socioeconomic integration of the former and their more frequent interaction with the local non-Jewish population.

Perceptions and experiences are interrelated (Rebhun, 2014). Due to the small number of Israelis who experienced physical attack, we focus from here onward only on verbal manifestations of antisemitism. Table 6.1 shows that among Israelis who experienced verbal antisemitism in the past year, 42.6 percent regard antisemitism in the German media as a fairly big or a big problem, compared to exactly half this rate, 21.3 percent, among those who did not experience such antisemitism. Larger variations were found for antisemitism in the public sphere: 51.9 percent of Israelis who experienced

Table 6.1. Relations between Perception and Experience of Antisemitism (Percentages)

Perceptions of Antisemitism	Verbal Experience of Antisemitism	
	No	Yes
Media		
Total	100.0	100.0
Not a problem at all	44.7	24.1
Not a very big problem	34.0	33.3
A fairly big problem	13.7	16.7
A very big problem	7.6	25.9
Index of dissimilarity	0.21	
Public Sphere		
Total	100.0	100.0
Not a problem at all	43.0	13.7
Not a very big problem	35.6	34.6
A fairly big problem	13.6	23.1
A very big problem	7.7	28.8
Index of dissimilarity	0.31	
Internet		
Total	100.0	100.0
Not a problem at all	28.6	16.7
Not a very big problem	37.3	18.8
A fairly big problem	19.4	22.9
A very big problem	14.7	41.7
Index of dissimilarity	0.31	

verbal insult deem antisemitism in the public sphere to be a fairly big or a very big problem versus only 21.3 percent of peers who had had no such experience. For antisemitism on the internet, the figures are 64.6 percent and 34.1 percent, respectively.

To summarize the overall differences in perceptions of antisemitism by experience, we created an index of dissimilarity. This index expresses the size of variations in perceptions of antisemitism between those who experienced a verbal antisemitic incident and those who did not. The index ranges from 0, perfect similarity, to 1, complete difference. The dissimilarity index for the media suggests that 21 percent of Israelis would have to move from one perception category to another in order to create perfect alignment in the distribution of perceptions of antisemitism between those who experienced antisemitism and those who did not. The dissimilarity indices for the other two manifestations of antisemitism—in the public sphere and online—are slightly larger at .31. Overall, our findings in table 6.1 point to rather strong relations between perceptions and experiences of antisemitism among Israelis in Germany.

Antisemitism and Individual Characteristics

How are perceptions and experiences of antisemitism associated with the three major dimensions: sociodemographic characteristics, group identification, and place of residence? To answer, we merged the manifestations of perceptions of antisemitism in the media, the public sphere, and the internet into a single index. Given that each manifestation has four categories ranging from 0 (not a problem at all) to 3 (a very big problem), the combination of all three manifestations yields scores in the 0–9 range. The average index for the perception of antisemitism among all Israelis in Germany is 3.42. To assess the experiencing of antisemitism, we stick to the single variable of verbal antisemitism expressed in percentages (with an average rate of 12.9 percent).

Sociodemographic Characteristics

Veterancy is positively associated with perceptions of antisemitism. While Israelis who immigrated to Germany over the preceding three years scored 3.17, counterparts who have six to ten years of veterancy assessed antisemitism at the level of 3.64, and those who settled in Germany more than twenty years ago had an even higher index score, 4.33 (see table 6.2).It stands

Table 6.2. Perceptions and Experiences of Antisemitism by Integration Characteristics

	Perceptions of Antisemitism (Index 0–9)	Experience of Verbal Antisemitism (%)
Total Israelis in Germany	3.42	12.9%
Veterancy		
1–3 years	3.17	8.7
4–5 years	3.51	16.3
6–10 years	3.64	18.4
11–20 years	3.30	8.3
21+ years	4.33	25.0
Proficiency in German		
None	3.55	9.1
Weak	3.73	11.5
Mediocre	3.39	10.6
Good	3.16	16.7
Very good	3.47	13.6
German Citizenship		
No	3.30	11.1
Yes	3.87	14.8
Education		
No diploma	3.31	14.8
Matriculation	3.64	15.8
Post-secondary	3.29	10.7
BA	3.04	14.7
MA+	3.84	8.6
Employment Status		
Student	2.56	16.9
Self-employed	3.15	9.6
Employee	3.59	13.0
Unemployed/retired/other	4.50	13.5
Marital Status		
Single	3.19	16.4
Married to a Jew	4.03	9.2
Married to a non-Jew	3.44	11.9
Jewish partner	4.30	5.6
Non-Jewish partner	2.76	7.8
Formerly married	3.21	27.6

to reason that as their veterancy in Germany increases, Israelis have more opportunities to be exposed to antisemitic manifestations in various arenas. Over time, too, although not in a totally linear way, Israelis in Germany also experience more antisemitism: from 8.7 percent among those with veterancy of 1–3 years who reported verbal antisemitism, the rate increased threefold to 25.0 percent among Israelis who have been living in Germany for more than two decades.

Similarly, Israelis who hold German citizenship scored half a point more on the measure of perceptions of antisemitism than did Israelis who lack such citizenship. Likewise, those with German citizenship are more vulnerable to self-experiencing of antisemitism. One possible reason for this is their specific family history: if they descend from German Jews or are naturalized, they have more frequent encounters with the German bureaucracy, which poses specific pitfalls for nonnative speakers because legal-administrative language differs strongly from standard German. We did not find a clear association between proficiency in German and perceptions of antisemitism. Fluency in German, however, seems to increase self-experiencing of antisemitism—possibly because fluent immigrants have better overall integration and more frequent interaction with non-Jews.

The nexus of education and perceptions is inconsistent, as it is for education and experiences. Still, the measure of perceptions is especially high among Israelis whose education is limited to a matriculation certificate (they also ranked highest in self-experience of antisemitism) and, contrastingly, those who have an advanced academic degree. These Israelis seem to suffer from the same phenomenon that local native-German-speaking Jews report: they rise in the ranks and allow their personal perceptions to interfere with the discourse. One such case, reported in our fieldwork, concerned an Israeli who works as a social scientist. She reports that her boss found her contributions off and rejected her input; he deemed the integration of her Israeli Jewish perspective to be undesirable within the touchy area of memory politics. Conflicts like this arose in particular within that sensitive domain but recurred in other fields, such as integration and migration, that carry strong emotional currency in German society.

The inconsistent outcomes of this part of our research may be associated with other characteristics of the Israelis, such as marital or employment status. Data not shown here suggest that Israelis who migrated to Germany for studies assess antisemitism in Germany as rather low. Interestingly, they are the group that experiences antisemitism most intensively. These Israelis appear to differentiate between their own experience in the academic environment, which is often a place of lively political activity, and German society at large. Concurrently, Israelis who have the strongest perceptions of antisemitism are the unemployed, who may attribute their failure to find a job to discrimination on the grounds of their Jewish extraction (whether this is factually true or not). Employees, who interact intensively with members of the general local society, rank antisemitism higher than do the self-employed, at 3.59 and 3.15, respectively. Substantial gaps between these two groups are also found in regard to the experiencing of antisemitism.

Israelis who live with or are married to a Jewish partner have a much higher assessment of the extent of antisemitism in Germany than do those who cohabit with or are married to a non-Jew or live alone (single or formerly married). In fact, living with someone who is Jewish, be this in marriage or in cohabitation, is associated with one of the highest scores of perception of antisemitism relative to any other sociodemographic characteristic. This happens, we propose, because these couples share information that they read, hear, or witness against Jews, thus strengthening (doubling) the impression of the extent of antisemitism in the country. At the same time, they score very low in experiencing verbal antisemitism. It is possible that endogamous couples/partners are more strongly involved than others in Jewish social networks and Jewish and Israeli cultural activities; perhaps, too, they live near their ethnic peers. All of these circumstances would lessen their encounters with non-Jews and, in turn, their experiencing of antisemitic incidents.

Group Identification

Next, we examined the relations between the three measures of identification—transnational, religio-ethnic, and local-German—and perceptions of the severity of antisemitism in Germany. We present the results in plot diagrams. Each dot in the diagram indicates the relation between a given value of the identificational variables and a value of the index of perceptions of antisemitism. When the dots escalate from the lower left-hand part of the diagram to its upper-right-hand sector, they attest to a positive correlation between the variables under investigation; if they slope from upper left to lower right, they suggest a negative correlation.

Despite some deviations, the findings show that strong transnational identification (see figure 6.3A) and strong religio-ethnic identification (see figure 6.3B) amplify perceptions among Israelis in Germany that antisemitism is a problem in the country; they also indicate that local-German identification weakens this assessment (see figure 6.3C). The dots in the diagram are

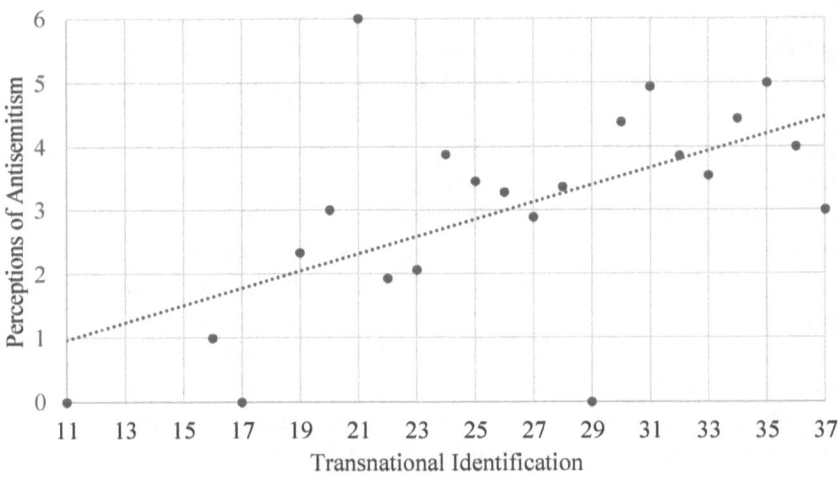

Figure 6.3A. Transnational Identification and Perceptions of Antisemitism among Israelis in Germany.

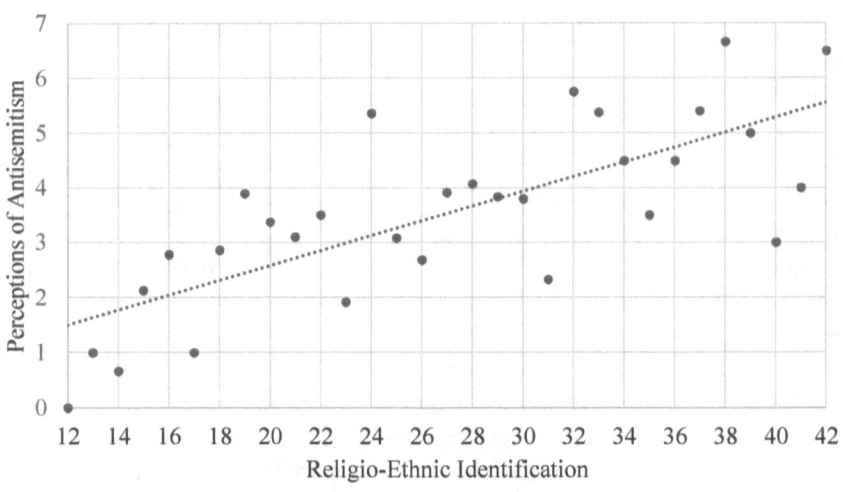

Figure 6.3B. Religio-Ethnic Identification and Perceptions of Antisemitism among Israelis in Germany.

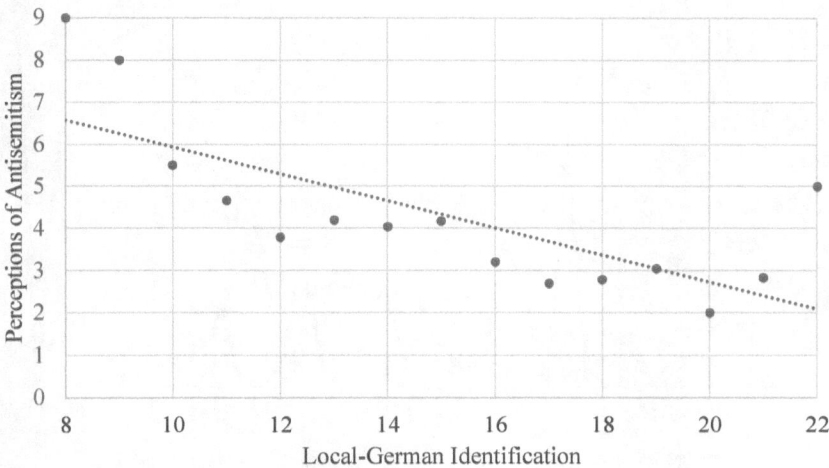

Figure 6.3C. Local-German Identification and Perceptions of Antisemitism among Israelis in Germany.

spread in a pattern that associates weak German identification with a high score of perceived antisemitism; as German identification gathers strength, the perception of antisemitism as a problem in the country declines.

The relation between group identification and experiencing verbal antisemitism is somewhat less robust. The curves of each manifestation—transnational, religio-ethnic, and local-German identification—fluctuate rather strongly and are characterized by sharp ups and downs (see Figure 6.4). This unfolding may be abetted by the small number of Israelis who experienced verbal antisemitism, in general, hence for each value of identification, in particular, turning the alterations across the identificational axis to be especially sensitive. Still, within this wave-like pattern one can see that the percentages of experiencing verbal antisemitism are relatively high in the segment of strong religio-ethnic identification. Low levels of local-German identification, in turn, are associated with rather high levels of antisemitic experiencing and vice-versa—experiences are generally less reported by Israelis who identify strongly with local Germans. This type of descriptive analysis did not reveal any meaningful relations between transnational identification and verbal experiencing of antisemitism.

192 | A Double Burden

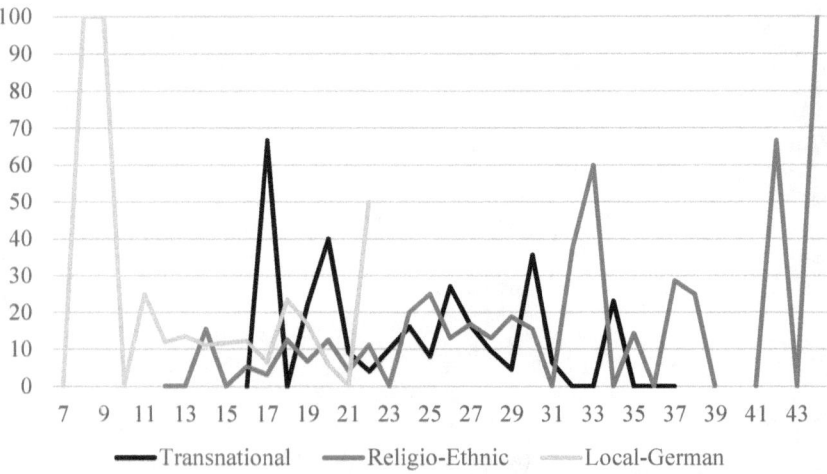

Figure 6.4 Group Identification and Experiences of Verbal Antisemitism among Israelis in Germany.

PLACE OF RESIDENCE

Figure 6.5 shows the means of perceptions of antisemitism and percentages of Israelis in Germany who experienced antisemitism, parsed by places of residence. Israelis' mean assessment of antisemitism in the media, in public places, and online is the lowest in Berlin, at 3.32, highest in other large cities (3.59), and in between in other places (3.47).

The proportion of Israelis who self-experienced verbal antisemitism is highest in other places. The inhabitants of small localities may often belong to low social and economic strata and be deficient in tolerance toward foreigners; they may even inhabit strong bases of neo-Nazi organizations. The share of Israelis in Berlin who experienced antisemitism is moderate and that in other large cities is the lowest among the three geographic categories. The relative paucity of antisemitic experiences in Berlin and other large cities may trace back to the very significant international populations of these urban localities and the diversity of the population to which Israelis connect. If so, Israelis there are less likely to encounter antisemitism of the kind found in small villages.

Overall, there are spatial differences, sometimes quite substantial, in antisemitism as assessed by the Israelis; they are reflected in the specific rankings that the Israelis gave them for each measure of perceptions and experiences.

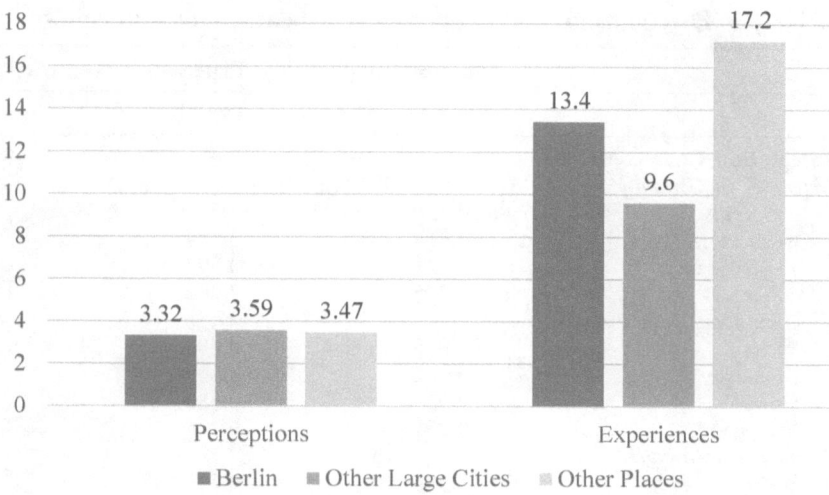

Figure 6.5 Perceptions (Index) and Experiences (Percentages) of Antisemitism by Place of Residence.

Determinants of Antisemitism in the Eye of the Beholder

To refine our view of the relations among the integration, identificational, and environmental factors, on the one hand, and antisemitism, on the other hand, we perform multivariate analyses. We present two models—one for perceptions of antisemitism and the other for verbal experiencing of antisemitism. Each dimension of antisemitism is explored using a specific technique appropriate to the nature of the variable: continuous and dichotomous, respectively.

All other factors controlled for, having a Jewish partner is significantly associated with an increased likelihood of considering antisemitism in Germany a big problem (see table 6.3). In contrast, self-employed Israelis and those who are students tend less to perceive antisemitism as a big problem in their new country, quite possibly because of the specific milieus in which they circulate. Notably, not only were very few of the integration variables found robust for perceptions of antisemitism, but those that do exhibit a statistically significant effect do so at the rather low level of $p < .10$. Group identification plays a much more central role in determining perceptions of antisemitism; stronger religio-ethnic identification amplifies the perceived severity of antisemitism. Conversely, Israelis who develop a local-German identity are less troubled by antisemitism in the country. Transnational

Table 6.3. Determinants of Perceptions and Experiences of Antisemitism

	Perceptions (OLS)[1]	Experiences (Logistic)[2]
	Unstandardized B	Exp (B)
Integration Characteristics		
Veterancy in Germany:		
4–5 years	0.638	2.568[i]
6–10 years	0.314	3.154[i]
11–20 years	0.322	3.594
21+ years	0.275	7.768*
German language proficiency:		
Weak	−0.016	0.695
Mediocre	−0.682	0.639
Good	−0.989	0.388
Very good	−0.951	0.228
German citizenship:		
Yes	0.583	0.648
Education:		
Matriculation	0.375	2.607
Post-secondary	−0.035	4.703[i]
BA	−0.106	2.399
MA+	0.254	3.260
Marital status:		
Jewish spouse	−0.336	0.189*
Non-Jewish spouse	0.207	1.287
Jewish partner	1.924[i]	0.720
Non-Jewish partner	−0.594	0.393
Formerly married	−0.391	2.322
Employment status:		
Employed	−0.728	1.165
Self-employed	−1.004[i]	0.251*
Student	−1.115[i]	1.152
Group Identification		
Transnational	0.061	0.859*
Religio-ethnic	0.078*	1.171*
Local-German	−0.257**	0.947
Place of Residence		
Other major cities	0.018	0.310*
Other places	0.431	0.808
Constant	4.936	
Explanatory Power	8.4%	26.9%

[1]Ordinary Least Squares.

[2]Logistic regression.

*Significant at least at the 0.05 level; [i]significant at $p < 0.10$.

Reference categories are: veterancy—1–3 years; German-language proficiency—none; citizenship—no; education—no diploma certificate; marital status—single; employment status—unemployed; place of residence—Berlin.

identification is not significantly associated with perceptions of antisemitism. Our model did not reveal any independent effect of place of residence on perceptions of antisemitism. Overall, it explained less than 10 percent of the variance in the way Israelis assess antisemitism in Germany.

The set of independent variables explained differences in experiencing (verbal) antisemitism much more effectively. Greater veterancy is associated with stronger likelihood of experiencing verbal antisemitism, especially among Israelis who have lived in Germany for more than two decades. Also, Israelis with post-secondary education report more exposure to antisemitism than their peers who failed to earn a matriculation certificate (the reference group). Conversely, being endogamously married and working as self-employed diminish the experiencing of antisemitism. Unlike the descriptive data, which are somewhat inconsistent, the multivariate analysis shows clearly that transnational identification weakens reportage of antisemitic experiences, whereas strong religio-ethnic identification is positively associated with such experiences. It stands to reason that Israelis who maintain strong Israeli identity circulate socially and culturally in an environment composed of national peers and secular orientation, lacking any marks that can attest to their Jewishness. In contrast, those who have strong religious and ethnic identification are likely to attend various events of the local Jewish community, affiliate with Jewish organizations, and, perhaps, express their Jewish identity in the public sphere—placing them at much higher risk of experiencing antisemitism. All else being equal, Israelis who reside in large cities are less likely to experience antisemitism than are Israelis in Berlin and, equally, Israelis in other places. This model succeeded in explaining 26.9 percent of why some Israelis self-experienced verbal antisemitism and others did not.

The "New Antisemitism": Hostility to Israel

Negative attitudes toward and hatred of Israel are escalating and expanding in Europe, Germany included. Often they are associated with the Israeli-Palestinian conflict and include not only criticism of Israeli military and political actions but also support of boycotting Israeli products, scientific relations and collaborations, and a fortiori visiting the country. This strategy is officially spearheaded by the BDS movement. As suggested above, it is not always possible to distinguish between hateful ideas and actions toward Israel that belong to the old antisemitism, which targets Jews, and those specifically aimed at the State of Israel, hence, "new antisemitism."

Be that as it may, we asked our respondents whether antisemitic reportage about Israel in the German media, the public sphere, and the internet is a problem and, if so, to what extent.

Slightly less than one-quarter (23.3 percent) of Israelis in Germany believe that the way the German media report about Israel is a fairly big problem, and another 14.1 percent were even more critical, defining it as a very big problem (see figure 6.6). A similar proportion, between one-fifth and one-quarter, also consider the way Israel is discussed in public places and online a fairly big problem. There are several significant differences in the rates of those who assessed the problem of Israel-related antisemitism as very big: 11.7 percent for the public sphere and 16 percent for the internet. Israelis in Germany consider antisemitism about Israel a more severe problem than general antisemitism toward Jews. This is especially salient in regard to the media and the public sphere; for the third manifestation, the internet, the share of respondents who see reportage about Jews as representing a fairly big or a big problem of antisemitism is very similar to the assessment of the problem of anti-Israeli reportage (see figures 6.1 and 6.6).

A strong relation exists between Israelis' perceptions of antisemitism about Jews and their perceptions of antisemitism directed toward Israel (see table 6.4). Among those Israelis who see no problem at all with antisemitism toward Jews in the German media, a very small proportion (1.3 percent)

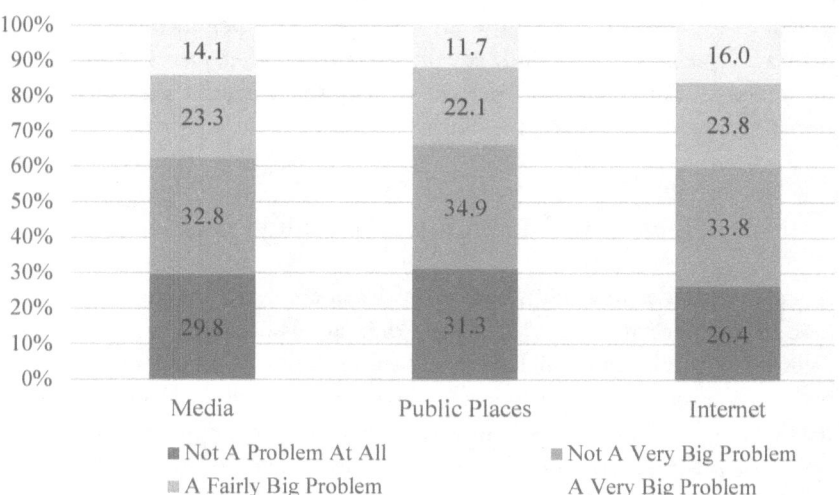

Figure 6.6. Perception of Extent of Antisemitism about Israel (Percentages).

Table 6.4. Relations between Perceptions of Antisemitism toward Jews and Antisemitism about Israel among Israelis in Germany

		Antisemitism about Israel			
Antisemitism about Jews	Total	Not a Problem At All	Not a Very Big Problem	A Fairly Big Problem	A Very Big Problem
Media (Pearson's R = .677)					
Not a problem at all	100.0	58.0	30.6	10.2	1.3
Not a very big problem	100.0	11.5	53.8	23.8	10.8
A fairly big problem	100.0	1.9	13.2	56.6	28.3
A very big problem	100.0	0.0	7.7	30.8	61.5
Public Sphere (Pearson's R = .672)					
Not a problem at all	100.0	62.8	27.6	8.3	1.4
Not a very big problem	100.0	15.0	55.6	26.3	3.0
A fairly big problem	100.0	10.7	16.1	51.8	21.4
A very big problem	100.0	0.0	12.5	22.5	65.0
Internet (Pearson's R = .754)					
Not a problem at all	100.0	74.4	20.5	3.8	1.3
Not a very big problem	100.0	12.9	70.3	15.8	1.0
A fairly big problem	100.0	6.9	15.5	62.1	15.5
A very big problem	100.0	3.6	10.7	21.4	64.3

consider Israel-related antisemitism to be a very big problem. The rate increases to 10.8 percent among those who think antisemitism toward Jews is not a very big problem, rises to 23.8 percent among those who assess antisemitism toward Jews as a fairly big problem, and peaks at 61.5 percent among Israelis who define antisemitism in the German media as a very big problem. Very similar trends are observed for the other two manifestations of antisemitism: in the public sphere and online. Complementary evidence of the strong relations noted above is the Pearson's correlation test, which allows a range of −1 (strong negative relation) to 1 (strong positive relation): for all three manifestations of antisemitism, the value of the Pearson's test is high and positive. Judged by this test, the relation between perceptions of antisemitism toward Jews and antisemitism about Israel is strongest in regard to the internet.

In sum, although not as significant as among all local Jews, a substantial proportion of Israeli immigrants in Germany consider antisemitism, both old (against Jews) and new (against Israel), to be a serious problem in various spheres of German society. These perceptions do not operate out of a context; rather, they are salient among Israelis who self-experienced antisemitism in Germany, which manifests mainly verbally and not physically. Likewise, both measure of antisemitism—perceptions of its severity and extent of its experiencing—are associated with individual characteristics. These relations are largely in concordance with the role of integration, group identification, and environment in determining prejudice and hatred in the eye of the beholder, with some specific factors more meaningful than others. What is apparent is that, insofar as the relations are significant, social and economic integration does not attenuate perceptions and experiences of antisemitism but rather strengthens them. Likewise, inward gathering, as in Jewish endogamy and strong religio-ethnic identification, amplifies subjective feelings about antisemitism. Only a deep conscious shift of adopting a local German identity, often a lengthy process if achieved at all in the first generation, can control for perceptions and experiences of antisemitism among Israelis in Germany. Much less consistent and clear is the effect of place. This requires further exploration with a larger sample and a better distinction among cities, taking into account their specific characteristics such as the population's religio-ethnic profile, local economic indicators, and local cultural and political patterns.

In the meantime, our findings have two major implications for policy: first, successful integration amplifies perceptions and experiences of antisemitism; here, local German authorities should make stronger efforts to combat negative views toward Jews, in general, and Israeli Jews, in particular, among the general German population.[1] Second, the strong link between Jewish identification and perceptions and experiencing of antisemitism should prompt local Jewish organizations and the established Jewish community to arrange ongoing Jewish/non-Jewish dialogues aimed at strengthening understanding between the two groups and, in turn, Israelis' confidence in their adjustment to their new lives in Germany.

Conclusion

People today are on the move. Migration, circular migration, and return migration are salient affinities of Western and free societies. Somewhat paradoxically, spatial movements and trends in residential lifestyles are unfolding amid growing similarities among countries, for specific social strata, with respect to access to sustainable products, cultural consumption, and opportunities for remote acquisition of human capital. This uneven harmonization may ease the migration of those who are lured to a new place due to education, work, family, or other personal considerations. Coupled with advanced technology that allows migrants to maintain intensive contacts with those who stayed behind, it may give them a sense of being home while away from home.

To a large extent, this explains present-day international migration among Jews. On the one hand, modern times have witnessed the convergence of the overwhelming majority of Jews into a small number of developed and liberal countries; on the other hand, every year several tens of thousands of Jews migrate or immigrate internationally, mainly to or from North and South America, Eastern and Western Europe, Australia, and Israel. In fact, one of the strongest flows of Jews in recent years is from Israel, encompassing more than ten thousands individuals annually. The predominant and long-standing destination of this migration is the United States but Israelis in smaller numbers also move to Canada, Australia, the UK, and France (Cohen, 2011; Rebhun and Pupko, 2010). Significant Israeli migration to Germany has evolved only in the past twenty-five years with the reunification of the country's western and eastern parts, the acceleration of German economic and cultural development, the stabilization of the European Union, generational changes among Israeli Jews, and the attenuation of the stigma attached to leaving Israel. These developments, among others, have made

Germany, and Berlin in particular, a magnet for a substantial number of immigrants from Israel (as from around the globe more generally). Israeli immigrants to Germany also benefit from special opportunities for citizenship if they are of German extraction and enjoy access to resident status if they hold any EU citizenship. Paired with generous governmental support of Jewish institutions and activities and special programs for Israelis, this makes Germany a desirable immigration destination from different complementary standpoints.

Israeli migration to Germany is another element in the dramatic sociodemographic changes that German Jewry has been undergoing. From the end of World War II to 1990, the country hosted a tiny Jewish community characterized by severe aging and challenges that may be characterized as long-term effects of the Shoah. In particular, surviving Jewish displaced persons of East European background lacked skills applicable to Germany, making for a difficult economic situation. Furthermore, the vast majority of members of this community suffered from grave (Holocaust) trauma (Grünberg, 1988), or, if among second-generation survivors, transmitted trauma (Grünberg, 2007; Hadar, 1991), causing ambiguities about being in Germany to cascade onto the third generation (Brumlik, 1998; Frerker, 1998; Kranz, 2015a; Mendel, 2010; Ranan, 2014). Despite this heavy freight, changes occurred among the second generation and more so among the third, so that as of this writing Jews in Germany have developed a forward-facing outlook (Kranz, 2019b; 2021). One of the most significant changes occurred when unexpected geopolitical developments in the Soviet bloc allowed Soviet Jews to leave what became the FSU. Some of them, largely attracted by Germany's economic and social incentives, choose to settle in this of all countries. This turned "German Jews," that is, local resident Jews of German or East European descent, into an exceptional, nay, a unique case of a Diaspora community that grew demographically at an unprecedented pace (DellaPergola, 2018; Schmelz and DellaPergola, 1990). Spurring the process, the German authorities, as well as world Jewish organizations, began investing in restoration and development of Jewish sites such as synagogues, schools, and other institutions, reviving religious and ethnic life across the country. This was accompanied by the massive presence of Holocaust memory and commemoration in the public sphere, which gained a particular momentum in the 1990s (Bodemann, 1996; Cronin, 2018). Thus, Jews in Germany swerve among past, present, and future: they are part of mythic time that merges all three.

Exposure in Germany to the Jewish tragedy of the Holocaust is stronger today than ever before. This exposure, not to say its performative manifestations, has become the subject of critical investigation (e.g., Bishop Kendzia, 2018; Bodemann, 1996; Dekel, 2013). This development coincides with the reshaping of Holocaust consciousness in Israel to include the life stories of survivors who in advanced age feel ready to share their experience with their loved ones. This, however, does not deter thousands of Israelis from visiting Germany, among whom many hundreds move to and settle in the country, marry local non-Jewish Germans, and obtain German citizenship. Many of these immigrants, even if they come from a background associated with the Holocaust, receive support from their immediate families for their decision. What was once the burden of leaving Israel and the double burden of settling in Germany (Webster, 1995) is viewed today by segments of Israeli society as acceptable behavior.

This may attest to wider trends both in Israel and in Germany, and, hence, also the relations between the two societies. Most Israelis who migrate to Germany today are young and, in greater part, the third generation of Jews who moved to Israel following statehood. They are distant from the immediate effects that the Holocaust had on the survivors and also from the trickle-down of these effects to their children. At the same time, if they are of German descent, they grew up with a binary that supports migration to Germany on both ends: either Germany was praised in their grandparents' memory or was portrayed as a damned and forbidden place. Both approaches piqued the descendants' curiosity and prompted some to migrate to Germany.

Concurrently, today's German society is overwhelmingly composed of people who had not been born at the time of World War II, let alone were old enough to take part in the destruction of European Jewry. Likewise, the Israeli migrants to Germany belong to the Y generation, for whom "national ideology does not constitute such a strong glue. [. . .] Emigration is not difficult and does not torment [them] as it did earlier generations because lifestyle has become global [and they] are not ashamed of their emigration" (Almog and Almog, 2016: 383–87). Like people in other Western societies, Israelis are becoming more and more individualistic, their personal aspirations often overcoming group solidarity and commitment and also reflected, among some, in deviations from behaviors that their close relatives and friends expect of them. Because the Jewish past is strongly tied to Germany, many young Israelis wish to acquaint themselves with German history and culture, both general and Jewish, including the local language. This creates among them a connection with Germany involving studies, work, and friendships, which may eventually lead to permanent settlement whether planned in advanced or not. Others, viewing the move to Germany as a challenge, may wish to help the revival of Jewish life there.

The migration that we researched above would not have been possible without Israel's rapprochement with (West) Germany, which owes its origins to John J. McCloy's warning to the first West German government in 1949. While antisemitism remained a problem in Germany and the reparation arrangements caused ongoing conflict in Israel (Platt, 2012), the first round of reparation negotiations and the economic relations that followed may be seen as paving the way to more comprehensive bilateral relations. They were cemented by the formation of diplomatic ties in 1965, which allowed official relations to develop further. Today, the official interaction may be described as growing, successful, and very comprehensive, spanning student exchange to business partnerships and specific visas for young Germans and Israelis to visit, work, and live in each other's countries. Beneath these initially superimposed official relations, however, individual Germans as well as individual Israelis reached out to each other. Initially, these were German non-Jews and German Jews who, among the latter, had become Israelis by default. Often they had been close before the Shoah, as the film *The Flat* (Goldfinger, 2011) evidences. In this documentary, grandparents—German Jews—hide their relations with non-Jewish Germans from their (Israeli) children and grandchildren. In other cases, German Jews cum Israelis were more open about their contacts with their country of birth and followed up on invitations to erstwhile hometowns (Nikou, 2020), for example, some taking their children and grandchildren along. These manifold opportunities to meet led to human contact. As Germans and Israelis encountered each other, they began to see each other beyond the categories. In some cases, this enabled migration to Germany (Oz-Salzberger, 2001), but in others the process worked in the opposite direction, German (non-Jews) becoming accidental migrants to Israel (Kranz, 2018b).

Be the reasons for migration as they may, most Israelis in Germany today see no difficulty in living in the country due to its past. Their assessment of the extent of antisemitism in Germany is modest (relative to that of local Jews) and they enjoy informal social relations with non-Jewish Germans. Although they distance themselves from Israel and many no longer see Israel as their home, they do not replace Israel with Germany and continue to regard themselves as Israelis. Arguably, then, they are Israelis who lack a "spiritual" home in the sense of Israel, as the Jewish state, being the "natural" spiritual home of Jewish Israelis. Perhaps, however, we should move away from this notion and also from the idea of these Israelis' being by necessity "post-Zionist" or "post-Israeli." Rather, we have reached a point in time where we witness a reframing of Israeli Jewish identities as increasingly hybrid and mobile (cf. Arviv, 2018, in the case of Canada). This is true for both veteran Israelis in Germany and those recently arrived: they have multiple or split identities and exhibit different levels of belonging (Lapidot and Ilany, 2015). The point made here is that these hybridities and possible alterities do not occur because of the location—Germany—on which we have focused. Instead, these multiple attachments are inherent to and informative of the identity praxes of immigrants. Many participants in our study do not intend to stay in Germany; as such, they epitomize a fluid connection with place and blurred group belonging in the present-day globalized world that is accessible to them. Their ability to live out this fluidity, however, also underscores the privileges of Israelis in Germany, who are far better educated and better off than their average counterparts back in Israel.

The Israeli migrants studied above are a distinct group within the Jewish community in Germany. Ostensibly, they could provide the local Jews, especially in Berlin and in several other cities, with a significant injection of young members, including some with families and children, diversify the community's range of social and cultural activities, and contribute to the critical mass that is needed to sustain educational and cultural Jewish activities. However, the very characteristics of these Israelis—their youth, their very secular orientation, and their cultural and linguistic distance from the majority of the Jews—deter such binding. If they forge ties with local Jews at all, they often do so outside of synagogues and established structures (Kranz, 2019b). Further, many of these Israelis consider leaving Germany within a few years and have nothing to gain by affiliating with the local Jewish community. Among those who intend to remain in Germany, a high proportion are married to or partnered to non-Jews, exhibit weak Jewish identity, and may be seen as "post-halachic," aka "Jews beyond Judaism," as the (German Jewish) historian George L. Mosse (1985) put it.

Nevertheless, Israeli migrants in Germany, most saliently in Berlin, initiate and practice Israel-oriented activities. Some are symbolic and intermittent, mainly on the private sphere, such as consuming Israeli food or celebrating major Jewish holidays in an Israeli style. Other activities, in the public sphere, are more ongoing and include enrolling children in Hebrew-speaking preschools, sending children to youth movements such as

Hashomer Hatzair, subscribing to a library of Hebrew books (as in HaSifriya HaIvrit BeBerlin), and so on. Israelis in Berlin are in the very early stage of Diaspora-building. As they grow numerically, crystallize socially and culturally, and strengthen their communal foundations, more Israelis may choose to move to and settle in Germany in general and Berlin in particular. It stands to reason that over time, as the veteran Jews in Germany, including those from the FSU, pass away, Israeli immigrants will make stronger inroads in established Jewish institutions and organizations, reshaping them in a new spirit that takes the multiplicity of subgroups into account—Ashkenazim and Sephardim, interfaith families, LGBTQI+s, and people of different views on the Israeli-Palestinian conflict. The result, in any case, will be a community that combines Israeliness with the challenges of Jewish life in twenty-first-century Germany.

Appendix

Correlations between Push Factors in Israel
and Pull Factors in Germany

	Push Factors					
Pull Factors	Political/ Security	Professional Development	Economic Development	Education	Religious Establishment	Family/ Friends
Education	.242	.360	.245	.815	.287	.042*
German culture	.395	.449	.382	.368	.415	.088
Professional/economic development	.354	.653	.643	.396	.390	.066*
Family origin	.084	.123	.092	.128	.105	.158
German Partner	.018*	-.090	-.011*	-.049*	.036*	.091
Seeking challenge	.219	.253	.253	.206	.210	.053*

*Not significant.

Notes

Chapter 1

1. We use the term *immigration* to denote entering a new country and *immigrant* for one who is in the midst of this act; *emigration* for leaving an origin country and *emigrant* for one in the midst of this act (and *émigré* for one who has completed it); and *migration* when the spatial movement is neutral with no reference either to "in" or to "out."

2. Since the early 1970s, anthropologists and other, qualitatively working, social scientists have been engaging with the researcher/researched role critically. Dell Hymes (1972) pushed forward the notion of candor, in terms of disclosure of the research to research participants. Previous research had referred to them as "informants." The complexity of the social relationships between researcher and researched had been blanked out to comply with the notions of "neutrality, objectivity, and reliability" that had guided empiricists and positivist social sciences. These notions came under challenge by the deconstructionist movement by scholars such as Bruno Latour and Steven Wolgar (1979), who outlined that research questions are underpinned by cultural configurations, and that interpretations of the—not neutral—data are also biased. Continuing in this vein, Renato Rosaldo (1988) critically examined the emotions of anthropologists in the field, while Lisa M. Tillmann-Healy (2003) was a forerunner of analyzing friendship as method, which remains a recurring topic within the area of the sociology—and anthropology—of knowledge (cf. Ramírez-i-Ollé, 2019). Furthermore, "intimate ethnography" was coined, which appreciates that fieldwork might take places with people who are intimately close to the researchers (Waterston and Rylko-Bauer, 2006). In order to do justice to the research we conducted, and against the backdrop of these developments, we use specific terms concerning our research. The qualitative research work was conducted in the shape of ethnography, that is, as participant observation among Israeli Jewish migrants. The Israelis we met in these situations are related to

as fieldwork partners, or fieldwork participants. Israelis who we conducted interviews with—either narrative or semistructured ones—are referred to as interview partners. Michael Angrosino (1989) stipulated that interviews are documents of interaction, which means that an exchange between the communication partners—interviewee and interviewer—took place. Respondents are individuals who responded to our quantitative survey, and with whom we did not have personal interactions.

Chapter 2

1. Also noteworthy in this regard is Esti Amarmi's semidocumentary film *Berlin Diary*, which deals with a video letter to Amarmi's grandparents, who left Germany for Mandate Palestine in the 1930s, and whose granddaughter has now emigrated to Berlin (Anderman, 2014).

Chapter 3

1. Notably, Ashkenazim (Jews of European-American origin) are overrepresented in central Israel; their superior social and cultural capital and the larger preponderance of EU passports among them, relative to Israelis in southern and northern peripheries, are supportive of migration.

2. Although our study is concerned with native Israelis only, it is noteworthy that German data on Israeli migrants' place of birth show that a significant number were born abroad, most commonly in former Soviet countries. Although these data are not available for each German city or county, they allude to Soviet Jews who came to Israel, found themselves in the West Bank, and left because they had gone there not for ideological reasons but for economic ones.

3. Numbers refer to our sample of Israelis in Germany.

4. However, with 2019 directives being in place that facilitated naturalization, we might see changes, but the directives, as well as the reported increased in applications for renaturalization, happened after we collected statistical data for this specific project.

5. Munich, Frankfurt, Stuttgart, Cologne, Hamburg, and Düsseldorf.

6. Multinomial regression.

Chapter 4

1. An important component of efficiency in learning a foreign language is the phonetic distance between the home language and the host language (Chiswick and Miller, 1995; 2007). Given that the population at issue is composed of

native-born Israelis, the distance between Hebrew and German and, in turn, the difficulty of learning a foreign language is the same for all of them. Moreover, German and Hebrew have the same set of sounds. Still, some of our respondents, although themselves born in Israel, may be products of families that arrived from elsewhere and spoke a language other than Hebrew at home. Insofar as the distance between that language and German is shorter than the distance between Hebrew and German, these Israelis should master German more quickly than the others would. Multilingualism also eases the learning of a new language. Regrettably, our data did not index information on either bilingualism or multilingualism.

2. The relative deficiency in language acquisition among Israelis above age thirty-five may be partly related to their life situation, as the ethnographic data evidences. Many are parents, deterring/delaying language acquisition due to parental duties, or had been sent to Germany as part of a global career track, meaning that they operated in English-speaking environments and had less need to master the local vernacular.

3. We found them in the face-to-face interviews, particularly in the highly and highest skilled brackets and among IT professionals as well as artists. Inability to speak German well, or at all, did not hinder their career trajectory.

4. That Jewish women may also cover their hair has never been debated in the German media or the German courts, while the issue of wearing a kippa (skullcap) has appeared alongside headscarf issues. Both the Jewish kippah and the Muslim headscarf are perceived as "religious" garb, although in terms of actual rituals neither is a ritual object for Jewish or Muslim women.

5. In the previous chapter, we classified occupations in greater detail. Here, due to the rather small number of married Israelis, we had to lump several categories together: professionals and artists, and blue collar together with sales/clerical/service and other.

Chapter 5

1. Notably, goodness of fit between observed coefficients and geometrical distances is measured by the coefficient of alienation (Amar and Toledano, 2001). This coefficient varies from 0 to 1, with 0 denoting a perfect fit (Borg and Lingoes, 1987). The coefficient of alienation obtained for the configuration of group identification is satisfactory at .16 (and with the external variables .11).

2. The individuals in question are *most likely* Muslim; migration background is coded in terms of countries, because neither Islam nor any other religion is a category in German statistics.

3. Notably, Cronbach's test further attests to the strong interrelations among the items of each measure (construct). Cronbach's Alphas are as follows: transnational index = .843; religio-ethnic index = .636; and local-German index = .707.

Chapter 6

1. However, it should be noted that antisemitism is not met with indifference by the majority of all Germans, and that it meets serious resistance across political and on social levels.

Bibliography

Abulof, Uriel. 2009. " 'Small Peoples': The Existential Uncertainty of Ethnonational Communities." *International Studies Quarterly* 53 (1): 227–48.
Aced, Miriam, Tamer Düyzol, Arif Rüzgar, and Christian Schaft. 2014. *Migration, Asyl und Post-Migrantische Lebenswelten in Deutschland.* Münster, Germany: LIT Verlag.
Alba, Richard. 2020. *The Great Demographic Illusion: Majority, Minority, and the Expanding American Mainstream.* Princeton, NJ and Oxford, UK: Princeton University Press.
Alba, Richard, and Victor Nee. 1997. "Rethinking Assimilation Theory for a New Era of Immigration." *International Migration Review* 31 (4): 826–74.
———. 2003. *Remaking the American Mainstream: Assimilation and Contemporary Immigration.* Cambridge, MA: Harvard University Press.
Alba, Richard, and Nancy Foner. 2014. "Comparing Immigrant Integration in North America and Western Europe: How Much Do the Grand Narratives Tell Us?" *International Migration Review* 48 (suppl. 1): S263–291.
Alba, Richard D., and J. R. Logan 1992. "Assimilation and Stratification in Homeownership Patterns of Racial and Ethnic Group." *International Migration Review* 26 (4): 1314–41.
Allmendinger, Jutta. 1994. *Lebensverlauf und Sozialpolitik. Die Ungleichheit zwischen Mann und Frau und ihr öffentlicher Ertrag.* Frankfurt am Main, Germany: Campus.
Allmendinger, Jutta, and Julia Haarbrücker. 2017. *Arbeitszeiten und die Vereinbarkeit von Beruf und Familie: Ergebnisse der Beschäftigtenbefragung der IG Metall 2017.* Berlin: Wissenschaftzentrum Berlin Aür Sozialforschung, Discussion Paper No. 2017-002.
Allmendinger, Jutta, and Dorothea Kübler. 2020. "Geschlechtergerechtigkeit: Viel erreicht und weit entfernt." *humboldt chancengleich* 11: 16–18.
Allport, Gordon W. 1954. *The Nature of Prejudice.* Boston, MA: Beacon Press.
Almog, Oz. 2000. *The Sabra: The Creation of the New Jew.* Berkeley: University of California Press.

Almog, Tamar, and Oz Almog. 2016. *As If There Is No Tomorrow: How Generation Y Is Changing the Face of Israel*. Moshav Ben Shemen, Israel: Modan Publishing House.

Almog, Yael. 2015. "Das Unbehagen in der Diaspora." *Heinrich Böll Stiftung* (blog). April 20. https://www.boell.de/de/2015/04/20/das-unbehagen-der-diaspora.

———. 2019. "Illusory Diasporas." *Shofar* 37 (2): 64–71.

Alon, Tal. 2012. "Community in the Making." [In Hebrew.] *Spitz* 1: 2–4.

———. 2013. "A Place of Their Own." [In Hebrew.] *Spitz* 6: 14–15.

———. 2014. "Divided." [In Hebrew.] *Spitz* 13: 8–9.

Amar, Reuven, and Shlomo Toledano. 2001. *Hudap Manual with Mathematics and Windows Interface*. Jerusalem, Israel: Hebrew University of Jerusalem.

Amersfoort, Hans V. 2004. "The Waxing and Waning of a Diaspora: Moluccans in the Netherlands 1950–2002." *Journal of Ethnic and Migration Studies* 30 (1): 151–74.

Amir-Moazami, Schirin, ed. 2018. *Der inspizierte Muslim: Zur Politisierung der Islamforschung in Europa*. Bielefeld, Germany: transcript.

Amit, Hagai. 2013. "In Berlin There Is no Gold on the Floor, but Those Who Work or Study—The State Takes Care of Them." [In Hebrew.] *Haaretz: Marker Week Supplement*, October 10, 18–22.

Amit, Hila. 2016 "Lisa Peretz: Let Us." [In Hebrew.] *Haaretz*. August 7, 2016. http://www.haaretz.co.il/opinions/.premium-1.3031476.

———. 2017. "The Revival of Diasporic Hebrew in Contemporary Berlin." In *Cultural Topographies of the New Berlin*, edited by Jennifer Ruth Hosiek and Karin Bauer, 253–71. Oxford, UK: Berg.

———. 2018. *A Queer Way Out*. Albany: State University of New York Press.

Amit, Vered. 2001. "A Clash of Vulnerabilities: Citizenship, Labor, and Expatriacy in the Cayman Islands." *American Ethnologist* 28 (3): 574–94.

———, ed. 2007. *Going First Class? New Approaches to Privileged Travel and Movement*. Oxford, UK: Berghahn.

Anderman, Nirit. 2014. "The Unpromised Land." [In Hebrew.] *Haaretz: Gallery Supplement*, July 28, 1–2.

Anderson, Bridget 2013. *Us & Them: The Danger of Immigration Controls*. Oxford, UK: Oxford University Press.

Angrosino, Michael. 1989. *Documents of Interaction*. Gainesville, FL: University of Florida Press.

Anidjar, Gil. 2003. *The Jew, the Arab: A History of the Enemy*. Stanford, CA: Stanford University Press.

———. 2015. "Christianity, Christianities, Christian." *Journal of Religious and Political Practice* 1 (1): 39–46.

Anti-Defamation League (ADL). 2014. *GLOBAL100: An Index of Anti-Semitism*. New York: ADL.

Arango, Joaquin. 2000. "Explaining Migration: A Critical View." *International Social Science Journal* 52: 283–96.

Arnold, Sina, and Jana König. 2016. *Flucht und Antisemitismus*. Berlin: Humboldt Universität—Berliner Institut für Integrations- und Migrationsforschung. https://www.bim.hu-berlin.de/media/Abschlussbericht_Flucht_und_Antisemitismus_SA_JK.pdf.

Arviv, Tamir. 2018. "Reframing Jewish Mobilities: De-Nationalized/Non-Territorialized, Racialized, and Hybrid Identities among Israeli Immigrants in Canada." *Mobilities* 14 (2): 173–87.

Atshan, Sa'ed, and Galor, Katharina. 2020. *The Moral Triangle: Germans, Israelis, Palestinians*. Durham, NC and London: Duke University Press.

Avineri, Shlomo, Liav Orgad, and Amnon Rubinstein. 2009. *Managing Global Migration: A Strategy for Immigration Policy in Israel*. Jerusalem, Israel: Metzilah.

Baeyer, Walter Ritter von, Heinz Haefer, and Karl Peter Kisker. 1964. *Psychiatrie der Verfolgten: Psychopathologische und Gutachtliche Erfahrungen an Opfern der Nationalsozialistischen Verfolgung und Vergleichbarer Extrembelastungen*. Berlin, Germany: Springer.

Balakrishnan, T. R., and Zheng, Wu. 1992. "Homeownership Patterns and Ethnicity in Selected Canadian Cities." *Canadian Journal of Sociology* 17 (4): 389–403.

Barkai, Avraham. 2002. *"Wehr Dich!" Der Centralverein deutscher Staatsbürger jüdischen Glaubens (C. V.) 1893–1938*. Munich, Germany: C. H. Beck.

Bartal, Ann P., and Marianne Koch. 1991. "Internal Migration of U.S. Immigrants." In *Immigration, Trade, and the Labor Market*, edited by John M. Abowd and Richard B. Freeman, 121–34. Chicago, IL and London: University of Chicago Press.

Basch, Linda Nina Glick Schiller, and Cristina Blanc-Szanton. 1994. *Nations Unbound: Transnational Projects, Postcolonial Predicaments, and Deterritorialized Nation States*. Basel, Switzerland: Gordon and Breach Publishers.

Bauböck, Rainer. 2002. "Political Community beyond the Sovereign State: Supranational Federalism and Transnational Minorities." In *Conceiving Cosmopolitanism: Theory, Context and Practice*, edited by S. Vertovec and R. Cohen, 110–36. Oxford, UK: Oxford University Press.

Bauman, Zygmunt. 1989. *Modernity and the Holocaust*. Ithaca, NY: Cornell University Press.

———. 1991. *Modernity and the Holocaust*. Cambridge, UK: Polity Press.

———. 1996. "From Pilgrim to Tourist or a Short History of Identity." In *Questions of Cultural Identity*, edited by Stuart Hall and Pauldu Gay, 18–36. London: Sage Publications.

———. 1997. "Allosemitism: Premodern, Modern, Postmodern." In *Modernity, Culture, and "The Jew,"* edited by Bryan Cheyette and Laura Marcus, 143–56. Cambridge, UK: Polity Press.

Beauftragte der Bundesregierung für Migration, Flüchtlinge und Integration. 2016. *Bericht der Beauftragten der Bundesregierung für Migration, Flüchtlinge und Integration. Teilhabe, Chancengleichheit und Rechtsentwicklung in der Einwanderungsgesellschaft Deutschland*. Berlin, Germany: Die Beauftragte der Bundesregierung für Migration, Flüchtlinge und Integration. https://www.bundesregierung.de/Content/Infomaterial/BPA/IB/11-Lagebericht_09-12-2016.pdf?__blob=publicationFile&v=6.

Beck, Ulrich. 1992. *Risk Society: Towards a New Modernity*. London: Sage Publications.

Becker, Franziska. 2001. *Ankommen in Deutschland*. Berlin, Germany: Dietrich Reimer Verlag.

Beenstock, Michael. 1996. "The Acquisition of Language Skills by Immigrants: The Case of Hebrew in Israel." *International Migration* 34 (1): 3–30.

Behar, Ruth. 1996. *The Vulnerable Observer: Anthropology that Breaks Your Heart*. Boston, MA: Beacon Press.

Beine, Michel, Anna Boucher, Brian Burgoon, Mary Crock, Justin Gest, Michael Hiscox, Patrick McGovern, Hillel Rapoport, Joep Schaper, and Eiko Thielemann. 2016. "Comparing Immigration Policies: An Overview from the IMPALA Database." *International Migration Review* 50 (4): 827–63.

Ben Yehuda-Sternfeld, S., and J. Mirsky. 2014. "Return Migration of Americans: Personal Narratives and Psychological Perspectives." *International Journal of Intercultural Relations* 42: 53–64.

Benson, Michaela, and Karen O'Reilly. 2016. "From Lifestyle Migration to Lifestyle in Migration: Categories, Concepts and Ways of Thinking." *Migration Studies* 4 (1): 20–37.

Benz, Wolfgang. 2020. "Wütende Abwehrreflexe: Warum es in der DDR keine Judenfeindschaft gegeben haben soll." In *Streitfall Antisemitismus: Anspruch auf Deutungsmacht und politische Interessen*, edited by Wolfgang Benz, 239–54. Berlin, Germany: Metropol.

Bernstein, Julia. 2018. *"Mach mal keine Judenaktion!" Herausforderungen und Lösungsansätze in der professionellen Bildungs- und Sozialarbeit gegen Antisemitismus*. Frankfurt, Germany: Frankfurt University of Applied Sciences. https://www.frankfurt-university.de/fileadmin/standard/Aktuelles/Pressemitteilungen/Mach_mal_keine_Judenaktion__Herausforderungen_und_Loesungsansaetze_in_der_professionellen_Bildungs-_und_Sozialarbeit_gegen_Anti.pdf.

Berry, John W. 1997. "Immigration, Acculturation, and Adaptation." *Applied Psychology* 46 (1): 5–34.

Bhagwati, Jagdish. 2003. "Borders beyond Control." *Foreign Affairs* 82 (1): 98–104.

Bilsborrow, Richard E. 2016. "Concepts, Definitions and Data Collection Approaches." In *International Handbook of Migration and Population Distribution*, edited by Michael J. White, 109–56. Dordrecht, the Netherlands: Springer.

Bishop Kendzia, Victoria. 2018. *Visitors to the House of Memory: Identity and Political Education at the Jewish Museum Berlin*. Oxford, UK: Berghahn Books.

Blaschke, Wolfgang, Karola Fings, and Cordula Lissner. 1997. *Unter Vorbehalt: Rückkehr aus der Emigration nach 1945*. Cologne, Germany: Emons Verlag.

Bloemraad, Irene, Anna Korteweg, and Gokce Yurdakul. 2008. "Citizenship and Immigration: Multiculturalism, Assimilation, and Challenges to the Nation-State." *Annual Review of Sociology* 34: 153–79.

Bloemraad, Irene, and Matthew Wright. 2014. "Utter Failure or Unity Out of Diversity? Debating and Evaluating Policies of Multiculturalism." *International Migration Review* 48 (suppl. 1): S292–334.

Bocquier, Philippe. 2016. "Migration Analysis Using Demographic Surveys and Surveillance Systems." In *International Handbook of Migration and Population Distribution*, edited by Michael J. White, 205–23. Dordrecht, the Netherlands: Springer.

Bodemann, Y. Michal. 1996. *Gedächtnistheater: Die jüdische Gemeinschaft und ihre Deutsche Erfindung*. Hamburg, Germany: Rotbuch Verlag.

———. 2006. "Between Israel and Germany from the 'Alien Asiatic People' to the new German Jewry." *Jewish History* 20 (1): 91–109.

———, ed. 2008. *The New German Jewry and the European Context*. Basingstoke, UK and New York: Palgrave Macmillan.

Bonjour, Saskia, and Laura Block. 2016. "Ethnicizing Citizenship, Questioning Membership: Explaining the Decreasing Family Migration Rights of Citizenship in Europe." *Citizenship Studies* 20 (6–7): 779–94.

Borg, Ingwer, and James Lingoes. 1987. *Multidimensional Similarity Structure Analysis*. New York: Springer-Verlag.

Borjas, George J. 1989. "Economic Theory and International Migration." *International Migration Review* 23 (3): 457–85.

———. 2002. "Homeownership in the Immigrant Population." *Journal of Urban Economics* 52 (3): 448–76.

Borneman, John, and Jeffrey M. Peck. 1995. *Sojourners: The Return of German Jews and the Question of Identity*. Lincoln, NE: University of Nebraska Press.

Boum, Aamar, and Sarah Abreyeva Stein, eds. 2018. *The Holocaust and North Africa*. Stanford, CA: Stanford University Press.

Boyd, Monica. 1989. "Family and Personal Networks in International Migration: Recent Developments and New Agenda." *International Migration Review* 23 (3): 638–70.

Boyd, Monica, and Joanne Nowak. 2012. "Social Networks and International Migration." In *An Introduction to International Migration Studies: European Perspectives*, edited by Marco Martiniello and Jan Rath, 80–105. Amsterdam, the Netherlands: Amsterdam University Press.

Brähler, Elmar, and Oliver Decker, eds. 2018. *Flucht ins Autoritäre—Rechtsextreme Dynamiken in der Mitte der Gesellschaft*. Leipzig, Germany: Universität Leipzig.

Brenner, Michael, ed. 2012. *Geschichte der Juden in Deutschland von 1945 bis zur Gegenwart*. Munich, Germany: C. H. Beck.

Brettell, Caroline B. 2016. "Perspectives on Migration Theory-Anthropology." In *International Handbook of Migration and Population Distribution*, edited by Michael J. White, 41–67. Dordrecht, the Netherlands: Springer.

Brinkerhoff, Jennifer M. 2009. *Digital Diasporas: Identity and Transnational Engagement.* New York: Cambridge University Press.

Brown, Susan K., and Frank D. Bean. 2016. "Conceptualizing Migration: From Internal/International to Kinds of membership." In *International Handbook of Migration and Population Distribution*, edited by Michael J. White, 91–106. Dordrecht, the Netherlands: Springer.

Brubaker, W. Rogers. 1989. "Membership without Citizenship: The Economic and Social Rights of Noncitizen." In *Immigration and the Politics of Citizenship in Europe and North America*, edited by W. Rogers Brubaker 145–62. Lanham, MD: University Press of America.

Brumlik, Micha. 1998. *Zu Hause, keine Heimat? Junge Juden und ihre Zukunft in Deutschland.* Gerlingen, Germany: Bleicher Verlag.

Brumlik, Micha, Doron Kiesel, Cilly Kugelmann, and Julius Schoeps, eds. 1988 *Jüdisches Leben in Deutschland seit 1945.* Frankfurt am Main, Germany: Jüdischer Verlag bei Athenaeum.

Bryman, Alan. 1988. *Quantity and Quality in Social Research.* London: Routledge.

Bund, Kerstin, Astrid Geisler, and Anne Kunze. 2019. "Der große Unterschied." *Die Zeit*, March 20. https://www.zeit.de/2019/13/gleichberechtigung-frauen-arbeitsmarkt-karriere-familie

Bundesagentur für Arbeit 2017. *Employment of Foreign Workers in Germany: Questions, Answers and Tips for Employees and Employers.* Nuremberg, Germany: Bundesagentur für Arbeit. https://www3.arbeitsagentur.de/web/wcm/idc/groups/public/documents/webdatei/mdaw/mtaw/~edisp/l6019022dstbai651347.pdf.

Burton, Elise K. 2015. "An Assimilating Majority? Israeli Marriage Law and Identity in the Jewish State." *Journal of Jewish Identities* 8 (1): 73–94.

Cadge, Wendy, and Elaine H. Ecklund. 2007. "Immigration and Religion." *Annual Review of Sociology* 33 (1): 359–79.

Cadwallader, Martin. 1992. *Migration and Residential Mobility: Macro and Micro Approaches.* Madison: University of Wisconsin Press.

Caponi, Vincenzo, and Miana Plesca. 2014. Empirical Characteristics of Legal and Illegal Immigrants in the USA." *Journal of Population Economics* 27 (4): 923–60.

Carens, Joseph H. 2010. *Immigrants and the Right to Stay.* Cambridge, MA: MIT Press.

Carliner, Geoffrey. 2000. "The Language Ability of U.S. Immigrants: Assimilation and Cohort Effects." *International Migration Review* 34 (1): 158–82.

Carrera, Sergio. 2006. *A Comparison of Integration Programs in the EU: Trends and Weakness.* CEPS CHALLENGE paper no. 1, March 1. http://aei.pitt.edu/6773/.

Cassel, Joan, ed. 1994. *Children in the Field: Anthropological Experiences.* Philadelphia, PA: Temple University Press.

Castaneda, Heide. 2008. "Paternity for Sale: Anxieties over 'Demographic Theft' and Undocumented Migrant Reproduction in Germany." *Medical Anthropology Quarterly* 22 (4): 340–59.
Castles, Stephen. 2004. "The Factors that Make and Unmake Migration Policies." *International Migration Review* 38 (3): 852–85.
Castles, Stephen, and A. Davidson. 2000. *Citizenship and Migration: Globalization and the Politics of Belonging*. Basingstoke, UK: Palgrave.
Castles, Stephen, Hein de Haas, and Mark J. Miller. 2009. *The Age of Migration: International Population Movements in the Modern World*, 5th ed. New York, NY: Palgrave Macmillan.
Chanes, Jerome A. 1999. "Antisemitisim and Jewish Security in Contemporary America: Why Can't Jews take Yes for an Answer?" In *Jews in America: A Contemporary Reader*, edited by Roberta Farber Rosenberg and Chaim I. Waxman, 124–50. Hanover, NH and London: Brandeis University Press.
Chauvin, Sébastien, and Blanca Garcés-Mascareñas. 2012. "Beyond Informal Citizenship: The New Moral Economy of Migrant Illegality." *International Political Sociology* 6 (3): 241–59.
Chiswick, Barry R., and Paul W. Miller. 1995. "The Endogeneity between Language and Earnings: International Analyses." *Journal of Labor Economics* 13 (2): 246–88.
———. 2001. "A Model of Destination-Language Proficiency Acquisition: Application to Male Immigrants in Canada." *Demography* 38 (3): 391–409.
———. 2007. *The Economic of Language: International Analysis*. London: Routledge.
Chiswick, Barry R., Y. L. Lee, and Paul W. Miller. 2004. "Immigrants' Language Skills: The Australian Experience in a Longitudinal Survey." *International Migration Review* 38 (2): 611–54.
Chiswick, Barry R., and Gustavo Repetto. 2000. "Immigrant Adjustment in Israel: Literacy and Fluency in Hebrew and Earnings." In *International Migration: Trends, Policy and Economic Impact*, edited by S. Slobodan, 204–28. New York: Routledge.
Chiswick, Barry R., and M. Wenz. 2006. "The Linguistic and Economic Adjustment of Soviet Jewish Immigrants in the United States, 1980 to 2000." In *The Economics of Immigration and Social Diversity*, edited by Solomon W. Polachek, Carmel Chiswick, and Hillel Rapoport, 179–216. *Research in Labor Economics*, Vol. 24. Bingley, UK: Emerald.
Clark, William A. V., and Regan Maas. 2015. "Interpreting Migration through the Prism of Reasons for Moves." *Population, Space and Place* 21 (1): 54–67.
Clerge, Orly, Gabriela Sanchez-Soto, Jing Song, and Nancy Luke. 2017. "I Would Really Like to Go Where You Go: Rethinking Migration Decision-Making among Educated Tied Movers." *Population, Space, and Place* 23 (2): 1–12.
Cohen, Asher, and Bernard Susser. 2009. "Jews and Others: Non-Jewish Jews in Israel." *Israel Affairs*, 15 (1): 52–65.

Cohen, Erez. 2008. "'We Are Staying in Our Country-Here': Israeli Mediascapes in Melbourne." *Journal of Ethnic and Migration Studies* 34 (6): 1003–19.

Cohen, Erik H., and Reuven Amar. 2002. "External Variables as Points in Smallest Space Analysis: A Theoretical, Mathematical and Computer-Based Contribution." *Bulletin de Methodologie Sociologique* 75 (1): 40–56.

Cohen, Hadas, and Dani Kranz. 2017. "Israeli Jews in the New Berlin: From Shoah Memories to Middle Eastern Encounters." In *Cultural Topographies of the New Berlin: An Anthology*, edited by Jennifer Ruth Hosek and Karin Bauer, 322–46. Oxford, UK: Berghahn.

Cohen, Nir. 2013. "From Nation to Profession: Israeli State Strategy toward Highly-Skilled Return Migration, 1949–2012." *Journal of Historical Geography* 42: 1–11.

Cohen, Yinon. 2011. "Israeli-Born Emigrants: Size, Destinations and Selectivity." *International Journal of Comparative Sociology* 52 (1–2): 45–62.

Connor, Phillip. 2010. "Contexts of Immigrant Receptivity and Immigrant Religious Outcomes: The Case of Muslims in Western Europe." *Ethnic and Racial Studies* 33 (3): 376–403.

Cornelius, Wayne A. 1998. "The Structural Embeddedness of Demand for Mexican Immigrant Labor: New Evidence from California." In *Crossings: Mexican Immigration in Interdisciplinary Perspective*, edited by Marcelo Suarez-Orozco, 115–55. Cambridge, MA: Center for Latin American Studies, Harvard University.

Constant, Amelie, Rowan Roberts, and Klaus F. Zimmermann. 2007. *Ethnic Identity and Immigrant Homeownership*. IZA discussion paper, no. 3050. Bonn, Germany: IZA.

Cronin, Joseph. 2018. "Wladimir Kaminer and Jewish Identity in 'Multikulti' Germany." *Skepsi* 9/10: 65–77.

Czaika, Mathias, and Hein de Haas. 2014. "The Globalization of Migration: Has the World Become More Migratory?" *International Migration Review* 48 (2): 283–323.

Czaika, Mathias, Jakub Bijak, and Toby Prike. 2021. "Migration Decision-Making and Its Key Dimensions." *The Annals of the American Academy of Political and Social Science* (forthcoming).

Czollek, Max. 2020. *Gegenwartsbewältigung*. Munich, Germany: Hanser.

Decker, Oliver, and Elmar Brähler, eds. 2018. *Flucht ins Autoritäre—Rechtsextreme Dynamiken in der Mitte der Gesellschaft*. Giessen, Germany: Psychosozial-Verlag.

Decker, Oliver, Johannes Kies, and Elmar Brähler, eds. 2016. *Die enthemmte Mitte. Autoritäre und rechtsextreme Einstellungen in Deutschland*. Giessen, Germany: Psychosozial-Verlag.

De Haas, Hein. 2009. "Migration System Formation and Decline: A Theoretical Inquiry into the Self-Perpetuating and Self-Undermining Dynamics of Migration Processes." IMI/DEMIG working paper, no. 19. Oxford, UK: International Migration Institute.

———. 2010. "Migration Transitions: A Theoretical and Empirical Inquiry into the Developmental Drivers of International Migration." IMI/DEMIG working paper, no. 24. Oxford, UK: International Migration Institut.
De Haas, Hein, Katherina Natter, and Simona Vezzoli. 2018. "Restrictiveness or Changing Selection? The Nature and Evaluation of Migration Policies." *International Migration Review* 52 (2): 324–67.
Dekel, Irit. 2013. *Mediation at the Holocaust Memorial in Berlin*. London: Palgrave Macmillan.
———. 2020. "'You Are My Liberty': On the Negotiation of Holocaust and Other Memories for Israelis in Berlin." In *Rebuilding Jewish Life in Germany*, edited by Jay Howard Geller and Michael Meng, 223–42. New Brunswick, NJ: Rutgers University Press.
Dekel, Irit, Bernhard Forchtner, and Ibrahim Efe. 2019. "Circumcising the Body: Negotiating Difference and Belonging in Germany." *National Identities* 22 (2): 193–211. DOI: 10.1080/14608944.2019.1603218.
DellaPergola, Sergio. 2018. "World Jewish Population." In *American Jewish Year Book 2018*, edited by Arnold Dashefsky and Ira M. Sheskin, 361–449. Cham, Switzerland: Springer.
Destatis (Statistisches Bundesamt). 2011. *Hochqualifizierte in Deutschland: Erhebung zu Karriereverläufen und internationaler Mobilität von Hochqualifizierten*. Wiesbaden, Germany: Statistisches Bundesamt. https://www.destatis.de/DE/Publikationen/Thematisch/BildungForschungKultur/Hochschulen/HochqualifizierteDeutschland5217205139004.pdf?__blob=publicationFile.
———. 2012. *Bevölkerung und Erwerbstätigkeit: Ausländische Bevölkerung Ergebnisse des Ausländerzentralregisters*. Wiesbaden, Germany: Statistisches Bundesamt.
———. 2015. *Bevölkerung und Erwerbstätigkeit: Ausländische Bevölkerung Ergebnisse des Ausländerzentralregisters*. Wiesbaden, Germany: Statistisches Bundesamt.
———. 2017a. *Migration and Integration*, Wiesbaden, Germany: Statistisches Bundesamt. https://www.destatis.de/DE/ZahlenFakten/GesellschaftStaat/Bevoelkerung/MigrationIntegration/MigrationIntegration.html.
———. 2017b. *Bevölkerung und Erwerbstätigkeit Einbürgerungen*. Wiesbaden, Germany: Statistisches Bundesamt. https://www.destatis.de/DE/Publikationen/Thematisch/Bevoelkerung/MigrationIntegration/Einbuergerungen2010210177004.pdf?__blob=publicationFile.
———. 2020. *Bau- und Immobilienpreise Preisindizes für Wohnimmobilien: Indizes und Veränderungsraten*. Wiesbaden, Germany: Stastisches Bundesamt. https://www.destatis.de/DE/Themen/Wirtschaft/Preise/Baupreise-Immobilienpreisindex/Tabellen/Haeuserpreise-Bauland.html.
Dietze, Gabriele. 2016. "Ethnosexismus: Sex-Mob-Narrative um die Kölner Sylvesternacht." *Movements: Journal for Critical Migration and Border Regime Studies* 2 (1): 177–85.

Docquier, Frederic, Giovanni Peri, and Ilse Ruyssen. 2014. "The Cross-Country Determinants of Potential and Actual Migration." *International Migration Review* 48 (suppl. 1): S37–S99.

Donath, Orna. 2015. "Regretting Motherhood: A Sociopolitical Analysis." *Signs: Journal of Women in Culture and Society*, 40 (2): 343–67.

Doughan, Sultan, and Tzuberi, Hannah. 2018. "Säkularismus als Praxis und Herrschaft: Zur Kategorisierung von Juden und Muslimen im Kontext säkularer Wissensproduktion." In *Der inspizierte Muslim: Zur Politisierung der Islamforschung in Europa*, edited by Schirin Amir-Moagami, 269–308. Bielefeld, Germany: transcript.

Eisenstadt, Shmuel N. 2010. *Multiple Modernities*. [In Hebrew.] Jerusalem, Israel: The Van Leer Jerusalem Institute and Hakibbutz Hameuchad.

El-Mafaalani, Aladin. 2018. *Das Integrationsparadox: Warum gelungene Integration zu mehr Konflikten führt*. Cologne, Germany: Verlag Kiepenheuer & Wietsch.

Espenshade, Thomas J., and Gregory A. Huber. 1999. Fiscal Impacts of Immigrants and the Shrinking Welfare State." In *The Handbook of International Migration: The American Experience*, edited by Charles Hirschman, Philip Kasinitz, and Josh DeWind, 360–70. New York: Russell Sage Foundation.

Ettinger, Shmuel. 1969. *History of the Jewish People: Modern Times*. Tel Aviv, Israel: Dvir.

European Union Agency for Fundamental Rights. 2013. *Discrimination and Hate Crime against Jews in EU Member States: Experiences and Perceptions of Anti-Semitism*. Vienna, Austria: European Union Agency for Fundamental Rights.

———. 2018. *Experiences and Perceptions of Anti-Semitism-Second Survey of Discrimination and Hate Crime against Jews in the EU*. Vienna, Austria: European Union Agency for Fundamental Rights.

Eurostat. 2017. "Gender Pay Gap in Unadjusted Form by NACE Rev. 2 Activity—Structure of Earnings Survey Methodology." Last updated March 7, 2019. https://bit.ly/2NrOwba.

Extra, Guus, Massimiliano A. Spotti, and Piet Van Averment, eds. 2009. *Language Testing, Migration, and Citizenship*. London and New York: Continuum.

Faist, Thomas. 2000. *The Volume and Dynamics of International Migration and Transnational Social Spaces*. London: Clarendon Press.

Faist, Thomas, Jürgen Gerdes, and Beate Rieple. 2004. "Dual Citizenship as a Path-Dependent Process." *International Migration Review* 38 (3): 913–44.

Fang, Di, and David Brown. 1999. "Geographic Mobility of the Foreign-Born Chinese in Large Metropolises, 1985–1990." *International Migration Review* 33 (1): 137–55.

Fasani, Francesco. 2015. "Understanding the Role of Immigrants' Legal Status: Evidence from Policy Experiments." *Economic Studies* 61 (3): 722–63.

Favell, Adrian. 2013. *The Changing Face of Integration in a Mobile Europe*. Council of European Studies 43, no. 1 (Spring).

Fechter, Anne-Meike. 2007. *Transnational Lives: Expatriates in Indonesia*. Ashgate, Farnham, UK.
Fischer, Shlomo, Yotam Hotam, and Philip Wexler. 2012. "Democracy and Education in Post-Secular Society." *Review of Research in Education* 36 (1): 261–81.
Fogiel-Bijaoui, Sylvie. 2016. "Navigating Gender Inequality in Israel: The Challenges of Feminism." In *Handbook of Israel: The Major Debates*, edited by Eliezer Ben-Rafael, Julius Schoeps, Yitzhak Sternberg, and Olaf Glöckner, 423–36. Berlin, Germany: De Gruyter.
Foroutan, Naika. 2017. "Herausforderungen der Forschung zu Integration und Migration." Paper given at InZentIM, January 31, Universität Duisburg-Essen, Campus Essen, Germany.
Frerker, Kathryn. 1998. "Junge Juden in Deutschland: Lebensentwürfe im Schatten des Holocaust." Unpublished master's thesis. Department of Psychology, University of Cologne, Germany.
Furtado, Delia, and Tao Song. 2015. "Intermarriage and Socioeconomic Integration: Trends in Earnings Premiums among U.S. Immigrants Who Marry Natives." *The Annals of the American Academy of Political and Social Science* 662: 207–22.
Gamlen, Alan. 2014. "Diaspora Institutions and Diaspora Governance." *International Migration Review* 48 (suppl. 1): S180–217.
Gamlen, Alan, Michael E. Cummings, and Paul M. Vaaler. 2017. "Explaining the Rise of Diaspora Institutions." *Journal of Ethnic and Migration Studies* 45 (4): 492–516.
Garner, Alan C. 1991. "Forecasting Consumer Spending: Should Economists Pay Attention to Consumer Confidence Surveys?" *Economic Review—Federal Reserve Bank of Kansas City* 76 (3): 57–71.
Geis, Jael. 1996. "Gehen oder Bleiben? Der Mythos von der "Liquidationsgemeinde." In *Gedächtnistheater: Die jüdische Gemeinschaft und ihre Deutsche Erfindung*, edited by Y. M. Bodemann, 56–79. Hamburg, Germany: Rotbuch Verlag.
Geist, Claudia, and Patricia A. McManus. 2012. "Different Reasons, Different Results: Implications of Migration by Gender and Family Status." *Demography* 49 (1): 197–217.
Geller, Jay Howard 2005. *Jews in Post-Holocaust Germany, 1945–1953*. Cambridge, UK: Cambridge University Press.
Ghanem, Asa'ad. 2011. "The Expanding Ethnocracy: Judaization of the Public Sphere." *Israel Studies Review* 26 (1): 21–27.
Glaser, Barney, and Anselm, Strauss. 1965. *Awareness of Dying*. Chicago, IL: Aldine.
Glick, Jennifer, and Julie Park. 2016. "Migration, Assimilation and Social Welfare." In *International Handbook of Migration and Population Distribution*, edited by Michael J. White, 505–24. Dordrecht, the Netherlands: Springer.
Gilbertson, Greta A. 1995. "Women's Labor and Enclave Employment: The Case of Dominican and Colombian Women in New York City." *International Migration Review* 29 (3): 657–70.

Gmelch, George. 1980. "Return Migration." *Annual Review of Anthropology* 9: 135–59.
Golan, Noa. 2014. "Packed Alone: I Played Footsie with Religion until I Got Kit-Kat." [In Hebrew.] *Spitz* 14: 16–17.
———. 2015a. "Packed Alone: There's No Such Thing as a Blank Page." [In Hebrew.] *Spitz* 16: 16–17.
———. 2015b. "Packed Alone: I Allowed Myself to Be in Many Colors." [In Hebrew.] *Spitz* 17: 12–13.
Gold, Steven. 2002. *The Israeli Diaspora*. London and New York: Routledge.
Goldfinger, Arnon, dir. 2011. *The Flat (הדירה)*. Hebrew with English subtitles. Ruth Diskin Films, Sundance Selects, Edition Salzgeber. DVD.
Goldscheider, Calvin. 2004. *Studying the Jewish Future*. Seattle and London: University of Washington Press.
Gomberg-Munoz, Ruth. 2017. *Becoming Legal: Immigration Law and Mixed-status Families*. Oxford: Oxford University Press.
Goodman, Yehuda C., and Nissim Mizrahi. 2008. "The Holocaust Does Not Belong to European Jews Alone: The Differential Use of Memory Techniques in Israeli High Schools." *American Ethnologist* 35 (1): 95–114.
Gordon, Milton M. 1964. *Assimilation in American Life: The Role of Race, Religion, and National Origins*. New York: Oxford University Press.
Gosewinkel, Dieter. 2016. *Schutz und Freiheit? Staatsbürgerschaft in Europa im 20. Und 21. Jahrhundert*. Berlin, Germany: Suhrkamp.
Graeber, David 2012. "Dead Zones of the Imagination: On Violence, Bureaucracy, and Interpretive Labor. The 2006 Malinowski Memorial Lecture." *HAU: Journal of Ethnographic Theory* 2 (2): 105–28. https://doi.org/10.14318/hau2.2.007.
Grenier, Gilles. 1982. "Language as Human Capital: Theoretical Framework and Application to Spanish-Speaking Americans." PhD dissertation. Princeton, NJ: Department of Economics, Princeton University.
Grigoleit-Richter, Grit. 2017. "Highly Skilled and Highly Mobile? Examining Gendered and Ethnicised Labour Market Conditions for Migrant Women in STEM-professions in Germany." *Journal of Ethnic and Migration Studies*, 43 (16): 2738–55.
Grin, François. 1990. "The Economic Approach to Minority Languages." *Journal of Multilingual and Multicultural Development* 11 (1–2): 153–72.
Gromova, Alina. 2013. *Generation "koscher light": Urbane Räume und Praxen junger russischspracher Juden in Berlin*. Bielefeld, Germany: Transcript Verlag.
Grossmann, Atina, and Lewinsky, Tamar. 2012. "Erster Teil: 1945–1949 Zwischenstation." In Brenner, Michael *Geschichte der Juden in Deutschland von 1945 bis zur Gegenwart*, 67–152. Munich, Germany: C. H. Beck.
Grünberg, Kurt. 1988. "Folgen des Holocaust bei Kindern von Überlebenden in der Bundesrepublik Deutschland." In *Reichsprogromnacht: Vergangenheitsbewältigung aus jüdischer Sicht*, edited by Micha Brumlik and Petra Kunik, 59–75. Frankfurt am Main, Germany: Brandes & Apsel.

———. 2000. *Liebe nach Auschwitz: Die Zweite Generation*. Frankfurt am Main, Germany: Sigmund-Freud-Institut.

———. 2007 "Contaminated Generativity: Holocaust Survivors and Their Children in Germany." *American Journal of Psychoanalysis* 67 (1), 82–97.

Guild, Elspeth. 2012. "Whither EU Immigration after the Lisbon Treaty?" In *An Introduction to International Migration Studies: European Perspectives*, edited by Marco Mertiniello and Jan Rath, 329–49. Amsterdam: Amsterdam University Press.

Gurak, Douglas T., and Maria Fe Caces. 1992. "Migration Networks and the Shaping of Migration Systems." In *International Migration Systems: A Global Approach*, edited by Mary Kritz, Lin Lean Lim, and Hania Zlotnik, 150–76. Oxford, UK: Clarendon Press.

Gurak, Douglas T., and Mary M. Kritz. 2000. "The Interstate Migration of U.S. Immigrants: Individual and Contextual Determinants." *Social Forces* 78 (3): 1017–39.

Guttman, Louis. 1959. "Introduction to Facet Design and Analysis." In *Proceedings of the Fifteenth International Congress of Psychology. Brussels—1957*, 130–32. Amsterdam, the Netherlands: North Holland.

———. 1968. "A General Nonmetric Technique for Findings the Smallest Coordinate Space for a Configuration of Points." *Psychometrika* 33 (4): 469–506.

Haan, Michael. 2005. "The Decline of the Immigrant Homeownership Advantage: Life-Cycle, Declining Fortunes and Changing Housing Careers in Montreal, Toronto and Vancouver, 1981–2001." *Urban Studies* 42 (12): 2191–212.

Hadar, Yossi. 1991. "Existentielle Erfahrung oder Krankheitssympton? Überlegungen zum Begriff der "Zweiten Generation." In *Schicksale der Verfolgten: Psychische und Somatische Auswirkungen von Terrorherrschaft*, edited by R. P. Beigel, N. Freudenberg, N. Schmitt, and H. Stoffels, 160–72. Berlin and Heidelberg, Germany and New York: Springer.

Hagan, Jacqueline, and Helen R. Ebaugh. 2003. "Calling upon the Sacred: Migrants' Use of Religion in the Migration Process." *International Migration Review* 37 (4): 1145–62.

Hagemann, Steffen, and Robby Nathanson. 2015. *Deutschland und Israel heute: Verbindende Vergangenheit, trennende Gegenwart*. Gütersloh, Germany: Bertelsmann Stiftung. https://www.bertelsmann-stiftung.de/fileadmin/files/BSt/Publikationen/GrauePublikationen/Studie_LW_Deutschland_und_Israel_heute_2015.pdf.

Halperin-Kaddari, Ruth, and Yaacov Yadgar. 2010. "Between Universal Feminism and Particular Nationalism: Politics, Religion and Gender (In)equality in Israel." *Third World Quarterly* 31 (6): 905–20.

Hamnett, Chris, Michael, Harmer and Peter, Williams. 1991. *Safe as Houses: Housing Inheritance in Britain*. London: P. Chapman.

Hannerz, Ulf. 2004. *Foreign News: Exploring the World of Foreign Correspondents*. Chicago, IL: University of Chicago Press.

Harari, Yuval Noah. 2018. *21 Lessons for the 21st Century*. New York: Spiegel & Grau.
Harpaz, Yossi. 2012. "The Demand for European Passports in Israel: Dual Citizenship as Intergenerational Transfer and Status Symbol." [In Hebrew.] *Megamot* 38 (3–4): 626–55.
———. 2019. *Citizenship 2.0: Dual Nationality as a Global Asset*. Princeton, NJ: Princeton University Press.
Harvey, David. 1969. "Conceptual and Measurement Problems in the Cognitive Behavioral Approach to Location Theory." In *Behavioral Problems in Geography: A Symposium*, edited by K. R. Cox and R. G. Golledge, 16–28. Evanston, IL: Northwestern University Press.
Haug, Sonja, and Peter Schimany. 2005. "Jüdische Zuwanderer in Deutschland: Ein Überblick über die Forschung. Working Papers des Bundesamts für Migration und Flüchtlinge." Nuremberg, Germany: Bundesamt für Migration und Flüchtlinge. http://www.bamf.de/SharedDocs /Anlagen/DE/Publikationen/ WorkingPapers/wp03-juedische-zuwanderer.pdf?__blob=publicationFile.
Hecht, Cornelia. 2003. *Deutsche Juden und Antisemitismus in der Weimarer Republik*. Bonn, Germany: J. H. W. Dietz.
Hegner, Victoria. 2015. " 'I Am What I Am. . . .' " In *Russisch-jüdische Gegenwart in Deutschland. Interdisziplinäre Perspektiven auf eine Diaspora im Wandel*, edited by Karen Körber, 82–106. Göttingen, Germany: Vandenhoeck & Ruprecht.
Heil, Simone. 2011. *Young Ambassadors: Youth Exchange and the Special Relationship between Germany and the State of Israel*. Baden-Baden, Germany: Nomos.
Hervieu-Leger Daniele. 2000. *Religion as a Chain of Memory*. Cambridge, UK: Polity.
Herzfeld, Michael. 1991. *The Social Production of Indifference: Exploring the Symbolic Roots of Western Bureaucracy*. New York: Berg.
Hestermann, Jenny. 2016. "Vor der Diplomatie: Deutsch-israelische Wissenschaftsbeziehungen als Brückenbauer?" *Jahrbuch des Simon-Dubnow-Instituts* 15: 399–419.
Hever, Shir. 2014. "Israel's Security Industry as a Business Model: Conflict-Management Industry." In *Human Rights, Human Security, and State Security*, edited by S. Takahashi, 195–221. Santa Barbara, CA; Denver, CO; and Oxford, UK: Praeger.
Hewstone, Miles, and Rupert Brown. 1986. "Contact Is Not Enough: An Intergroup Perspective on the 'Contact Hypothesis.' " In *Contact and Conflict in Intergroup Encounters*, edited by Miles Hewstone and Rupert Brown, 1–44. New York: Basil Blackwell.
Higley, John, and John, Nieuwenhuysen. 2009. "Introduction." In *Nations of Immigrants: Australia and the USA Compared*, edited by John Higley and John Nieuwenhuysen, 1–21. Cheltenham, UK and Northampton, MA: Edward Elgar.
Hirschfeld, Na'aman. 2014. "Becoming Post-Israeli: Why I Immigrated to Berlin." *Haaretz*. October 25. http://www.haaretz.com/opinion/.premium-1.622536.

Hirschman, Charles. 1983. "America's Melting Pot Reconsidered." *Annual Review of Sociology* 9: 397–423.
———. 2004. "The Role of Religion in the Origins and Adaptation of Immigrant Groups in the United States." *International Migration Review* 38 (3): 1206–33.
Hirschman, Charles, Philip Kasinitz, and Josh DeWind. 1999. "Theories and Concepts of International Migration." In *The Handbook of International Migration: The American Experience*, edited by Charles, Hirschman, Philip Kasinitz, and Josh DeWind, 13–20. New York: Russell Sage Foundation.
Hollifield, James F. 2004. "The Emerging Migration States." *International Migration Review* 38 (3): 885–913.
Horst, Heather, and Miller, Daniel. 2012. *Digital Anthropology*. Oxford, UK: Berg.
Hotam, Yotam, and Philip Wexler. 2014. "Education and Religion in Israel: Blurring the Boundaries of 'Secular' and 'Religious.'" In *International Comparative Perspectives on Religion*, edited by C. Wolhuter, 9–27. Bloemfontein, South Africa: Sun Press.
Huddleston, Thomas, and Jan Niessen. 2011. *Migration Integration Policy Index III*. Brussels, Belgium: British Council and Migration Policy Group.
Hymes, Dell. 1972. *Reinventing Anthropology*. New York: Pantheon.
Inkeles, Alex, and David H. Smith. 1974. *Becoming Modern: Individual Change in Six Developing Countries*. Cambridge, MA: Harvard University Press.
Iredale, Robyn R. 2001. "The Migration of Professionals: Theories and Typologies." *International Migration* 39 (5): 7–25.
Israel Central Bureau of Statistics. 2015. *Statistical Abstract of Israel*. Jerusalem: Central Bureau of Statistics of Israel.
Israel Democracy Institute. 2011. *A Portrait of Israeli Jews: Beliefs, Observance, and Values of Israeli Jews, 2009*. Jerusalem: Israel Democracy Institute.
Izraeli, Dafna N. 2004. "Gender Military Service in the Israel Defence Forces." In *Stratification in Israel: Class, Ethnicity, and Gender*, edited by Moshe Semyonov and Noah Lewin-Epstein, 281–311. New Brunswick, NJ and London: Transaction Publishers.
Jewish People Policy Institute (JPPI). 2017. "Comprehensive Three-Dimensional Anti-Semitism Index." In *Annual Assessment: The Situation and Dynamics of the Jewish People 2017*, edited by the JPPI, 83–93. Jerusalem, Israel: JPPI.
Joppke, Christian. 1998. "Why Liberal States Accept Unwanted Immigration." *World Politics* 50 (2): 266–93.
———. 1999. *Immigration and the Nation-State: The United States, Germany, and Great Britain*. Oxford, UK: Oxford University Press.
———. 2005. *Selecting by Origin: Ethnic Migration in the Liberal State*. Cambridge, MA: Harvard University Press.
Joppke, Christian, and Ze'ev Rosenhek. 2002. "Contesting Immigration: Germany and Israel Compared." *Archives Europeennes de Sociologie* 43 (4): 301–35.

Judaken, Jonathan. 2018. "Rethinking Anti-Semitism." *American Historical Review* 123 (4): 1122–38.
Kalmijn, Matthijs. 1998. "Intermarriage and Homogamy: Causes, Patterns, Trends." *Annual Review of Sociology* 24: 395–421.
———. 2015. "The Children of Intermarriage in Four European Countries: Implications for School Achievement, Social Contacts, and Cultural Values." *Annals of American Academy of Political and Social Science* 662, November 2015: 246–78.
Kalmijn, Matthijs, Paul M. de Graaf, and Jacques P. G. Janssen. 2005. "Intermarriage and the Risk of Divorce in the Netherlands: The Effects of Differences in Religion and Nationality, 1974–1994." *Population Studies* 59 (1): 71–85.
Kantor Center for the Study of Contemporary European Jewry. 2018. *Antisemitism Worldwide 2018: General Analysis*. Tel Aviv, Israel: Tel Aviv University.
Katz, Guy. 2011. *Intercultural Negotiation*. Norderstedt, Germany: Books on Demand.
Kauders, Anthony D. 2007. *Unmögliche Heimat: Eine deutsch-jüdische Geschichte der Bundesrepublik*. München, Germany: Deutsche Verlags-Anstalt.
———. 2010. "West German Jewry: Guilt, Power, and Pluralism." *Quest. Issues in Contemporary Jewish History. Journal of Fondazione CDEC* 1: 15–33.
Kemp, Adriana, and Nelly Kfir. 2016. "Wanted Workers but Unwanted Mothers: Mobilizing Moral Claims on Migrant Care Workers' Families in Israel." *Social Problems* 50 (1): 82–116.
Kessler, Judith. 1997. "Jüdische Immigration seit 1990. Resümee einer Studie über 4000 jüdische Migranten aus der ehemaligen Sowjetunion in Berlin." *Zeitschrift für Migration und soziale Arbeit* 3–4: 40–46.
———. 2002. Umfrage 2002: "Mitgliederbefragung der Jüdischen Gemeinde zu Berlin." Unpublished research report.
Khasani, Shila. 2005. "Eine Minderheit in der Minderheit: Das Engagement der linksorientierten Juden in der Frankfurter Jüdischen Gruppe." *Trumah* 14: 55–74.
Khoo, Siew-Ean, Graeme Hugo, and Peter McDonald. 2008. "Which Skilled Temporary Migrants Become Permanent Residents and Why?" *International Migration Review* 42 (1): 193–226.
Kidron, Carole. 2004. "Surviving a Distant Past: A Case Study of the Cultural Construction of Trauma Descendant Identity." *Ethos* 31 (4): 513–44.
King, Russell, Tony Warnes, and Allan M. Williams. 2000. *Sunset Lives: British Retirement Migration to the Mediterranean*. Oxford, UK: Berg.
Kivisto, Peter. 2005. *Incorporating Diversity: Rethinking Assimilation in a Multicultural Age*. Boulder, CO: Paradigms.
Klekowski von Koppenfels, Amanda. 2014. *Migrants or Expatriates? Americans in Europe*. London: Palgrave Macmillan.
Knaul, Susanne. 2017. "Die Digitale Supermacht." *taz*, January 10. http://www.taz.de/!5369118/

Körber, Karen. 2018. "Muss es gleich Heimat sein?" Paper presented at Heimat, Konferenz der Bildungsabteilung des Zentralrats der Juden in Deutschland, Frankfurt am Main, Germany, March 7–9.

———. 2021. *Lebenswirklichkeiten. Junge russischsprachige Juden in der deutschen Einwanderungsgesellschaft*. Göttingen, Germany: Vandenhoeck & Rupprecht.

Kosnick, Kira. 2007. *Migrant Media: Turkish Broad Casting and Multicultural Politics in Berlin*. New Anthropologies of Europe Series. Bloomington, IN: Indiana University Press.

Kranz, Dani. 2009. *"Shades of Jewishness: The Creation and Maintenance of a Liberal Jewish Community in Post-Shoah Germany."* PhD Dissertation, University of St. Andrews.

———. 2015a. "Where to Stay and Where to Go? Ideas of Home and Homelessness amongst Third Generation Jews Who Grew Up in Germany." In *The Shadows of the Shadows of the Holocaust: Narratives of the Third Generation*, edited by Esther Jilovsky, Jordy Silverstein, and David Slucki, 179–208. London: Vallentine Mitchell.

———. 2015b. *Israelis in Berlin, Report for the Bertelsmann Foundation for the 50th Anniversary of German Israeli Diplomatic Relationships*. Gütersloh: Bertelsmann Stiftung. https://www.bertelsmann-stiftung.de/en/publications/publication/did/israelis-in-berlin/.

———. 2015c. "Expressing Belonging through Citizenship—Are We Talking Third Generation Israelis, Third Generation Yekkes, or Third Generation Diasporic German Citizens?" In *The Meaning of Citizenship*, edited by Richard Marback and Marc W. Kruman, 95–125. Detroit, MI: Wayne State University Press.

———. 2016a. "Forget Israel—the Future Is in Berlin! Local Jews, Russian Immigrants and Israeli Jews in Berlin and across Germany." *Shofar* 34 (4): 5–28.

———. 2016b. "Changing Definitions of Germanness across Three Generations of *Yekkes* in Palestine/Israel." *German Studies Review* 39 (1): 99–120.

———. 2016c. "Quasi-Ethnic Capital vs. Quasi–Citizenship Capital: Access to Israeli Citizenship." *Migration Letters* 13 (1): 64–83.

———. 2017. "Changing Measures of the Quantum of Sufficient Germanness: Access to German Citizenship of Children of German/Non-German Parentage, and Children Eligible Under Jus Solis Provisions." *Journal of Comparative Family Studies* 18 (3): 367–79.

———. 2018a. "Anthropological Perspectives on German NGOs in Israel/the Palestinian Territories." In *Between Jerusalem, Ramallah and Tel Aviv: German Political Foundations Abroad: A Kaleidoscope of Perspectives*, edited by Anna Abelmann and Katharina Konarek, 53–64. Wiesbaden, Germany: Springer.

———. 2018b. "German, Non-Jewish Spousal and Partner Migrants in Israel: The Normalisation of Germanness and the Dominance of Jewishness." *Journal of Israeli History* 36 (2): 171–87.

———. 2018c. "Ein Plädoyer für den Alloismus: Historische Kontinuitäten, Zeitgeist und transkultureller Antisemitismus." In *Flucht ins Autoritäre—Rechtsextreme Dynamiken in der Mitte der Gesellschaft*, edited by Oliver Decker & Elmar Brähler, 177–92. Leipzig: Universität Leipzig.

———. 2018d. "Vom Ort des Traumas zum Ort der Sehnsüchte: Anthropologische Beobachtungen zur intergenerativen Tradierung von Trauma und Deutschsein unter *Jeckes* in Israel." *Psychotherapie im Alter* 15 (3): 277–92.

———. 2019a. "The Global North Goes to the Global North Minus? Intersections of Integration of Non-Jewish, Highly Skilled, Female Partner/Spousal Migrants from the Global North in Israel." *International Migration* 57 (3): 192–207.

———. 2019b. "It Took Me a Few Years until I Understood that I Am, as a Matter of Fact, Jewish": The Third Generation (Writ Small) Going Large as a Generaction." In *Trauma, Resilience and Empowerment*, edited by Adina Dymczyk, Jost Rebentisch, and Thorsten Fehlberg, 105–25. Frankfurt, Germany: Mabuse Verlag.

———. 2020a. "Notes on Embodiment and Narratives Beyond Words." In *Translated Memories: Transgenerational Perspectives in Literature on the Holocaust*, edited by Bettina Hoffmann and Ursula Reuter, 347–69. Lanham, MD: Lexington Books.

———. 2020b. "Towards an Emerging Distinction between State and People: Israeli Diasporas between Self-Management and Coveted Citizens." "Diaspora Management." Special issue *Migration Letters* 17 (1): 91–101.

———. 2021. "Navigating Mythical Time: Israeli Jewish Migrants and the Identity Play of Mirrors." In *The Future of the German-Jewish Past: Memory and the Question of Antisemitism*, edited by Gideon Reuveni and Diana Franklin, 163–78. West Lafayette, IN: Purdue University Press.

Kranz, Dani, and Hani Zubida. 2019. "Working Hand or Humans? Temporary Migrants in Israel and Germany: Between Acceptance and Rejection in the Social and Legal Spheres." In *Citizenship between Inclusion and Exclusion*, edited by Andreas Kewes, 221–42. Heidelberg, Germany: Springer.

Kranz, Dani, Yotam Hotam, and Avihu Shoshana. 2019. "Big Baggage on Small Shoulders? Children of Israeli/German Interparentage in Germany." In *Les mariages mixtes dans les sociétés Européennes, XVIIIe-XXIe siècles. Pour une histoire sociale de la mixité matrimoniale*, edited by Michael Gasperoni, Cyrile Grand, and Vincent Gourdon, 286–312. Rome: Vialla.

Kringelbach, Helene N. 2013. "Mixed Marriages." In *Citizenship and the Policing of Intimacy in Contemporary France*. IMI/DEMIG working paper no. 77. Oxford, UK: International Migration Institute.

Kritz, Mary M., and Douglas T. Gurak. 2015. "U.S. Immigrants in Dispersed and Traditional Settlements: National Origin Heterogeneity." *International Migration Review* 49 (1): 106–41.

Kulkarni, Veena S., and Xiaohan, Hu. 2014. "English Language Proficiency among the Foreign Born in the United States, 1980–2007: Duration, Age, Cohort Effects." *International Migration Review* 48 (3): 762–800.
Lapidot, Elad, and Ofri Ilany. 2015. "We're Only Someone Else's Fantasy." [In Hebrew.] *Spitz* 19: 4–5.
Latour, Bruno, and Steven Wolgar. 1979. *Laboratory Life: The Construction of Scientific Facts*. Beverly Hills, CA: Sage Publications.
Lavsky, Hagit. 2011. "German Jewish Interwar Migration in a Comparative Perspective: Mandatory Palestine, the United States, and Greater Britain." In *Ethnicity and Beyond: Theories and Dilemmas of Jewish Group Demarcation*, edited by Eli Lederhendler, 115–44. Oxford, UK: Oxford University Press.
Lee, Everette S. 1966. "A Theory of Migration." *Demography* 3 (1): 47–57.
Lee, Jennifer, Jorgen Carling, and Pia Orrenius. 2014. "The International Migration Review at 50: Reflecting on Half a Century of International Migration Research and Looking Ahead." *International Migration Review* 48 (suppl. 1): S3–36.
Lerner, Daniel. 1958. *The Passing of Traditional Society: Modernizing the Middle East*. Glencoe, IL: Free Press.
LeVine, Robert A., and Donald T. Campbell. 1972. *Ethnocentrism: Theories of Conflict, Ethnic Attitudes, and Group Behavior*. New York: Wiley.
Levitt, Peggy, Josh DeWind, and Steven Vertovec. 2003. "International Perspectives on Transnational Migration: An Introduction." *International Migration Review* 37 (3): 565–75.
Levitt, Peggy, and Nina Glick Schiller. 2004. "Conceptualizing Simultaneity: A Transnational Social Field Perspective on Society." *International Migration Review* 38 (3): 1002–39.
Levitt, Peggy, and B. Nadya Jaworsky. 2007. "Transnational Migration Studies: Past Developments and Future Trends." *Annual Review of Sociology* 33: 129–56.
Levy, Shlomit. 1985. "Lawful Roles of Facet in Social Theories." In *Facet Theory: Approaches to Social Research*, edited by David Canter, 59–69. New York: Springer.
Light, Ivan, and Steven Gold. 2000. *Ethnic Economies*. Cambridge, MA: Academic Press.
Löw-Beer, Martin. 1996. "From Nowhere to Israel and Back: The Changing Self-Definition of German-Jewish Youth since 1960." In *Germans, Jews and Memory: Reconstructions of Jewish Life in Germany*, edited by Y. M. Bodemann, 101–30. Ann Arbor: University of Michigan Press.
London Assembly 2017. *EU Migration Report*. Economy Commission of the London Assembly Reports. London: London Assembly. https://www.london.gov.uk/sites/default/files/eu_migration_report_final_2.pdf
Long, Michael H. 1990. "Maturational Constrains on Language Development." *Studies in Second Language Acquisition* 12 (3): 251–85.

Lopez, David E. 1999. "Social and Linguistic Aspects of Assimilation Today." In *The Handbook of International Migration: The American Experience*, edited by Charles Hirschman, Philip Kasinitz, and Josh DeWind, 212–22. New York: Russell Sage Foundation.

Lowie, Robert H. 1954. *Towards Understanding Germany*. Chicago: University of Chicago Press.

Lustick, Ian S. 2017. "The Holocaust in Israeli Political Culture: Four Constructions and Their Consequences." *Contemporary Jewry* 37 (1):125–70.

Luthra, Renee, Lucinda Platt, and Justyne Salamonska. 2018. "Types of Migration: The Motivations, Composition, and early Integration Patterns of 'New Migrants' in Europe." *International Migration Review* 52 (2): 368–403.

Lutz, Helma. 2017. "Was #MeToo und die Kölner Silvesternacht eint." *Mediendienst Integration* (blog). Published December 14. https://mediendienst-integration.de/artikel/was-metoo-und-die-koelner-silvesternacht-eint.html.

Macedo, Stephen. 2007. "The Moral Dilemma of U.S. Immigration Policy: Open Borders versus Social Justice." In *Debating Immigration*, edited by Carol M. Swain, 63–81. Cambridge, UK: Cambridge University Press.

Mai, Nicola, and Russell King. 2009. "Love, Sexuality and Migration: Mapping the Issue(s)." *Mobilities* 4 (3): 295–307.

Mandel, Ruth Ellen. 2008. *Cosmopolitan Anxieties: Turkish Challenges to Citizenship and Belonging in Germany*. Durham, NC: Duke University Press.

Maor, Harry. 1961. "Über den Wiederaufbau der jüdischen Gemeinden in Deutschland seit 1945." Unpublished PhD dissertation. Philosophy Department, University of Mainz. Accessed October 23, 2006. http://harrymaor.com/download.htm#item1.

Marcus, George E. 1995. "Ethnography in/of the World System: The Emergence of Multi-Sited Ethnography." *Annual Review of Anthropology* 24: 95–117.

Marcus, L. Kenneth. 2015. *The Definition of Anti-Semitism*. New York and Oxford: Oxford University Press.

Martiniello, Marco, and Jan, Rath. 2012. "An Introduction to International Migration Studies: European Perspectives." In *An Introduction to International Migration Studies: European Perspectives*, edited by Marco Martiniello and Jan Rath, 15–24. Amsterdam, the Netherlands: Amsterdam University Press.

Masri, Mazen. 2013. "Love Suspended: Demography, Comparative Law and Palestinian Couples in the Israeli Supreme Court." *Social and Legal Studies* 22 (3): 309–34.

Massey, Douglas S. 1988. "Economic Development and International Migration in Comparative Perspective." *Population and Development Review* 14 (3): 383–413.

———. 1990. "Social Structure, Household Strategies, and the Cumulative Causation of Migration." *Population Index* 56 (1): 3–26.

Massey, Douglas S., Joaquin Arango, Graeme Hugo, Ali Kouaouci, Adela Pellegrino, and J. Edward, Taylor. 1993. "Theories of International Migration: A Review and Appraisal." *Population and Development Review* 19 (3): 431–66.

McCray, Jacquelyn W., Margarete J. Weber, and P. L. Claypool. 1987. "A Housing Decision Framework: Development and Application." *Housing and Society* 14 (1): 51–69.
McKinnish, Terra. 2008. "Spousal Mobility and Earnings." *Demography* 45 (4): 829–49.
Meiering, Kerstin. 1998. *Die christlich-jüdische Mischehe in Deutschland, 1840–1933*. Hamburg, Germany: Dölling und Galitz Verlag.
Mende, Tugrul. 2020. "The Moral Triangle: Germans, Israelis and Palestinians in Berlin: An Interview with Sa'ed Atshan and Katharina Galor about the Difficult, Complex Relationship of These Three Communities." *openDemocracy*, April 30. https://www.opendemocracy.net/en/north-africa-west-asia/moral-triangle-germans-israelis-and-palestinians-berlin/.
Mendel, Meron. 2010. *Jüdische Jugendliche in Deutschland: Eine Biographisch-Narrative Analyse zur Identitätsfindung*. Norderstedt, Germany: Books on Demand.
Merkur, Lianne. 2019. *Pillars of Salt: Israelis in Berlin and Toronto*. Leiden, the Netherlands and Boston, MA: Brill.
Meyer, Beate 2002. *"Jüdische Mischlinge" Rassenpolitik und Verfolgungserfahrung*. Hamburg, Germany: Dölling und Galitz.
Michalos, Alex C. 1997. "Migration and the Quality of Life: A Review Essay." *Social Indicators Research* 39 (2): 121–166.
MIPEX. 2015. *Migrant Integration Policy Index 2015*. Barcelona/Brussels: CIDOB / Migration Policy Group. http://mipex.eu/sites/default/files/downloads/files/mipex-2015-book-a5.pdfu.
Mitchell, Robert E. 1971. "Some Social Implications of High Density Housing." *American Sociological Review* 36 (1): 18–29.
Mollenkopf, John, and Jennifer, Hochschild. 2010. "Immigrant Political Incorporation: Comparing Success in the United States and Western Europe." *Ethnic and Racial Studies* 33 (1): 19–38.
Moore, Eric G., and Mark W. Rosenberg. 1995. "Modeling Migration Flows of Immigrant Groups in Canada." *Environment and Planning A: Economy and Space* 27 (5), 699–714.
Morawska, Ewa. 1990. "The Sociology and Historiography of Immigration." In *Immigration Reconsidered: History, Sociology, and Politics*, edited by Virginia Yans-McLaughlin, 187–240. New York: Oxford University Press.
———. 2012. "Historical Structural Models of International Migration." In *An Introduction to International Migration Studies: European Perspectives*, edited by Marco Martiniello and Jan Rath, 57–77. Amsterdam: Amsterdam University Press.
Morris, Earl W. and Mary, Winter. 1978. *Housing, Family, and Society*. New York: John Wiley and Sons.
Mosse, George L. 1985. *German Jews beyond Judaism*. Pittsburgh, PA: Hebrew Union College.
Munch, Allison, J. Miller McPherson, and Lynn Smith-Lovin. 1997. "Gender, Children, and Social Contact: The Effects of Childrearing for Men and Women." *American Sociological Review*, 62 (4): 509–20.

Muttarak, Raya, and Anthony Heath. 2010. "Who Intermarries in Britain? Explaining Ethnic Diversity in Intermarriage Patterns." *British Journal of Sociology* 61(2): 275–305.

Myers, Dowell. 2005. "Cohorts and Socioeconomic Progress." In *The American People: Census 2000*, edited by Farley Reynolds and Haaga John, 139–66. New York: Russell Sage Foundation.

Myrdal, Gunnar. 1957. *Rich Lands and Poor: The Road to World Prosperity.* New York: Harper.

Naar, Devin E. 2016. *Jewish Salonica: Between the Ottoman Empire and Modern Greece.* Stanford, CA: Stanford University Press.

Näsholm, Malin H. 2011. *Global Careerists' Identity Construction: A Narrative Study of Repeat Expatriates and International Itinerants.* Umeå, Sweden: Umeå School of Business. http://www.diva-portal.org/smash/get/diva2:403920/FULLTEXT02.pdf.

Newbold K. Bruce. 1996. "Internal Migration of the Foreign-Born in Canada." *International Migration Review* 30 (3): 728–47.

Nikou, Lina. 2020. *Besuche in der alten Heimat: Einladungsprogramme für ehemals Verfolgte des Nationalsozialismus in München, Frankfurt am Main und Berlin.* Berlin, Germany: Neofelis.

Noy, Chaim. 2008. "Sampling Knowledge: The Hermeneutics of Snowball Sampling in Qualitative Research." *International Journal of Social Research Methodology* 11 (4): 327–44.

Noyman, Efrat. 2013. "Poland Is Back to Fashion." [In Hebrew.] *Haaretz: TheMarker* (Economic Supplement), March 25, 2–5.

Oberschall, Anthony. 1973. *Social Conflict and Social Movements.* Englewood Cliffs, NJ: Prentice-Hall.

O'Dochartaigh, Pol. 2007. "Philo-Zionism as a German Political Code: Germany and the Israeli-Palestinian Conflict Since 1987." *Debatte* 15 (2): 233–55.

———. 2016. *Germans and Jews since the Holocaust.* London: Palgrave.

OECD. 2018. "Fertility Rates." OECD. Accessed February 16, 2021. Data.oecd.org/pop/fertility-rates.htm.

Okely, Judith. 1996. *Own or Other Culture.* London: Routledge.

Ong, Aihwah. 1999. *Flexible Citizenship: The Cultural Logics of Transnationality.* Durham, NC: Duke University Press.

Onger, Maya. 2013. "An Intensive Integrative Course." [In Hebrew.] *Spitz* 6: 6–7.

Oppenheimer, Walter W. Jacbob. 1967. *Jüdische Jugend in Deutschland.* Munich, Germany: Juventa.

O'Reilly, Karen, and Michaela Benson. 2009. "Lifestyle Migration: Escaping to the Good Life?" In *Lifestyle Migration: Expectations, Aspirations, and Experiences*, edited by Karen O'Reilly and Michaela Benson, 1–14. Farnham, UK: Ashgate.

Ostergaard-Nielsen, Eva. 2012. "Transnational Migration." In *An Introduction to International Migration Studies: European Perspectives*, edited by Marco Mertiniello and Jan Rath, 107–29. Amsterdam, the Netherlands: Amsterdam University Press.

Ostow, Robin 1989. *Jews in Contemporary East Germany: The Children of Moses in the Land of Marx.* London: Palgrave Macmillan.

Owen, David. 2011. "Migrant Communities and Quality of Life in European Neighborhoods." Paper presented at the international conference on Population Geographies, Umeå, Sweden.

Oz-Salzberger, Fania. 2001. *Israelis in Berlin.* Berlin, Germany: Jüdischer Verlag.

Panagiotidis, Jannis. 2012. "The Oberkreisdirektor Decides Who Is a German: Jewish Immigration, German Bureaucracy, and the Negotiation of National Belonging, 1953–1990." *Geschichte und Gesellschaft* 38 (3): 503–33.

———. 2015. "A Policy for the Future: German-Jewish Remigrants, Their Children, and the Politics of Israeli Nation-Building." *Leo Baeck Institute Year Book* 60: 191–206.

———. 2019. *The Unchosen Ones: Diaspora, Nation, and Migration in Israel and Germany.* Indianapolis: Indiana University Press.

Papastergiadis, Nikos. 2000. *The Turbulence of Migration.* Cambridge, UK: Polity Press.

Parisi, Rosa. 2014. "Practices and Rhetoric of Migrants' Social Exclusion in Italy: Intermarriage, Work, and Citizenship as Devices for the Production of Social Inequalities." *Identities: Global Studies in Culture and Power* 21 (5): 1–18. doi:10.1080/1070289X.2014.950967.

Paul, Anju M. 2011. "Stepwise International Migration: A Multistage Migration Patterns for the Aspiring Migrant." *American Journal of Sociology* 116 (6): 1842–886.

Peck, Jeffrey M. 2006. *Being Jewish in the New Germany.* Piscataway, NJ: Rutgers University Press.

Pew Research Center. 2016. *Israel's Religiously Divided Society.* March 8. Washington, DC: Pew Research Center. https://www.pewforum.org/wp-content/uploads/sites/7/2016/03/Israel-Survey-Full-Report.pdf.

———. 2018. *Being Christian in Western Europe, 2018.* May 29. Washington, D.: Pew Research Center. http://assets.pewresearch.org/wp-content/uploads/sites/11/2018/05/14165352/Being-Christian-in-Western-Europe-FOR-WEB1.pdf.

Piore, Michael J. 1979. *Birds of Passage: Migrant Labor in Industrial Societies.* Cambridge, UK: Cambridge University Press.

Platt, Kristin. 2012. *Bezweifelte Erinnerung, Verweigerte Glaubhaftigkeit. Überlebende des Holocaust in den Ghettorenten-Verfahren.* München, Germany: Wilhelm Fink.

Plotke, David. 1999. "Immigration and Political Incorporation in the Contemporary United States." In *The Handbook of International Migration: The American Experience,* edited by Charles Hirschman, Philip Kasinitz, and Josh DeWind, 294. New York: Russell Sage Foundation.

Portes, Alejandro. 1995. *The Economic Sociology of Immigration: Essays on Networks, Ethnicity and Entrepreneurship*. New York: Russell Sage Foundation.
———. 1997. "Immigration Theory for a New Century: Some Problems and Opportunities." *International Migration Review* 31 (4): 799–825.
Portes, Alejandro, and Josh, DeWind. 2007. *Rethinking Migration: New Theoretical and Empirical Perspectives*. New York and Oxford, UK: Berghahn Books.
Portes, Alejandro, Luis E. Guarnizo, and Patricia Landolt. 1999. "The Study of Transnationalism: Pitfalls and Promise of an Emergent Research Field." *Ethnic and Racial Studies* 22(2): 217–37.
Portes, Alejandro, and Ruben G. Rumbaut. 2006. *Immigrant America: A Portrait*, 3rd ed. Berkeley: University of California Press.
Portes, Alejandro and Min Zhou. 1993. "The New Second Generation: Segmented Assimilation and Its Variants." *Annals of the American Academy of Political and Social Science* 530: 74–96.
Preuss, Urlich K. 2003. "Citizenship and the German Nation." *Citizenship Studies* 7 (1): 37–56.
Radu, Dragos, and Thomas, Straubhaar, 2012. "Beyond 'Push-Pull': The Economic Approach to Modelling Migration." In *An Introduction to International Migration Studies: European* Perspectives, edited by Marco Martiniello and Jan Rath, 25–55. Amsterdam, the Netherlands: Amsterdam University Press.
Ramírez-i-Ollé, Meritxell. 2019. "Friendship as a Scientific Method." *Sociological Review Monographs*, 67 (2): 299–317.
Ranan, David. 2014. *Die Schatten der Vergangenheit sind noch lang: Junge Juden über ihr Lebend in Deutschland*. Berlin, Germany: Nicolai.
Rapaport, Lynn. 1997. *Jews in Germany after the Holocaust*. Cambridge, UK: Cambridge University Press.
Rau, Vanessa. 2016. "Exotisierung, Faszination, und Befremdung: Ein Blick auf Migration und Befremdung zwischen Israel und Deutschland." In *Deutschland, die Juden und der Staat Israel: Eine politische Bestandaufnahme*, edited by Olaf Glöckner and Julius H. Schoeps, 216–46. Hildesheim, Germany: Olms.
Ravenstein, Ernst G. 1885. "The Laws of Migration." *Journal of the Statistical Society of London* 48 (2): 167–235.
Raymer, James. 2016. "Migration in Europe." In *International Handbook of Migration and Population Distribution*, edited by Michael J. White, 371–88. Dordrecht, the Netherlands: Springer.
Rebhun, Uzi. 2006. "Nativity Concentration and Internal Migration among the Foreign-Born in Israel, 1990–1995." *Revue Européennee des Migrations Internationales* 22 (1): 107–32.
———. 2009. "Immigration, Ethnicity, and Housing-Success Hierarchies in Israel." *Research in Social Stratification and Mobility* 27 (4): 219–43.
———. 2014. "Correlates of Experiences and Perceptions of Anti-Semitism among Jews in the United States." *Social Science Research* 47: 44–60.

———. 2015. "English-Language Proficiency among Israeli Jews and Palestinian Arabs in the United States, 1980–2000." *International Migration Review* 49 (2): 271–317.

Rebhun, Uzi, and Israel Pupko. 2010. *Far Nearby: Migration, Jewish Identity, and Attachment to Homeland among Israelis Abroad*. Research Report. Jerusalem: Hebrew University of Jerusalem, Israel Ministry for Immigration and Absorption, and the Jewish Agency for Israel.

Rebhun, Uzi, and Lilach Lev Ari. 2010. *American Israelis: Migration, Transnationalism, and Diasporic Identity*. Leiden, the Netherlands and Boston, MA: Brill.

Remennick, Larissa. 2002. "'All My Life Is One Big Nursing Home': Russian Immigrant Women Speak about Caregiver Stress," *Women's Studies International Forum* 24 (6): 685–700.

———. 2019. "The Israeli Diaspora in Berlin: Back to Being Jewish?" *Israel Studies Review* 34 (1): 88–109.

Riano, Yvonne. 2011. "'He's the Swiss Citizen, I'm the Foreign Spouse': Binational Marriages and the Impact of Family-Related Migration policies on Gender Relations." In *Gender, Generations and the Family in International Migration*, Albert Kraler, Eleonore Kofman, Martin Kohli, and Camille Schmol, 265–84. Amsterdam, the Netherlands: Amsterdam University Press.

RIAS 2018. *Antisemitische Vorfälle Januar bis Juni 2018*. Berlin, Germany: VDK / RIAS. https://report-antisemitism.de/media/Bericht-antisemitischer-Vorfaelle-Jan-Jun-2018.pdf.

Ritchey, P. Neal. 1976. "Explanations of Migration." *Annual Review of Sociology* 2: 363–404.

Rodriguez-Garcia, Da. 2015. "Intermarriage and Integration Revisited: International Experience and Cross-Disciplinary Approaches." *Annals of the American Academy of Political and Social Science* 662: 8–36.

Rogers, Andrei, and Sabine, Henning. 1999. "The Internal Migration Patterns of the Foreign-Born and Native-Born Populations in the United States: 1975–80 and 1985–90." *International Migration Review* 33 (2): 403–29.

Rosaldo, Renato. 1988. *Culture & Truth: The Remaking of Social Analysis*. Boston, MA: Beacon Press.

Roy, Olivier. 2017. *Jihad and Death. The Global Appeal of Islamic State*. London: Hurst.

Rumbaut, Ruben G. 1997. "Assimilation and Its Discontents: Between Rhetoric and Reality." *International Migration Review* 31 (4): 923–60.

Saberdlov, Shira. 2013. "Being a Refugee Is the Right Place for Me." [In Hebrew.] *Spitz* 4: 26–27.

Salloum, Rainah. 2014. "Hype um Israelischen Facebook-Post: Auf ins Pudding-Paradies!" *Spiegel Online*, October 11. http://www.spiegel.de/politik/ausland/israel-und-berlin-auf-facebook-starten-pudding-proteste-a-996337.html.

Salzborn, Samuel. 2018. *Globaler Antisemitismus: Eine Spurensuche in den Abgründen der Moderne. Mit einem Vorwort von Josef Schuster*. Weinheim, Germany: Beltz Juventa.

Sand, Shomo. 2014. "I Wish to Resign and Cease Considering Myself a Jew." *Guardian Weekly*, October 10. https://www.theguardian.com/world/2014/oct/10/shlomo-sand-i-wish-to-cease-considering-myself-a-jew.

Sapir, Yoav. 2012a. "Packed Alone: One Morning You Realize You Can't Leave So Easily." [In Hebrew.] *Spitz* 1: 8–9.

———. 2012b. "Packed Alone: To Experience Every Place as It Is." [In Hebrew.] *Spitz* 2: 10–11.

———. 2012c. "Packed Alone: I Feel Guilty that I have It." [In Hebrew.] *Spitz* 3: 12–13.

———. 2013a. "Packed Alone: I Didn't Want to Move at All." [In Hebrew.] *Spitz* 4: 20–21.

———. 2013b. "Packed Alone: Netanya-Berlin-Netanya." [In Hebrew.] *Spitz* 5: 18–19.

———. 2013c. "Packed Alone: There's No Sense of Foreignness Here." [In Hebrew.] *Spitz* 6: 16–17.

———. 2014a. "Even the Bureaucracy Do Me Good." [In Hebrew.] *Spitz* 9: 16–17.

———. 2014b. "Packed Alone: Don't Tell Her 'Ahla.'" [In Hebrew.] *Spitz* 10: 18–19.

———. 2014c. "It Took Me 13 Years to Buy a Sofa." [In Hebrew.] *Spitz* 13: 22–23.

Sarbin, Theodore R., ed. 1986. *Narrative Psychology: The Storied Nature of Human Conduct*. Westport, CT and London: Praeger.

Saunders, Peter. 1990. *A Nation of Home Owners*. London: Unwin Hyman.

Scham, Paul. 2018. "A Nation that Dwells Alone: Israeli Religious Nationalism in the 21st Century." *Israel Studies* 23 (3): 207–15.

Schaum, Ina. 2020. *Being Jewish (and) in Love: Two and a Half Stories about Jews, Germans and Love*. Leipzig, Germany: Hentrich & Hentrich.

Scheller, Bertold. 1987. *Die Zentralwohlfartsstelle: Der jüdische Wolfahrtsverband in Deutschland. Eine Selbstdarstellung*. Frankfurt am Main, Germany: ZWST. https://www.zwst.org/medialibrary/pdf/ZWST_Mitgliederstatistik_1955–1985.pdf.

Schmalhausen, Bernd. 2002. *Josef Neuberger (1902–1977): Ein Leben für eine menschliche Justiz*. Baden-Baden, Germany: Nomos.

Schmelz, Uziel O., and Sergio DellaPergola. 1990. "World Jewish Population, 1990." *American Jewish Year Book* 90, 484–512.

Schütze, Yvonne. 1997. "Warum Deutschland und nicht Israel?" *BIOS—Zeitschrift für Biographieforschung* 10 (2): 186–208.

Schwander, Hanna, and Philip Manow. 2017. "It's Not the Economy, Stupid! Explaining the Electoral Success of the German Right-Wing Populist AfD." CIS working paper no. 94. Zürich: Center for Comparative and International Studies (CIS), ETH Zurich. https://www.ethz.ch/content/dam/ethz/special-interest/gess/cis/cis-dam/CIS_DAM_2017/WP94_A4.pdf.

Schwarz-Friesel, Monika. 2018. *Antisemitismus 2.0 und die Netzkultur des Hasses*. Berlin: Technische Universität Berlin. https://www.linguistik.tu-berlin.de/fileadmin/fg72/Antisemitismus_2-0_kurz.pdf.

Senfft, Alexandra. 2020. "Deutschland und Israel: Dynamik einer komplexen Beziehung." In *Streitfall Antisemitismus: Anspruch auf Deutungsmacht und politische Interessen*, edited by Woflgang Benz, 269–83. Berlin, Germany: Metropol.

Shapira, Avner. 2014. "Searching for a Pink Future." *Haaretz* Gallery Supplement, June 10, 2.

Shavit, Sivan. 2012. "The Tribal Bonfire." [In Hebrew.] *Spitz* 1: 4.

Sheffer, Gabriel. 2003. *Diaspora Politics: At Home Abroad*. Cambridge, MA: Cambridge University Press.

———. 2006. "Transnationalism and Ethno-National Diasporism." *Diaspora: A Journal of Transnational Studies* 15 (1): 121–45.

Shemoelof, Mati. 2014. "Here I Sit, with Two Refugees from Mashad." *Haokets*, April 12, 2014. Accessed March 12, 2017. http://www.haokets.org/2014/04/12/.

Shenhav, Yehuda. 2008. "An Invitation for a Post-Secular Outline for the Study of Society in Israel." [In Hebrew.] *Israeli Sociology* 10 (1): 161–88.

Shohat, Ella. 1999. "The Invention of the Mizrahim." *Journal of Palestine Studies* 29 (1): 5–20.

Shooman, Yasemin. 2012. "Islamfeindlichkeit und Antisemitismus: Diskursive Analogien und Unterschiede." *JMB Journal* 7: 17–20.

———. 2014. ". . . weil ihre Kultur so ist": Narrative des antimuslimischen Rassismus. Bielefeld, Germany: Transcript.

Shoshana, Avihu. 2016. "'Ethnicity without Ethnicity': Reeducation and (new) Ethnic Identity." *Social Identities* 22 (5): 487–501.

Shye, Samuel. 1978. *Theory Construction and Data Analysis in the Behavioral Sciences*. San Francisco, CA: Jossey-Bass.

Silber, Marcos. 2008. "Immigrants from Poland want Go Back in the 1950's." *Journal of Israeli History* 27 (2): 201–19.

Simonsen, Kristina Bakker. 2018. "Inclusive or Exclusive? How Contact with Host Nationals May Change Immigrants' Boundary Perceptions and Foster Identity Compatibility." *International Migration Review* 52 (4): 1011–39.

Sjaastad, Larry A. 1962. "The Costs and Returns of Human Migration." *Journal of Political Economy* 70: 80–93.

Skeldon, Ronald. 1997. *Migration and Development: A Global Perspective*. Harlow, UK: Addison Wesley Longman.

Slater, Don. 1997. *Consumer Culture and Modernity*. Cambridge, UK: Polity Press.

Slyomovic, Susan. 2014. *How to Accept German Reparations*. Philadelphia: University of Pennsylvania Press.

Smith, Michael P. 2005. "Transnational Urbanism Revisited." *Journal of Ethnic and Migration Studies* 31 (2): 235–44.

Sobel, Zvi. 1986. *Migration from the Promised Land*. New Brunswick, NJ: Transaction Books.

Speier, Sammy. 1988. "Von der Pubertät zum Erwachsenendasein: Bericht einer Bewußtwerdung." In *Jüdisches Leben in Deutschland seit 1945*, edited by Micha Brumlik, Doron Kiesel, Cilly Kugelmann, Julius Schoeps, 182–93. Frankfurt am Main, Germany: Jüdischer Verlag bei Athenäum.

Staetsky, L. Daniel. 2019. "Is Criticism of Israel Antisemitic? What Do British and French Jews Think about the Link between Antisemitism and Anti-Israel Attitudes among Non-Jews?" In *Unity and Diversity in Contemporary Antisemitism: The Bristol-Sheffield Hallam Colloquium on Contemporary Antisemitism*, edited by Jonathan G. Campbell and Lesley D. Klaff. Brookline, MA: Academic Studies Press.

Stark, Oded, and David E. Bloom. 1985. "The New Economics of Labor Migration." *American Economic Review* 75 (2): 173–78.

Statistisches Bundesamt 2015. *Statistisches Jahrbuch 2015*. Wiesbaden, Germany: Statistisches Bundesamt. https://www.statistischebibliothek.de/mir/servlets/MCRFileNodeServlet/DEAusgabe_derivate_00000229/StatistischesJahrbuch2015.pdf.

Stauber, Shuki. 2017. *Israelis in Berlin: A Community in the Making*. [In Hebrew.] Tel Aviv, Israel: Yedioth Ahronoth.

Stern, Frank. 1991. "Philosemitismus. Stereotype über den Feind, den man zu lieben hat." *Babylon. Beiträge zur jüdischen Gegenwart* 8: 15–26.

Stevens, Gillian. 1999. "Age at Immigration and Second Language Proficiency among Foreign-Born Adults." *Language in Society* 28 (4): 555–78.

Stevens, Gillian, and Gray Swicegood. 1987. "The Linguistic Context of Ethnic Endogamy." *American Sociological Review* 52 (1): 73–82.

Sünker, Heinz. 2016. "Community's Discontent: The Ideology of the Volk Community in National Socialism." *Policy Futures in Education* 4 (3): 306–319.

Sünker, Heinz, and Hans-Uwe Otto, eds. 1997. *Education and Fascism: Political Formation and Social Education in German National Socialism*. London and New York: Routledge.

Sweid, Yousef. 2016. "My Two Mothers." *Spitz*, October 5 https://spitzmag.de/culture/8935. [In Hebrew.]

Süssmuth, Rita, and Werner Weidenfeld. 2005. "Introduction: The Integration Challenge: Living Together in a Europe of Diversity." In *Managing Integration: The European Union's Responsibilities Towards Immigrants*, edited by Rita Süssmuth and Werner Weidenfels, XI–XVIII. Washington, DC: Bertelsman Stiftung/Migration Policy Institute.

Tajfel, Henri, and John, Turner. 1986. "The Social Identity Theory of Intergroup Behavior." In *Psychology of Intergroup Relations*, 2nd ed., edited by S. Worchel and W. G. Austin, 7–24. Chicago, IL: Nelson-Hall Publishers.

Terdy, Dennis, and David, Spener. 1990. *English Language Literacy and Other Requirements of the Amnesty Program*. Washington, DC: ERIC National Clearing-House on Literacy Education.

Thorn, Jennifer Kaye. 2008. "Flight of the Kiwi: An Exploration of Motives and Behaviours of Self-Initiated Mobility." PhD thesis. Massey University, Auckland, New Zealand.

Tillmann-Healy, Lisa M. 2003. "Friendship as Method." *Qualitative Inquiry* 9 (5): 729–49.

Tobin, Gary A. 1988. *Jewish Perceptions of Antisemitism*. New York and London: Plenum Press.

Tonkens, Evelien, and Jan Willen Duyvendak. 2016. "Introduction: The Culturalization of Citizenship." In *The Culturalization of Citizenship: Belonging and Polarization in a Globalizing World*, edited by Jan Willen Duyvendak, Peter Geschiere, and Evelien Tonkens, 1–20. London: Palgrave Macmillan.

Turner, John C. 1991. *Social Influence*. Milton Keynes, UK: Open University Press.

Ullrich, Peter 2008. "Neuer Antisemitismus von links? Der Nahostkonflikt, Antizionismus, Antisemitismus und die Linke in Großbritannien und der BRD." In *Die Natur der Gesellschaft: Verhandlungen des 33. Kongresses der Deutschen Gesellschaft für Soziologie in Kassel 2006*, edited by Karl-Siegbert Rehberg. Frankfurt am Main, Germany and New York: Campus.

———. 2010. Der Nahostkonflikt: Spielfeld für einen neuen Antisemitismus von links? Ein internationaler Diskursvergleich. In *Der Nahostkonflikt: Befindlichkeiten der deutschen Linken*, edited by Marcus Hawel and Moritz Blanke, 67–80. Berlin, Germany: Dietz.

———. 2012. "Antisemitismus, Antizionismus und Kritik an Israel in Deutschland: Dynamiken eines diskursiven Feldes." *Jahrbuch für Antisemitismusforschung* 23: 105–20.

Ulrich, Andreas, Melanie Amann, und Martin Knobbe 2019. "Diffamierend, antisemitisch, rassistisch." *Spiegel Online*, January 17. https://www.spiegel.de/politik/deutschland/afd-verfassungsschutz-gutachten-nennt-partei-diffamierend-rassistisch-a-1248537.html.

United Nations. 1989. *Handbook of Social Indicators*. New York: United Nations.

———. 2015. *International Migration 2015*. New York: United Nations. www.unpopulation.org.

Van Hear, Nicholas. 2014. "Reconsidering Migration and Class." *International Migration Review* 48 (suppl. 1): S100–21.

Van Tubergen, Frank, and Matthijs Kalmijn. 2005. "Destination-Language Proficiency in Cross-National Perspective: A Study of Immigrant Groups in Nine Western Countries." *American Journal of Sociology* 110 (5): 1412–57.

Vertovec, Steven. 2001. "Transnationalism and Identity." *Journal of Ethnic and Migration Studies* 27 (4): 573–82.

Voutira, Eftihia. 2012. "*Jus Sanguinis* and *Jus Soli*: Aspects of Ethnic Migration and Immigration Policies in EU States." In *An Introduction to International Migration Studies: European Perspectives*, edited by Marco Mertiniello and Jan Rath, 131–54. Amsterdam, the Netherlands: Amsterdam University Press.

Wagner Constantin. 2014. "Wer sind 'wir'? Weißsein und Strukturen, Institutionen und Praktiken der Herrschaft." In *Migration, Asyl und (Post-)Migrantische Lebenswelten in Deutschland*, edited by Miriam Aced, Tamer Düzyol, Arif Rüzgar, and Christian Schaft, 177–200. Münster, Germany: LIT Verlag.

Waldinger, Roger. 2001. "Strangers at the Gates." In *Strangers at the Gates: New Immigrants in Urban America*, edited by Roger Waldinger, 1–29. Berkeley: University of California Press.

———. 2011. "Immigration: The New American Dilemma." *Daedalus* 140 (2): 151–65.

———. 2015. *The Cross-Border Connection: Immigrants, Emigrants, and Their Homelands*. Cambridge, MA: Harvard University Press.

Wallerstein, Immanuel. 1974. *The Modern World-System, vol. I: Capitalist Agriculture and the Origins of the European World-Economy in the Sixteenth Century*. London and New York: Academic Press.

Waters, Mary C., and Tomas R. Jimenez. 2005. "Assessing Immigrants' Assimilation: New Empirical and Theoretical Challenges." *Annual Review of Sociology* 31 (1): 105–25.

Waterston, Alisse, and Rylko-Bauer, Barbara. 2006. "Out of the Shadows of History and Memory: Personal Family Narratives and Ethnographies of Rediscovery." *American Ethnologist* 33 (3): 397–412.

Webster, Ronald. 1995. "Jüdische Rückkehrer in der BRD nach 1945: Ihre Motive, ihre Erfahrungen." *Aschkenas* 5 (1): 47–77.

Weiss, Yfaat, and Daniel Levy, eds. 2002. *Challenging Ethnic Citizenship: German and Israeli Perspectives on Immigration*. Oxford, UK: Berghahn Books.

Weißmann, Markus, and Amrei Maddox. 2016. "Early Ethnic Partner Choice among Natives and Descendants of Immigrants in Germany: The Role of Personal Preferences and Parental Influence." Working paper no. 164. Mannheim: Mannheimer Zentrum für Europäische Sozialforschung. http://www.mzes.uni-mannheim.de/publications/wp/wp-164.pdf.

Welch, Susan, Lee Sidelman, Timothy Bledsoe, and Michael Combs. 2001. *Race and Relations in an American City*. Cambridge, UK: Cambridge University Press.

Weller, Marc-Philippe, and Markus Lieberknecht. 2019. "Antisemitismus—Antworten des Privatrechts." *JuristenZeitung* 74 (7): 317–26.

White, Michael J., and Colin, Johnson. 2016. "Perspectives on Migration Theory-Sociology and political Science." In *International Handbook of Migration and Population Distribution*, edited by Michael J. White, 69–89. Dordrecht, the Netherlands: Springer.

White, Michael J., and Peter R. Mueser. 1994. "Changes in the Demographic Determinants of U.S. Population Mobility: 1940–1980." *Review of Regional Studies* 24 (3): 245–64.

Wilczynski, Martha. 2012. *Wie die Pizza in den Ruhrpott kam*. Cologne, Germany: WDR.

Winders, Jamie. 2014. "New Immigrant Destinations in Global Context." *International Migration Review* 48 (suppl. 1): S149–79.
WirtschaftsWoche. 2019. "Städteranking." Accessed June 8, 2022. https://web.archive.org/web/20200305105259/https://www.wiwo.de/politik/deutschland/staedteranking/.
Wistrich, Robert S. 2010. *A Lethal Obsession: Anti-Semitism from Antiquity to the Global Jihad*. New York: Random House.
Wodak, Ruth. 2018. "The Radical Right and Antisemitism." In *The Oxford Handbook of the Radical Right*, edited by Jens Rydgren, 61–85. Oxford, UK: Oxford University Press.
Wolpert, Julian. 1965. "Behavioral Aspects of the Decision to Migrate." *Papers of the Regional Science Association* 15, 159–69.
World Jewish Congress. 2019. *Germany Anti-Semitism Assessment Study: General Population Survey*. New York: World Jewish Congress.
Worman, Curt. 1970. "German Jews in Israel: Their Cultural Situation since 1933." *Yearbook of the Leo Baeck Institute* 1970, 73–103.
Wright, Fiona. 2018. *The Israeli Radical Left: An Ethics of Complicity*. Philadelphia: University of Pennsylvania Press.
Yagar, Hanna. 2012. *"Ovdei Etzot"* (עובדי עצות). [In Hebrew.] *Spitz* 2: 5. (The faulty Hebrew spelling in the original title of the paper is deliberate.)
Yadgar, Yaacov. 2010. *Masortim in Israel: Modernity without Secularization. Jerusalem.* [In Hebrew.] Moshav Ben Shemen, Israel: Bar-Ilan University/Keter Publishing.
Yair, Gad. 2015. *Love Is Not Praktish: The Israeli Look at Germany*. [In Hebrew.] Tel Aviv, Israel: Hakibbutz Hameuchad.
Yakobson, Alexander, and Amnon, Rubinstein. 2008. *Israel and the Family of Nations: Jewish Nations-State and Human Rights*. London: Routledge.
Yarris, Kristin, and Heide, Castaneda. 2015. "Special Issue Discourse of Displacement and Deservingness: Interrogating Distinctions between 'Economic' and 'Forced' Migration: Introduction." *International Migration* 53 (3): 64–69.
Yehudai, Ori. 2020. *Leaving Zion: Jewish Emigration from Palestine and Israel after World War II*. Cambridge, UK: Cambridge University Press.
Yurdakul, Gökçe. 2016. "Jews, Muslims and the Ritual Male Circumcision Debate: Religious Diversity and Social Inclusion in Germany." *Social Inclusion* 4 (2): 77–86.
Zagorski, Krzysztof, and John. S. McDonnell. 1995. "Consumer Confidence Indexes as Social Indicators." *Social Indicators Research* 36 (3): 227–46.
Zolberg, Aristide R. 1999. "Matters of State: Theorizing Immigration Policy." In *The Handbook of International Migration: The American Experience*, edited by Charles Hirschman, Philip Kasinitz, and Josh DeWind, 71–93. New York: Russell Sage Foundation.
Zimmermann, Moshe. 2008. "Rezension zu: Kauders, Anthony: Unmögliche Heimat. Eine deutsch-jüdische Geschichte der Bundesrepublik. München 2007." *H-Soz-*

u-Kult, February 20. Accessed May 12, 2008. http://hsozkult.geschichte.hu-berlin.de/rezensionen/2008-1-142.

Zuckermann, Moshe. 2007. *Israel—Deutschland—Israel: Reflexionen eines Heimatlosen*. Vienna, Austria: Passagen Verlag.

Index

Allosemitism, 175
Alternative für Deutschland (Alternative for Germany), 39
Anti-Defamation League, 177
Antisemitism: individual characteristics, 186–192; antisemitic attitudes, 89, 96, 172; context and concept, 175–177; IHRA definition, *see* International Holocaust Remembrance Alliance); in contemporary Germany, 180–182; in East Germany (*Deutsche Demokratische Republik*), 17, 180; measurements of, 177; perceptions of, 183–186, 193–195, 204; perpetuators of, 182; the "new" antisemitism, 195–199; theoretical considerations, 177–180
Arendt, Hannah, 178
Ausländers (Foreigners), 179

Babylon (magazine), 17
Balkan Wars, the, 10
Basic Law of Germany (1949), 129; Section 5, 176; Section 16, 10; Section 116, 13, 27, 65, 129
Bennett, Naftali, 38
Berlin, 38, 40, 47, 68, 105, 142; antisemitism in, 179, 181, 182, 192, 195; East Berlin, 14; Israelis in Berlin, 13, 39, 40, 41, 46, 53, 54, 55, 60, 75, 76–84, 88, 91, 94, 106, 120–121, 157, 163, 164; West Berlin, 15
Berlin Wall, the, 64
Berlin Diary (film), 210n1
Boycott, Diversification, and Sanctions campaign, the, 41, 101, 176–177, 195

Capital: cultural capital, 51; human capital, 6, 58, 102, 108, 123, 135, 137, 138, 143, 145, 201; social capital, 5, 26, 75, 210n1
Circumcision, 9, 115, 178
Citizenship, 3, 10, 11, 12, 23, 31, 44, 45, 67, 116–117, 122, 126–134, 138, 139, 145, 172, 188, 202; dual citizenship, 5, 7, 27–28, 29, 50, 57, 65, 66, 106, 128, 136; naturalization, 129, 130
Citizenship Law of Germany, 10, 13, 27, 28, 65, 129; renouncing or relinquishing dual citizenship, 5, 94; renaturalization and restitution of citizenship, 27, 68. *See also* Basic Law of Germany

Deutscher Akademischer Austausch Dienst (DAAD; the German Academic Exchange Service), 33

Displaced Persons (DPs), 14, 15, 28, 124, 178, 202

Educational stratification, 138, 167
European Union, the: citizenship of, 87; elections, 101; freedom of movement, 4, 12, 75

Gastarbeiter ("Guest workers"), 8–9, 47
Gelsenkirchen, 47
"German Middle East conflict," the, 18
German language, the: acquisition of, 90, 96, 106, 107, 109, 111; and perceptions of antisemitism, 31–32, 55; proficiency in, 101–114
Germany: as a migration destination, xiii, 4, 8–13, 47, 178; birthrate, 36; boycott of, 27; christo-normativity of, 96, 115, 121; *Einheitsgemeinde* (Unified Jewish community of), 15; "Germanness," 9, 93, 111, 130, 173; Jews in post-war Germany, 13–20, 126; *Kontingentflüchtlinge* ("quota refugees") 3, 11; labor migration to, 6, 8–9, 178; reunification of, 64, 181; *Spätaussiedler* ("late resettler"), 10, 11; Weimar Republic, the, 16, 20. *See also* Berlin; Gastarbeiter
Globalization, 2, 6, 57, 127
Grundgesetzt, *see* Basic Law of Germany

Ha'aretz (newspaper), 158
HaShomer Hatzair, 206
Hirschfeld, Na'aman, 158
Hebrew language, the, 20, 84, 88, 89, 91, 113, 157, 159, 172, 205; decolonization of, 94
Heimat, 141

Hertha Berlin Football Club, 102
High Commissioner for Jewish Life in Germany and in the Fight against Antisemitism (*Beauftragter der Bundesregierung für jüdisches Leben in Deutschland und den Kampf gegen Antisemitismus*), 182
Holocaust, the, 15, 23, 24, 26, 30, 31, 54, 55, 67, 94, 102, 163, 164, 166, 172, 203; denial of, 176; jokes about (as a coping mechanism), 33; survivors of, 16, 28–31; trauma (collective and individual), 13, 16, 19, 29, 31, 32–33, 54, 163, 166, 202
Homeownership in Germany 100, 134–145

Identity, 147–173, 205: group identification 16, 59, 149, 189–192; religio-ethnic identity, 147–149, 154, 160–164, 168–173, 195, 198; transnational identity, 4, 7, 24, 82, 147, 148–149, 152, 153, 155–160, 168, 171, 193–195; Zionism as, 22, 93. *See also* Antizionism, Transnationalism
"Integration paradox," the, 9
Intermarriage, 14, 32, 68, 100, 115–126, 139, 140, 144–155; and assimilation, 100, 172; binational vs interfaith marriages, 116, 145
International Holocaust Remembrance Alliance, the (IHRA), 176. *See also* Antisemitism, Holocaust
Intifada, the, 38, 47
Islamophobia, 96, 115
Israel: birthrate, 36; conscription in, 36; economic pressures in, 36, 75; ethnic identity in, 38, 39, 178; gender and gendered perspectives in, 36–37, 40, 82, 96, 171; Jewish

population of, 26, 29; labor market, 36, 37, 42, 47; migration to, 16; political/security situation, 18, 37, 41, 54, 71; "post-Israelism," 17–18; single women in, 72, 96, 113; "ultra Tel-Avivians," 63, 121. *See also* Yekkes

Israeli emigres, 17, 33–44, 87, 124, 126, 139, 203; chronology of migration, 64–76; reasons for migration, 40–41, 91–93, 96; responses to decision to migrate, 51–56, 117–118; sociodemographic characteristics, 44–51, 60–64, 112–113, 131–132

Jews: and German identity, 13, 21, 23, 27, 29, 51, 65, 164, 193, 198; *Geschichte der Juden in Deutschland von 1945 bis zur Gegenwart*, 14; and "Israeliness," 119, 121; Jewish identity, 30, 42, 55, 145, 195; Jewish Education, 172, 180, 205; and matrilineal descent, 122; Jewish migration to Germany, 149; Jewish refugees, 11, 33, "Jewish Renaissance," 18; Jewishness and Israeli identity, 29, 40, 119, 145, 179; Jewishness and rabbinical law, 122, 205; Jews in post-1945 Germany, 13–20, 202; Organized Jewish community, 16, 171, 179, 182, 195, 202; religio–ethnic identification of, 160–164, 168, 171, 198; secular Jews, 38, 39, 63, 119, 121, 160, 163. *See also* Identity, Judaism

Joint Distribution Committee, 16

Judaism, 115, 126; and civic life in Israel, 71, 94, 139; Jewish values, 38; Jewish festivals and celebrations, 160, 162–163, 164, 172, 195

Kantor Center for the Study of Contemporary European Jewry, 177

Luxemburg Treaties, 15
Luxembourg Reparation Agreement (1952), 29

McCloy, John C, 180, 204
Migrants: destination cities in Germany, 58, 76–87; family reunification and, 2, 10, 12, 47, 116; future migration intentions, 68, 87–97; guest laborers, 2, 7, 8–12, 47; and homeownership, 134–145; international migration today, 1–13; language acquisition, 99, 101–114; "lifestyle" migrants, 46, 50, 58, 72, 76, 78, 84, 86, 91, 123, 138; muslim migrants, 9, 12, 39, 168; and parallel societies, 9; *Passdeutsche* ("Passport Germans"), 11; refugees and asylum seekers, 2, 3, 10, 27, 33; social and cultural assimilation of, 99–101. *See also* Migration, Germany

Migration: chronology of, 64–76; chain migration, 6, 7, 47; forced and voluntary, 25; to Germany, 8–13, 15, 31, 60–64; internal migration, 58, 181; to Israel, 16, 26, 40; legal and undocumented migration, 100; legislation 3–5; reasons for migration, 6, 33–44, 47, 50, 69–76, 171; remigration, 14, 17, 59, 91; religious homophily, 9; theories of migration, 5–8, 149. *See also* Citizenship Law, Migrants

Migration Integration Policy Index (MIPEX), 101

Mikrozensus (Microcensus Act, MZG), 65

Netanyahu, Benjamin, 38

Oz-Salzberger, Fania, 13, 53

Palestine, Occupied Territories of, 19, 41
Palestine, British Mandate of, 15, 28, 33, 210n1
Patriotische Europäer gegen die Islamiserung des Abendlandes (Patriotic Europeans against the Islamisation of the Occident, PEGIDA), 39
Philosemitism, 17, 180. See also Antisemitism

Refugee Crises, the, 10, 33, 96
Religion, 9, 25, 37, 48, 62, 116, 121, 160, 172, 176, 202; ethno-religious institutions and networks, 7, 17, 26, 127, 147, 148; and marriage *see* Intermarriage; religious practices, 4, 5, 20, 36, 100, 160, 164, 211n4; religious prejudices, *see* Antisemitism; and secularity, 163; state protected religions in Germany (*Körperschaft des öffentlichen Rechts*), 115. See also Religiosity in Israel
Religiosity in Israel, 29, 34, 35, 38, 39, 42, 48, 55, 69, 71, 94, 134, 139, 159
RIAS (*Recherche und Informationsstelle Antisemitismus*), 115, 179, 180

Sand, Shlomo, 159

Shoah, the: pre-Shoah, 15, 54; post-Shoah, 14. See also Holocaust
Schengen Agreement, the, 57. See also European Union
Spitz (*newspaper*), 21, 40, 60, 105, 138

The Flat (film), 204
Transnationalism, 24, 148, 152, 155–160, 171

United Nations Population Division, 1

Wie die Pizza in Ruhrgebiet kam ("How Pizza came to the Ruhr Area") (Film), 47
Wirtschafts-Woche (newspaper), 90
Wissenschaftszentrum Berlin (WZB; Berlin Social Science Centre), 96
World War II, xiv, 3, 26, 29, 52, 55, 97, 178, 202, 203
World Jewish Congress, 177
World Union of Progressive Judaism, 11

Yekkes, xiv, 13, 31, 47, 64, 66, 68; Yekkishkeit, 93
Yishuv, the, 26. See also Palestine, British Mandate of
Ynet (website), 37

Zionism, xiv, 22, 35, 72, 93–94, 163; anti-Zionism, 40; philo-Zionism, *see* Philosemitism; post-Zionism, 56, 205. See also Post-Israelism

www.ingramcontent.com/pod-product-compliance
Lightning Source LLC
Chambersburg PA
CBHW020645230426
43665CB00008B/318